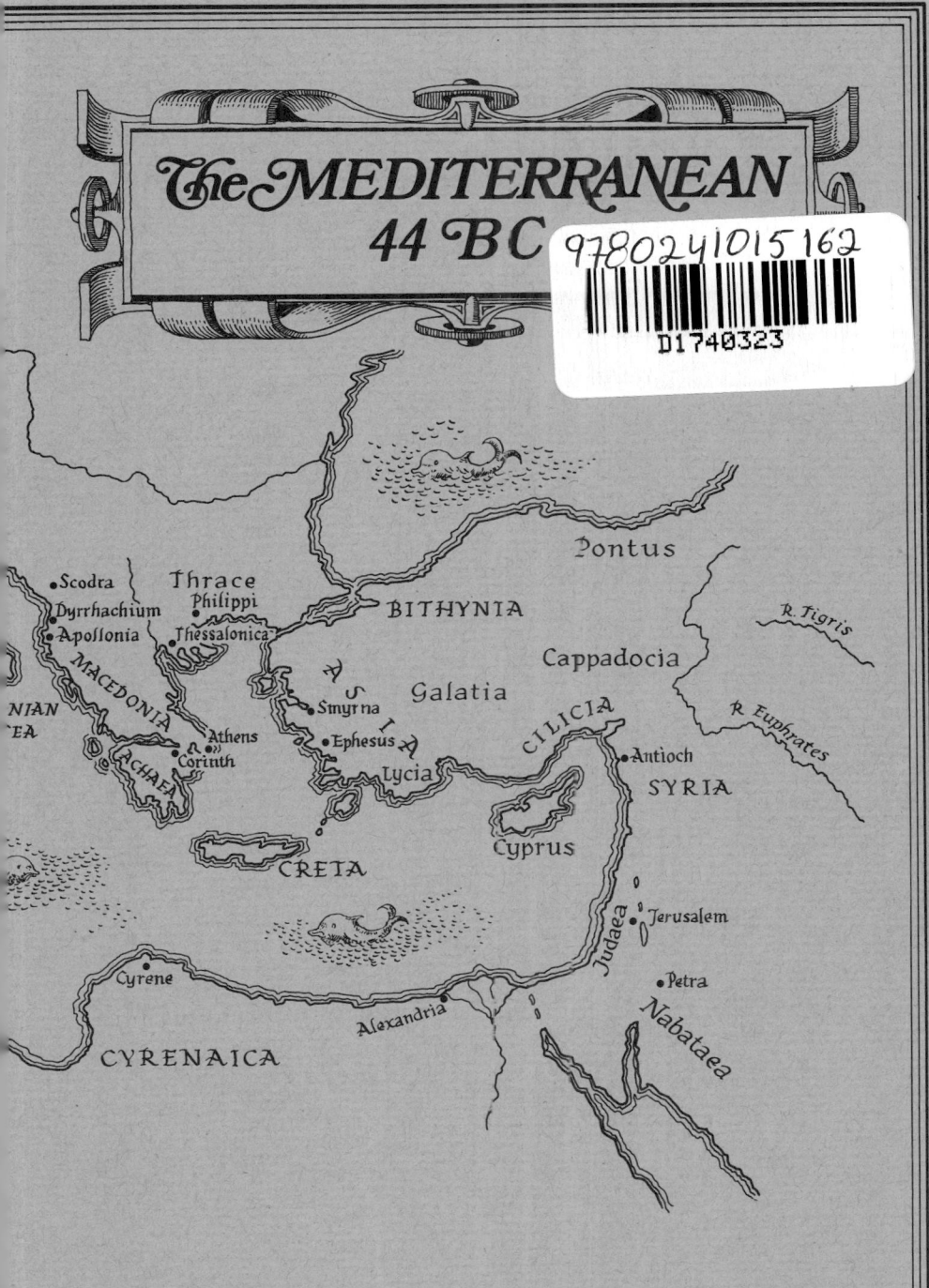

The MEDITERRANEAN
44 BC

Scodra
Dyrrhachium
Apollonia
Thrace
Philippi
Thessalonica
MACEDONIA
NIAN
EA
ACHAEA
Athens
Corinth
Pontus
BITHYNIA
A S I A
Smyrna
Galatia
Ephesus
Lycia
Cappadocia
CILICIA
Antioch
SYRIA
Cyprus
R. Tigris
R. Euphrates
CRETA
Judaea
Jerusalem
Petra
Cyrene
Alexandria
Nabataea
CYRENAICA

THE BATTLE OF ACTIUM

Photo: *Musée Lapidaire d' Art Païen, Arles*

OCTAVIAN

TURNING POINTS IN HISTORY

General Editor: SIR DENIS BROGAN

THE BATTLE OF ACTIUM

*THE RISE & TRIUMPH
OF AUGUSTUS CAESAR*

BY

JOHN M. CARTER

HAMISH HAMILTON

LONDON

First published in Great Britain, 1970
by Hamish Hamilton Ltd
90 Great Russell Street London WC1
Copyright © 1970 John M. Carter

SBN 241 01516 2

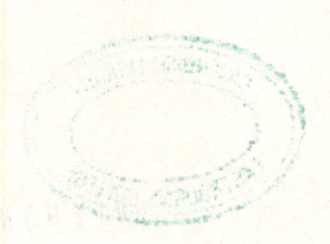

Printed in Great Britain
by Western Printing Services Ltd
Bristol

CONTENTS

ILLUSTRATIONS

Chapter I

THE IDES OF MARCH

IT IS still possible to see where Caesar died. Alongside the Largo Argentina, in the area of Rome which lies opposite St. Peter's between the Corso and the river Tiber, stands a row of four temples of the republican era. Behind them, embedded in the later buildings of the Christian city, can be made out traces of a hall which was evidently part of a much larger complex. The temples have so far defied identification; but the hall—though conclusive proof is lacking—can hardly be anything except the Curia Pompei, the place where the senate met on the morning of March 15, 44 B.C.

It formed part of what was once an imposing scheme, facing on to a tree-lined, porticoed square that was dominated by the back wall of a great open-air theatre on the opposite side. At that time the theatre was the first and only one in Rome; and theatre, porticoes, and hall together constituted the most splendid public building then to be seen in the city. The porticoes served for a foyer, and the hall, according to Plutarch, was designed as 'an additional ornament to the whole'.

All three carried the name of Gnaeus Pompeius, and all were his gift to the Roman people. Pompey had been called 'the Great' sarcastically in his youth, but it had not been long before the sarcasm had been forgotten. Since the legendary days of early Rome no man had enjoyed such prestige and influence as had been Pompey's at the height of his fame. In the traditional manner of the Roman noble, he had returned thanks to the people and ensured a lasting memorial to himself by erecting these magnificent buildings. He had started them in 55 B.C., when the unofficial compact between himself, Caesar, and Crassus by which they were able to dominate the state had been recently renewed. By 52 B.C., when the work was finished, Crassus had been killed in the Syrian desert, Julia, Caesar's daughter and Pompey's beloved wife, had died in childbirth, and it was already a possibility that Pompey might desert his ally and join the conservative group in the senate that both men had hitherto

I

opposed; as indeed happened. Caesar's political opponents won Pompey over and manoeuvred him, not entirely against his will, into leading them in the civil war they forced on Caesar. Defeated on the field of Pharsalus, he fled to Egypt and was ignominiously butchered by men who hoped to win the favour of his former father-in-law. It was ironical that the chain of events should end with Caesar stabbed to death in Pompey's hall, at the feet of Pompey's statue.

The irony was not missed by the historians of antiquity, but it remains no more than a bizarre coincidence. The senate did not usually meet so far from the centre of the city. Pompey's Theatre was in the Campus Martius, land which had originally served as a military exercise-ground, but which as the city grew in size became a place for sports and recreation for the ever-increasing urban population. March 15 was a feast-day, sacred to Anna Perenna, a mysterious minor deity connected with the springtime renewal of the year. Her festival went back deep into the past of Rome, and it was traditional for Roman families to come out of the crowded city and enjoy themselves beside the banks of the Tiber. The poet Ovid describes the scene:

> 'The people come, and scattered on the grass
> They drink, each lad reclining by his lass . . .
> Well-warmed, they pray for life, a year per cup,
> And keep the count as cups and years mount up.'

Doubtless the most dignified and important men in Rome did not enjoy themselves in quite this way. But the festival must have been the reason why Caesar chose the Curia Pompei as the senate's meeting-place on this particular day. As for the conspirators, Suetonius tells us: 'At first they hesitated whether to kill him in the Campus Martius on an Assembly day, when he was summoning the tribes to give their votes, by dividing their forces and throwing him off the bridge* and getting hold of him then, or whether to attack him on the Sacred Way or as he was on his way in to the theatre; but after a meeting of the senate was proclaimed for March 15 in the Curia Pompei, they had no doubts about preferring that time and place.'

The advantages were clear: Caesar would be alone as he went to the presiding consul's chair; it would be easy for the conspirators— all senators and numbering more than sixty—to gather without

* This was a bridge over a small stream, that played some part in the ceremony.

suspicion and crowd around their victim; and the senate was likely to be a more sympathetic audience than the people of Rome, who were much less interested in who governed them than in the tangible results of that government. On the face of it, Caesar's senate was a very different body from the one which had been unable to prevent its factional struggles from erupting into civil war in 49 B.C. Much of the diehard conservative opposition had perished—from natural causes or on the battlefields of the civil war—and Caesar had done more than fill their places in the traditional way from the ranks of the wealthy in Rome. He had enlarged the senate by half so that it now numbered about nine hundred. More significantly he had drawn some of his new men from farther afield, from the country districts of Italy and even from Gaul (probably Cisalpine Gaul, the Po Valley). A mock decree was placarded in Rome, 'In the name of God: no person may show a new senator the way to the senate-house' and there was a doggerel verse which ran:

> 'Caesar led the Gauls in triumph,
> Led them where the senate-house is;
> Now it's full of Gauls all wearing
> Purple robes instead of trousers.'

Exaggerated and unfair as this was, like all political lampoons, there was something in it. Trousered Gauls or not, Caesar's new men counted for very little. The rules of procedure in the senate ensured that debate was virtually confined to the consulars (the ex-consuls) and to those who currently held the higher magistracies. The senior senators had an importance and authority that bore no relationship to their numbers. Between them and the new men came a large number of the up-and-coming, the unambitious, and the mediocre or uninfluential who had reached their ceiling—the bulk in fact, of the senate. Broadly speaking, they were for Caesar. Some had been on his side from the beginning, some had taken the side of Pompey (and strict constitutional legality) and been pardoned. But all had entered the senate when the republic was still a reality, albeit a chaotic one. Many came from families that had been senatorial for centuries. Many expected, in the end, to achieve their consulships. They had assimilated in their youth the values and traditions which shaped, and finally destroyed, the republic. Their purpose in life was to serve the state and confer honour upon their family names by persuading the Roman people to elect them at the appropriate intervals to that sequence of magistracies which culminated in a consulship. There was nothing automatic about the sequence: each year eight praetors were elected, but there were only two consulships for them to go on to, and it was the same at the lower levels. Competition was the essence of the system. But once a man had reached the top, as consul and ex-consul he belonged to the small group which in effect controlled the state. He was his own master, and by the skilful deployment of his friendship, his patronage, and his family's marriages, he could perhaps manage for a time to guide the destinies of Rome. All this he did not in virtue of any office, for he probably held none, but by the possession of the authority, dignity, and prestige that his career had conferred on him. Men respected his views and, if he had arranged things properly, acted upon them. But he remained *primus inter pares*, and the shifting coalitions of families and interests ensured that no one man could monopolize power. This was what was meant by the 'free republic' and this was the tradition within which the vast majority of Caesar's senate had grown up. They may have owed their position and their advancement to Caesar, but this did not stop them from realizing that he had broken the framework of republican politics.

Caesar's power was, in effect, absolute. As victor in a civil war, he owed his position to no man—except his soldiers. The constitutional source of his power was the dictatorship, an ancient office whose enormous and overriding authority was tolerable only because it was conferred in an emergency and for a specific period or a particular task. But Caesar's dictatorship was different. Granted originally for one year at the beginning of the civil war by the partisan rump of the senate, it had been first extended to ten years and finally given for *life* in the autumn of 45—by a senate whose legal competence could not be questioned now that the war was over. Caesar could afford to dispense with the republican theory that the senate was a repository of collective wisdom. It continued to exist, even to meet. But no real decisions lay in its hands, and it seemed intent on turning itself into a body whose sole function was to confer ever more extravagant honours on its master.

Caesar responded in kind. He created a sensation in October 45 by remaining seated when the whole senate in procession came to inform him of the new honours they had just voted him. Apart from the dictatorship in perpetuity, these included continuous tenure of the consulship, the title 'Father of his Country', a golden throne, the inclusion of his statue amongst those of the ancient kings of Rome, and a number of privileges that were appropriate to a deity. Honoured thus, even if only by implication, as god and king, he continued to treat the institutions of the republic with contempt. 'The Republic,' he said, 'is nothing but a name lacking form and substance.' This is Cicero's wry account of a notable episode, from a letter to his friend Curius written early in January 44:

> It may be unpleasant to hear about what's happening here, but it's much worse to see it. At any rate you weren't there in the Campus Martius, when at seven a.m. at the beginning of the election of quaestors the ceremonial chair of Quintus Maximus—whom the Caesarians called consul—was put in position; but news came that he was dead, and the chair was removed. Our friend Caesar then held a consular election, though he had gone through the constitutional preliminaries for no such thing; and at one o'clock he announced a consul to hold office until the first of January, which was next morning. So be it known that in Caninius's consulship, no one had lunch. However, nothing went wrong while he was consul; for his vigilance was astounding and he took not a wink of sleep the entire time he held office. You may laugh; but you aren't here.

This farce apart, Caesar nominated the consuls for years ahead, depriving the people of their right to choose among the nobility and the nobility of their right to compete with their peers. He made no secret of his attitude to power, remarking that Sulla (who had been in an analogous position a generation earlier) 'didn't know his ABC', because he voluntarily laid down his dictatorship. Master Caesar was, and master he intended to remain.

The dictator's mistress was a queen: Cleopatra of Egypt, installed in a villa across the Tiber and mother of an infant son commonly held to be the dictator's. The only thing lacking to mark the end of the Republic and the return of monarchy to Rome was the name of king itself. And this, it was rumoured, was the purpose of the meeting convened for March 15: the aged and respected Aurelius Cotta, doyen of the consulars, would reveal that there had come to light an important prophecy in the Sibylline Books, the ancient collection of oracles which were consulted when divine guidance was needed—or when normal methods of persuasion were failing. This prophecy said that the Parthians, against whom Caesar was about to march, could only be conquered by a king. For five centuries the name and institution of monarchy had been anathema at Rome—ever since Lucius Junius Brutus had driven the arrogant and lecherous last Tarquin from the city and become first consul of the new republic. But it would be almost impossible for the senate to refuse to grant the title to Caesar on the eve of his departure. In the eyes of the superstitious populace, they would be condemning thousands of Roman citizens to their deaths in the deserts of the East.

They were, in fact, going to be manoeuvred into conferring on Caesar the status that public opinion had been unwilling to give a month before at the festival of the Lupercalia. On that occasion Caesar had appeared dressed for the first time in the magnificent garb decreed him at the end of the previous year. He wore a plain purple cloak, high red boots, and sat on his golden throne. These were the ornaments of the old Roman kings and their predecessors, the legendary rulers of Alba Longa from whom Caesar's family claimed its descent. The festival likewise went back into the pastoral prehistory of the city and was celebrated by an aristocratic and exclusive brotherhood wearing nothing more than goatskin girdles. Caesar's fellow-consul Mark Antony was one of the participants, and when they reached the forum he came forward, not in his purple-bordered robe of office, but in the semi-nudity of this archaic religious order, to place on Caesar's head the unmistakable badge of contemporary monarchy: a diadem. The tableau of old Rome was suddenly brought into the present. Even those closest to Caesar seemed uneasy. Marcus Lepidus, his current Master of Horse, betrayed discomfort. The people appear to have been taken by surprise, and when Caesar snatched off the diadem and flung it in front of him, the more distant section of the crowd applauded. A claque near by urged him to accept it, chanting 'Hail, King', while Antony made a second attempt to place it on Caesar's head. But it was clear that the people as a whole were not yet reconciled to the idea of King Caesar. So Caesar, dictator, consul, and high priest, laid aside the token of kingship and ordered it to be hung up in the temple of Jupiter on the Capitol; while in the official records of the state the entry was to be made that '*on the Lupercalia, by the wish of the people M. Antonius, consul, offered the kingship to Caesar, dictator for life; Caesar refused it*'.

It must have been at about that time that the conspiracy began to take real shape. Of the three leaders Marcus Brutus was the one who counted most, though the last to make up his mind. Brutus was high-minded, idealistic, a notable orator, and imbued with an inherited hatred of tyranny that was reinforced by his study of the Greek philosophers. He was a direct descendant of the first consul of Rome and very conscious that his family name was associated in the popular mind with the idea of freedom. Forty-one years old, he held the

office of urban praetor, the most senior magistracy after the consulship. Caesar thought highly of him and had him in mind for the
consulship in 41—in spite of the fact that he had taken Pompey's side
at the outbreak of the civil war and had not sought pardon until after
the battle of Pharsalus. There was even an ill-founded rumour that
Brutus was Caesar's son, for the dictator's affair with Brutus's
mother Servilia was one of the more notorious of his many liaisons.
The adherence of such a man to their cause placed the conspirators'
motives above suspicion. As Plutarch says: 'When Cassius sought to
induce his friends to conspire against Caesar, they all agreed to do so
if Brutus took the lead, arguing that the undertaking demanded not
violence or daring, but the reputation of a man like him, who should
consecrate the victim, as it were, and ensure by the mere fact of his
participation the justice of the sacrifice.'

Gaius Cassius was the moving force. His nature was darker and
more passionate than Brutus's, and he had dared to speak out openly
against Caesar in the senate. Like Brutus, he had been pardoned and
then promoted by Caesar. He was Brutus's contemporary and rival,
held the next-ranking praetorship, and was possibly intended to be
Brutus's colleague as consul in 41. The two men were linked by more
than age and career, for Cassius had married Brutus's half-sister
Junia. He had thus been drawn into the network of relationships that
centred on Brutus's uncle and father-in-law, Marcus Porcius Cato.
Cato had been a lifelong opponent of Caesar and had committed
suicide at Utica in 46 rather than surrender to his enemy. Stubborn,
upright, proud, and self-righteously conservative, Cato rather than
Pompey had been the true heart of the opposition to Caesar. He was
a dinosaur in Roman politics. Cicero complained of him that he
behaved as though he were living in Plato's Republic instead of on
the dunghill of Romulus. But he lived, and died, by his Stoic
principles, and his influence and example were powerful even after
his death. Through his kinsmen, he had his revenge on Caesar.

Suetonius names Decimus Brutus as the third of the conspiracy's
leaders. In spite of bearing the same family names as Marcus,
Decimus was only very distantly related to him, and had been Caesar's
man all along. He had served under Caesar during the years in Gaul
and had undertaken important operations for him afterwards in the
civil war. He reaped his reward with the praetorship in 45, and was
designated consul for 42. Caesar admitted him to his confidence,
honoured him conspicuously (by placing him alongside his great-
nephew Octavius, the future Augustus, in the carriage behind his

own when he returned to the city after the Spanish campaign), and named him in his will as one of his heirs. The future held even greater promise for him than for Marcus Brutus. Yet still he turned against his patron and benefactor: such was the strength of the republican traditions whose influence a man born into the Roman aristocracy could not escape.

The conspirators needed to do no elaborate planning. A dagger was easily hidden under the voluminous folds of a toga, and they could naturally and without comment meet in the porticoes outside the Curia Pompei before the senate went in to conduct its business. The nearness of the theatre was an advantage, too. As it was a feast-day, there was a show on. Decimus Brutus owned a troop of gladiators, and without arousing any suspicion he was able to arm them and station them beside the stage exit from the theatre, at the opposite end of the square from the Curia. Anyone who noticed them would assume that they were waiting to give a performance. But otherwise the plot was very simple—too simple, as it turned out —and there was nothing the conspirators had to do except make their way to the chamber and hope that no accident occurred to prevent the meeting from taking place.

Most of the conspirators (all except Brutus, if we are to believe Plutarch) gathered at Cassius's house. He had a son who was about to come of age; and it was the custom on such an occasion for the father to muster as large and imposing a group of friends as he could to accompany the boy down to the Forum to mark his debut in public life. So they all escorted the young Cassius to the forum, and then went on to the Curia Pompei. No one seeing these men together would have guessed what they had in mind. Certainly some of them, like Cassius himself, and the tribune Pontius Aquila who had incurred Caesar's sarcastic wrath by remaining firmly seated when the dictator rode past in triumph, were known opponents of Caesar; and some, like Minucius Basilus, who had been refused a provincial governorship, had personal grudges against him; but there were as many whose loyalty should have been beyond question—notably Decimus Brutus and Gaius Trebonius, a man whose career bore a marked similarity to that of Decimus and had already brought him a consulship.

Trebonius was the only consular in the plot. On the other hand, Cicero, who made no particular secret of his feelings and might have been expected to be in the group, was not among them. The great orator seemed to be a spent force in politics. Many years ago, as consul, he had saved Rome from a dangerous coup engineered by discontented members of the governing class; and in a stable and peaceful society Cicero's wit, ability, and respect for the established order would have made him a man to be listened to. But armies and influential connections had become essential to political success, and Cicero possessed neither. So he had retreated into philosophy, finding in it a refuge from the battle he was not equipped to fight. The furthest he had gone in opposing Caesar was to write a pamphlet in praise of Cato to which the dictator, who enjoyed literary warfare also, found time to reply from his campaign tent in Spain. Cicero was too cautious, too timid, too meticulous, for the conspirators; and so they had decided to exclude him.

In the portico, they received an unpleasant surprise. One Popillius Laenas, who was not in the plot, greeted Brutus and Cassius and enigmatically wished them well in their enterprise. Time was short for them in any case, since Caesar meant to depart in a few days for Dyrrhachium on the other side of the Adriatic, where his legions were waiting to set out on the campaign against the Parthians. But if Popillius Laenas knew what they intended, so must others, and it would be a matter of hours at most before the news reached Caesar's ears. However, there was nothing they could do. They could only wait, and pretend to be unconcerned.

The consuls were late. The time for the meeting went past, and there was still no sign of Caesar and Antony. Then there came a rumour that Antony was being sent to dismiss the senate. Caesar was quite capable of such high-handed behaviour, and the conspirators had to prevent it. Decimus Brutus, the closest of them all to Caesar, went to see what he could do. When he reached Caesar's house he discovered that the omens were unfavourable. Caesar, as chief priest and consul, was forever having to take the omens to ensure that the moment was auspicious for whatever official action he was about to perform. Ancestral custom died hard in Rome, and there were powerful men who had a vested interest in interpreting the will of the gods as shown by thunder, the flight of birds, the shape of a beast's liver, and so forth. Only a handful of reactionaries still believed in this archaic nonsense, and Caesar was not one of them. But for once, he was paying attention to the omens—perhaps because he was not feeling very well that morning and was glad of an excuse to defer state business, perhaps because his wife Calpurnia had had a strange dream that boded him no good, and was begging him not to leave the house.

Decimus pleaded with him, successfully. A bad dream, he said, was no reason for the conqueror of Gaul to stay at home, and if he intended to dismiss the senate because of the unfavourable omens, he should at least come and do so in person. So Caesar set out, carried in a litter and accompanied by Antony. It was now about eleven in the morning and the news of the conspiracy had had time to spread. Just after Caesar left his house a slave arrived with an urgent message that never reached him; and as he was on his way someone gave him a note warning him of his danger which was discovered still unread in his hand afterwards.

Outside the Curia, the consuls prepared to go through the routine formality of taking the auspices. Before they did so, Popillius Laenas approached Caesar and spoke to him privately. The conspirators must have been sure that he was telling Caesar of the plot, but it was merely some personal matter. The senators moved in to the chamber while the consuls and the augur watched the sacred chickens pecking and scratching at their corn. The augur interpreted their behaviour as unpropitious. Caesar asked him to repeat the procedure, but the birds were still unco-operative. Caesar was on the point of postponing the meeting; but at this moment attendants informed him that there was a quorum present, and Decimus Brutus for the second time that morning urged him not to let ritualistic scruple stand in his way.

Antony was detained at the door by Trebonius on some pretended business, and Caesar went in alone—tall, pale-faced and dark-eyed, wearing the laurel wreath that he prized so much because it hid his baldness. As he made his way up the aisle between them, the senators rose to their feet in respect. He had barely seated himself in the presiding magistrate's chair when Tillius Cimber and a number of others crowded round him, pleading with him to permit Cimber's exiled brother to return. Caesar made it plain by a gesture that the matter should be left to a more suitable occasion, but Cimber did not accept this. He took hold of Caesar's toga as though about to make a solemn entreaty. Caesar looked annoyed, and his annoyance changed to anger as Cimber pulled the toga harder. The rest crowded closer. The toga came right off Caesar's shoulders, and suddenly he realized what was happening. Shouting 'This is violence' he struggled to get up, but the toga hindered him. One of the brothers Casca, from behind him, tried to plunge a dagger into his neck. The blade skidded. Caesar drove the stylus he had in his hand into Casca's arm, wrenched his toga violently out of Cimber's grasp, then saw that all the others had daggers too. It was hopeless, and covering himself with the toga he gave a single groan and sank under a rain of frenzied, indiscriminate blows. Of the twenty-three wounds, only one was fatal, and in the confusion some of the conspirators themselves were stabbed.

There was uproar in the senate. Every man present had sworn an oath of personal loyalty to the dictator, yet only two men—Calvisius Sabinus and Censorinus—attempted to honour it. Against such odds, though, they had no chance, and fled lest they too should suffer the same fate. This should have been Marcus Brutus's great moment. His dagger dripping with the tyrant's blood, he had re-enacted the feat of his other famous ancestor Servilius Ahala, who four centuries earlier had rid the state of the upstart Spurius Maelius. Caesar had been struck down before the senate not simply because he was unguarded there—with his tremendous self-confidence he had dismissed his bodyguard some weeks previously and could have been attacked elsewhere almost as easily—but because this had to be a public killing. Brutus and his friends were solemnly and with the loftiest sanctions afforded by the history and traditions of Rome ridding the city of an oppressor who had taken away their freedom. It was not an act to be carried out privately and efficiently by a few men. The more who saw it and approved it, the more who were seen to have associated themselves with it, the greater and more splendid was the deed. This was no *putsch* but a vindication of liberty, and where could liberty be more gloriously vindicated than before the eyes of the most august assembly of the state?

The tyrant slain, it only remained for the senate to approve the slaying. Brutus attempted to address the churning, shouting, elbowing mass of frightened men trying to get out of the chamber, but none stopped to listen. None knew that Caesar was to be the only victim. None knew how many were in the conspiracy. They saw known favourites of Caesar among them and concluded that previous loyalties and friendships were poor guides at this moment. Escape was the paramount thought. It was so long since anyone had acted solely on moral principle in Rome (Cato always excepted) that nobody stopped to appreciate the noble Brutus in the role he had cast for himself: hero, tyrannicide, liberator of the Roman people.

Brutus had planned that the senate, protected by the gladiators of Decimus Brutus against any disturbance from outside following the report of Caesar's death, should formally declare him a tyrant and all his acts illegal, and set the seal on their verdict by having his body dragged to the Tiber on the executioner's hook and cast without ceremony, like a criminal's, into the river. His dictatorship had been a malignant growth upon the body of the state. Now that it had been cut away, the normal organs of government could start to function again forthwith. If Antony, as surviving consul and therefore head of state, were unwilling to preside, Brutus himself was the next senior magistrate and could legally see the business through in the absence of the consul. But Brutus had relied too much on the favourable reception of the murder. He had cogitated so long upon it himself that he had forgotten that those not privy to the plot were more likely to feel shock and terror than rapture and rejoicing. The gladiators should have been stationed to keep the senators in, not the people out; and as the chamber emptied, Brutus's chance slipped away. He tried again, outside, to make a speech, but it was useless. The best chance of legalizing the murder was gone with the vanishing senators.

The conspirators were at something of a loss. Excited by the prospect of action, convinced of the rightness of their cause, misled by the apparent simplicity of their remedy for oppression, and trusting in the strength of their numbers, they had failed to lay their plans carefully enough and to think what the consequences might be if the senate refused to support them. So they decided to retreat to the Capitol hill. This was a decision which made more sense as a symbolic act than as a constructive way out of the impasse. The Capitol had long ago lost the military significance it had possessed in the heroic days of the early republic. To occupy the Capitol was, if anything, to emphasize the conspirators' isolation from the people whom they claimed to be liberating. The scene is described by Nicolaus, the Greek from Damascus who became secretary to Herod and a friend of Augustus and must have talked to men who saw it all: 'The whole place was full of people trying to get away and shouting. There was a crowd, too, which had got up and poured out of the theatre (there were gladiatorial contests taking place) in no sort of order, not knowing precisely what had happened but disturbed by the shouting all around. Some said that the senate was being butchered by the gladiators, others that Caesar had been murdered and that the army had turned to loot the city; everyone had a different idea. Nothing could be heard clearly or distinguished in the tumult until they saw the assassins and Marcus Brutus trying to quiet the din and exhorting the people to take courage, for no disaster had occurred. . . . Then hurrying off, the assassins ran in flight through the Forum to the Capitol, their drawn swords in their hands, proclaiming that they had acted on behalf of the freedom of all.'

Chapter II

AFTER THE MURDER

THE INHABITANTS of Rome were used to riots: street battles and broken heads had been the accompaniment of the violent political warfare of the dying republic. The crowd dispersed as quickly as they could, taking refuge in the tenement blocks and pulling the heavy shutters across the open fronts of the shops. Antony himself, lucky not to have shared the dictator's fate, hurriedly shed his consular garb and slipped away through the side streets to the safety of his house—which had once been Pompey's. There he prepared for a siege. He had no more idea than anyone else of the extent and nature of the conspiracy. Of one thing, however, he could be certain: the conspirators could not possibly have the support of Caesar's veterans. The senate might, perhaps, condone the murder and seek to cast a veil of constitutional approval over it; but if there were men of influence and standing whose loyalty or interests would not permit them to acquiesce in such a course, once again it might be necessary to resolve the conflict by force. Then he would be in a strong position. As consul, he had the dignity and authority of the legitimately elected head of state; as a soldier, he possessed experience and ability; and as a Caesarian general, he could command the loyalty of the troops who had once been Caesar's. But he had no wish to plunge the state into another bout of armed strife. The losers in such a struggle could only be the class to which he himself belonged, the old senatorial nobility already decimated on the battle-fields of the civil war.

The conspirators themselves passed through the Forum and on up to the Capitol. They had been joined by a number of sympathizers from the senate, men who in Appian's tart phrase 'had not shared in the deed, but wanted the glory . . . and did not share in the glory, but suffered punishment with the guilty'. He names half a dozen of them, most notably P. Cornelius Dolabella, a young aristocrat of unstable and profligate character whom Cicero had unwillingly accepted and thankfully got rid of as a son-in-law. Yet Dolabella had been singled out by Caesar, whose judgment was seldom wrong, and had commanded troops for him in the campaigns of Pharsalus and Munda. In the interval, in 47 B.C., he had been a tribune of the people and had attempted to model himself on his erstwhile father-in-law's deadly enemy, the infamous and unlamented P. Clodius, employing Clodius's twin tactics of demagoguery and organized violence. He was alleged to have carried on an affair with Antony's wife, and it must have given Antony some little satisfaction to have been compelled, in his capacity as Caesar's Master of Horse with responsibility for keeping public order in Rome during the dictator's absence in the east, to intervene with armed force against him. Nevertheless Caesar continued to favour him, and had designated him to take his place as substitute (or suffect) consul once he had left the city to take over preparations for the forthcoming Parthian expedition. Others who enthusiastically joined the Liberators, as they liked to think of themselves, were L. Staius Murcus, a man of central Italian origin, who owed his advancement to Caesar, and was now the governor-designate of Syria; and, by the way of contrast, P. Cornelius Lentulus Spinther, a Roman of the Romans, whose father had held a consulship in the fifties and had died fighting for the Pompeian cause. Such was the fluidity of the political situation created by the murder. Loyalties were unpredictable, motives obscure.

The Liberators shared this general loss of orientation. Their object in going up to the Capitol was certainly in part to secure some sort of base; but they also wished to obtain the approval of Jupiter for their deed. His temple on the Capitol, where he was worshipped as Jupiter Best and Greatest, was to the Romans of this epoch much what St. Peter's is to their descendants: the holiest, most venerable, and most conspicuous of the city's temples. It had been consecrated in the first year of the republic by Brutus's ancestor, the first consul, after the expulsion of the Tarquins; and it was the repository of the greatest spoils and most solemn offerings of the Roman people and its commanders.

The Liberators' sense of historical appropriateness was impressive, their grasp of political realities less so. They took no action to seize the initiative. Their adherents assembled a crowd in the Forum, buying the support of a number of demobilized veterans and city poor—in the true tradition of late republican politics. The praetor L. Cornelius Cinna, brother of Caesar's first wife, came forward, laid aside his praetorian robe, and praised the Liberators for their services in ridding the state of a tyrant. The crowd was lukewarm, shouting only for peace. Then Dolabella spoke. He did not allow any consciousness of his own great debt to Caesar to deter him from attacking the memory and the acts of the murdered man. He even proposed (according to some reports) that this day be solemnized as the birthday of the republic. His words had greater effect because he had already assumed the consular insignia. The legality of this was dubious: Caesar certainly intended Dolabella to succeed him, and Dolabella had been elected for this purpose in proper form by the Roman people. But Antony had found (as he had announced in advance he would) technical religious grounds for annulling the election. Cicero later claimed that Antony's own procedure was strictly incorrect, and no doubt Caesar would have treated this republican obstructionism with the contempt that in his view it deserved. However, Caesar was arbiter no longer, Antony was undeniably consul, and Dolabella was his personal enemy. No wonder that Dolabella, claiming the consulship, threw in his lot with the Liberators at this moment. But Dolabella's tawdry personal ambitions accorded ill with the noble intentions of Marcus Brutus, and the Liberators made no attempt to turn to their own advantage the authority to which the new consul, however questionably, might lay claim.

After Dolabella's speech, Brutus and Cassius came down into the Forum in response to the shouts of the crowd. They complimented each other and the city on their good fortune and exhorted their audience to be like their ancestors who had expelled the kings. But the crowd, though not actively hostile, was far from enthusiastic. Historical analogy and the cry of liberty meant little to them. Political liberty was an upper-class luxury: to them it made little difference whether Cornelii and Antonii held their magistracies by Caesar's fiat or by election in an assembly heavily biased towards wealth and nobility. They knew that Caesar had brought some measure of order into public life at Rome and taken practical steps towards providing work and resettlement for large numbers of the unemployed urban rabble. Amongst the crowd were many veterans of Caesar's armies who had been discharged and were in Rome waiting to be led out, in quasi-military fashion, to one of the new settlements that were being founded in various parts of Italy. There they would enjoy the standard pension of the Roman soldier—the peasant smallholding. Fresh conflict might mean that they would lose their hard-earned plots of land. But beyond this, they still felt a strong personal loyalty to their one-time commander. They had all sworn a military oath of allegiance to him, an oath that did more than bind the soldier during his period of service; it created a relationship of mutual trust and obligation between him and his commander that continued even after discharge. They were, in the Roman term, his clients, and he their patron; and even if their personal interests had not been threatened by his murder they would still have felt it their duty to honour his memory and lend their support to those who claimed to be his political and material heirs. As it happened, Caesar was particularly likely to receive this sort of veneration, for he was both popular and respected by his men, and had the mystique attached to a general who had never yet lost a campaign. The Liberators would have an uphill fight to turn public opinion in their favour while there were many veterans present in Rome. This was their best opportunity, while all was still uncertain. But they failed to win the acclamation which might have encouraged them to more positive action, and withdrew again to the Capitol.

There they were visited by friends, relatives, and sympathizers. Cicero gave them excellent advice: to summon the senate there and then. Antony was in hiding, and if there were doubts about the legality of Dolabella's position as consul, Brutus himself as senior praetor was empowered to issue the necessary summons. But fear of a possibly needless clash with Antony prevailed, and messengers were sent to establish contact with the consul and with M. Lepidus. The burden of the messages was that the Liberators wished to avoid plunging the state into further bloodshed, and requested Antony and Lepidus to treat with them to this end. To Antony, this was a clear indication that any immediate danger was over, and he made a non-committal answer and at once got in touch with Lepidus and other Caesarian leaders, notably Balbus, the wealthy and influential citizen of Gades in Spain who had become one of Caesar's most trusted agents, and A. Hirtius, consul-designate for 43, who had the uncomplicated loyalty to Caesar of the outsider—his father being a prominent citizen of Ferentinum, and his own chief diversion gastronomy.

Lepidus commanded the only troops in Rome, one legion stationed on the island in the Tiber. His position was anomalous in that such authority as he had derived directly from the dictator. Now that the dictator was dead, the constitutional base of Lepidus's authority was gone. Nevertheless, his troops were scarcely likely to see things in quite this light, and, predictably, they continued to obey his orders.

He had already transferred them to the Campus Martius ready for trouble, and at first light on the 16th he seized the Temple of Ops, which served as the state treasury, and occupied the Forum. He was bent on vengeance, but Antony placated him with the promise of the vacant Chief Pontificate. Of the manner in which Antony was able to fulfil this substantial and irregular promise, history records only that it was underhand. Meanwhile the consul had ordered or persuaded Calpurnia to turn over to him all the state papers and the very large quantities of money that were in her husband's house.

The Liberators also had been in communication with their friends, to no profit, and all Brutus was able to do on the 16th was to call a public meeting on the Capitol. But his restrained and elegant style of oratory was hardly what was required, and his speech fell flat—not that this prevented him publishing it afterwards. Events had already moved beyond his control, as Cicero saw with the clarity of a man whose advice has not been taken. Nevertheless compromise was still possible and bloodshed had certainly been averted.

That evening Antony issued a summons to the senate to meet next morning, March 17, in the Temple of Tellus which lay conveniently close to his house. Public opinion, powerfully assisted by the leaders of the veterans, was already starting to swing against the conspirators, and when the praetor Cinna appeared wearing the robe of office he had previously cast aside he was pursued into a near-by house and would have been burnt there by the mob if it had not been for Lepidus's soldiers. On the other hand, the majority of the senate appear to have sympathized with the Liberators. Antony's handling of this delicate situation compels admiration. He neutralized Dolabella by recognizing his usurpation of the vacant consulship, and allowed the debate to produce all shades of support for the absent heroes. The staunchly republican Ti. Claudius Nero proposed special honours for the tyrannicides; others simply that they should be honoured as public benefactors; the diplomatic L. Munatius Plancus, governor-designate of the important military province of Transalpine Gaul, spoke, like Cicero, in favour of an amnesty. To the proposal advanced by the extremists, that Caesar's acts be annulled, Antony made a simple and effective counter. He pointed out that not merely had many important schemes been initiated by Caesar which it would be difficult or foolish to cancel, but that the vast majority of those assembled in the senate at that moment owed their past advancement, present status, and even future offices to

Caesar's decision. Prudence and self-interest won the day, and it was resolved that the murderers should not be prosecuted and that Caesar's acts and decrees should be confirmed 'for the good of the state'. 'And so,' says Plutarch, 'Antony went out of the senate the most illustrious of men; for he seemed to have removed the threat of civil war and to have handled a difficult and exceptionally confused situation in a most sensible and statesman-like way.'

Antony and Lepidus, as was normal, communicated the decision to the large crowd that had naturally gathered outside while the debate was taking place. They then invited the Liberators to descend from the Capitol, sending their own children up as hostages, and were publicly reconciled. That evening Brutus dined with his brother-in-law Lepidus, Cassius with Antony.

The result of the debate, and the official parade of goodwill, were almost inevitable, given the reluctance of either side to provoke a fresh civil war. Most of the senate were prepared to forgive if not actively to praise the Liberators, and a large number of them will have been friends or connections of the sixty-odd men involved. On the other hand, military force, and the sentiments of the veterans, were on the side of the Caesarian leaders. Cicero's correspondence makes it quite plain where his sympathies lay, and also why he contented himself with advocating an amnesty only: 'Who could have helped coming to the senate on the 17th? Suppose that were, somehow, possible: even when we *had* come, was there any chance of speaking freely? Didn't we have to protect ourselves somehow or other against the veterans who were standing there with arms in their hands while we were quite defenceless?'

Here already Cicero strikes one of the keynotes of the thirteen years to follow. The soldiers were possibly the only social group who saw clearly where their own interests lay. Roman citizens, but not from Rome, they were unimpressed by the traditions of urban politics. Sons of the soil, from the smallholdings of Picenum and Samnium and Umbria and Cisalpine Gaul, they had little in common with a city plebs heavily adulterated with servile and Oriental stock. They asked only that their years of service, dangerous and ill-paid, should at least earn them the reward which they expected: namely, their own little farm and what counted for security by the standards of their time. Their ears were deaf to the political catchwords surrounding the spasms of the moribund republic. The lack of political programmes, the insistence on personal claims to office and influence, the shifting alliances dictated by self-interest and expediency—these features of noble politics held no charms, indeed no interest, for Italian peasants.

The Roman nobility had continued to struggle for personal prestige with an almost total disregard for the changes which had overtaken the Roman state in the past century or more. Roman power had expanded over almost the whole Mediterranean and its surrounding countries; there had developed gradually what amounted to a standing professional army; and the Roman citizenship had been granted to the whole Italian peninsula. These were the symptoms and the agents of a political revolution. The primacy of the city of Rome was at an end, but the Roman nobility refused to acknowledge the fact. The strength of the Roman state lay in the peoples of Italy, and had done, if the truth was to be told, ever since the black day of Cannae when only the loyalty of the Italians saved Rome from Hannibal. Now at last the insatiable appetite of the Roman noble for power had woken forces beyond his control, forces which were to reshape the state in accordance with the new realities. And the interests of Italy, the basically apolitical interests of the Italian people outside Rome, found their representatives above all in the soldiers.

The soldiers served Rome, and they expected Rome to recognize their services. What they wanted was peace, stability, and a just reward for toil. To attain them, they were prepared to fight: that was their professional competence. They had not cared much whether Pompey, or Caesar, was master in Rome, so long as there was a master, so long as they and theirs were not made pawns in the political feuding of oligarchic cliques. Now that Caesar was dead, they would support his successor. This was at heart a matter neither of principle nor of sentiment, but of necessity, the same necessity that had driven them to fight for the rival dynasts in the Civil War. Had Pompey been victorious in that struggle, had Pompey quelled the factious nobles, his name and memory might have had the same power as Caesar's now. Cicero would indeed have liked to have 'spoken freely'; but the amnesty for which the sight of the veterans' swords induced him to plead was by far the better course. There were people outside the spotlit circle of the senatorial and business classes in Rome whose lives and prosperity were interlinked with that of the privileged and wealthy few in a way that these did not comprehend. To 'speak freely' was to return to the old ways, to the narrow, self-centred, and above all *Roman* politics which had already been found wanting. It was to take thirteen more years of civil war before the conflict of old and new was finally resolved.

The appearance of concord was short-lived. Caesar's own career might be cut short by a knife-thrust, but the forces which had made that career possible were not so easily tamed. All too soon the pressures generated by ambition, by the calculation of personal advantage, by the appearance of some sort of political balance, ruptured the momentary harmony. Caesar's father-in-law, L. Calpurnius Piso, was the guardian of the dictator's will. Some sympathizers of the Liberators, guessing its nature, asked him not to make it public. When the senate met, early next morning, he announced that he had no intention of complying with these requests. He can hardly have been ignorant of the contents of the document; and when it was unsealed and read out in Antony's house, the Roman people learnt that Caesar had left them three hundred sesterces each, and his gardens beside the Tiber. His chief heir was his sister's grandson, the eighteen-year-old C. Octavius. He named several of his assassins as guardians of his son, if one should be born to him, and amongst the heirs of second degree figured both Antony and Decimus Brutus. The generosity of the benefaction and the reminder of the treachery of the Liberators filled the fickle mob once more with enthusiasm for Caesar and hatred for his murderers.

A consul who died during his year of office was customarily given a public funeral, and it had therefore been decided, in accordance with the spirit of the amnesty, that this honour be granted to Caesar. His body was to be carried by magistrates and ex-magistrates in solemn procession, by way of the Forum, to the Campus Martius, there to be cremated alongside the tomb of his only child, his daughter Julia. In the absence of close male relatives, it fell to Antony to deliver the usual *laudatio*, the funeral eulogy pronounced to the people when the cortège stopped on its way through the Forum. Antony's business *was* to praise Caesar, but his manner of doing it was traditionally Roman and politically convenient. A Roman noble's glory lay in his deeds, not in his character, his beliefs, or his influence. Thus Antony did all that was required of him, and at the same time escaped the charge of being irresponsibly partisan, by having a herald recite first the decrees passed in Caesar's honour by the senate and people of Rome—not omitting to recall the personal oath of loyalty sworn to his inviolable person by every senator—and then his wars and battles, totals of captives and booty sent home, names of princes and nations defeated, and thanksgivings voted at Rome for his victories. To do so was only fitting. By anyone's reckoning, Caesar stood among the great men of Roman history. 'Do you remember,' wrote Cicero to Atticus a month later, 'how you cried that we were done for if Caesar had a public funeral?' If there were any sympathy for Caesar among the people of Rome, it was at his funeral that they would show it. Antony himself added some words of his own, becoming, according to Appian's account, visibly more moved as he proceeded. He made an attempt to control himself and cool the wild emotion sparking through the crowd. They might have mocked Caesar when he was alive; but dead, all was forgiven. Their anger and sorrow was ready to erupt in cathartic violence. A dirge-like chant paralysed their weakening self-control, then someone near the bier cried out the line of the old poet Pacuvius so that Caesar himself seemed to speak:

'Saved I these men that they should undo me?'

The breaking-point was reached when a wax effigy of the dead man was raised by unseen hands and rotated above the heads of the crowd, showing the twenty-three wounds and the mutilated face. The funeral procession went no farther. The crowd seized railings, benches, shutters, anything that would burn, and built a funeral pyre for Caesar there in the Forum. It was a spectacular and not inappropriate end for one who had burst the rotten republic apart. Cicero remained unimpressed: the same spontaneous honour had been paid to the gangster Clodius only eight years before. As the pyre blazed, the more violent and pro-Caesarian elements sought out the houses of the murderers and were barely prevented by the efforts of the domestic slaves and by the pleas of soberer citizens from setting fire to them. The whole city might have gone up in flames. The attackers withdrew, promising to return with more conventional weapons on the morrow. A mob of them, who met with the tribune Helvius Cinna and mistakenly took him for the praetor Cinna, vented their feelings by lynching him.

Whether Antony's conduct had been based on shrewd political calculation, or whether he too had been carried away, like the crowd, by the occasion and by genuine sentiment, there could no longer be any doubt where the sympathies of the people lay. The consul need fear no challenge to his position of authority. It was said that he had hoped to be named Caesar's heir in the will, but this hardly seemed a matter of any great importance. He was the natural leader of the Caesarian party, even without the prestige of his office. He had shown his loyalty and his worth to Caesar as soldier, as politician, and as deputy. He had commanded the left wing at the battle of Pharsalus, interposed a crucial veto as tribune in the days before

Caesar crossed the Rubicon, and governed Italy in 49 and 47. His only possible rival was Lepidus. Admittedly, Lepidus had held the office of Master of Horse to the dictator since April 46. But Lepidus was the older man, his family and connections more impressive—and less reliable. Such a supporter was apt to require the highest offices as his price. Furthermore, he had been designated governor of Narbonese Gaul (Provence) and Nearer Spain, where the activities of Pompey's surviving son Sextus demanded his attention. There is little indication that he had any other policy than to co-operate with Antony to keep public order and ensure the continued dominance of the Caesarian party. Antony, secure in his consular authority, in his standing as a Caesarian, and in the newly demonstrated loyalty of the Roman people to the memory of Caesar, could devote his attention to the task of restoring some normality to public life and preserving his own position in it.

The idealism of Brutus had succeeded all too well. The republic *was* free; free to become once again a battle-ground for the forces which had created the dictatorship of Caesar. It is easy for us to see how these forces were bound to act in the same way a second time. None of the ingredients of the situation had altered since Caesar had been manoeuvred by his enemies into crossing the Rubicon with an army at his back. Senators still lusted for personal power and wealth, the rural proletariat still regarded service under a successful general, regardless of who the enemy might be, as the quickest way of bettering themselves, and the urban plebs still knew their votes were worth a price. Even the principal actors in the drama were largely the same. Antony himself had taken a leading part in precipitating the final crisis in the first days of January 49; Cassius had commanded a fleet for Pompey; Cn. Domitius Ahenobarbus, the great-grandfather of the emperor Nero, had been with his father at Corfinium when that obstinate aristocrat had lost an army to Caesar. There had not been time either for the dictator's clemency to work any real change in the hearts of those who opposed him, or for his policies to heal the instability of the state. And so, when he was removed, it was inevitable that the struggle for power, which he had brought to an end by emerging as the victor, should break out again with fresh protagonists. That it did is a bitter and ironic proof that the Liberators were completely successful. Brutus had set his face against a *coup d'etat*, although Cassius had wanted to kill Antony, and Cicero lamented the omission; but it would have done no good. The Caesarian party had many heads, and could only be destroyed by removing its basis of support amongst the ordinary people of Rome and of all Italy.

Brutus was right to keep bloodshed to a minimum. But he and his associates were damned by their action. They had freed the republic from the constraints of autocratic rule, but their manner of doing it handicapped them grossly in the subsequent political situation. Their action was itself part of that situation, and they could scarcely complain if they were not at once given positions of special influence in the newly liberated state, or if the people of Rome treated them as worse than common murderers. If they expected otherwise, that was part of their miscalculation. The consul Antony and the senate were generous to them, as was the way of Roman nobles with their peers; but Antony could not fly in the face of the evident sentiments of the people he was supposed to be governing, nor could he be blamed for looking to his own position and political future at the same time as he attempted to avert the possibility of further bloodshed and the breakdown of legitimate authority. He accomplished this tricky task with great skill, neither forfeiting his position as leader of the Caesarians, nor exacerbating the deep divisions within the senate.

The scenes at Caesar's funeral were a warning of what might have been, but Antony showed that he would not allow popular demonstrations to get out of hand. There sprang up in the days after the funeral a cult of Caesar. It attracted especially Caesar's freedmen, who even under more normal circumstances would have paid a special debt of honour and reverence to their patron and erstwhile master. In the present situation their feelings were ripe for exploitation, and this was done with considerable effect by one Amatius, a Greek from Southern Italy who had Latinized his original name of Herophilos and claimed to be a grandson of the great Marius and therefore a kinsman of Caesar. This man erected an altar and a pillar in the Forum at the spot where Caesar's body had been burnt, and collected a gang whose avowed purpose was to take vengeance with their own hands on the murderers. Antony was not unwilling to see life made difficult for the Liberators, and at first he tolerated the activities of Amatius. The populace likewise can hardly have disapproved.

The climate of public opinion in Rome was such that Brutus and Cassius, praetors in office though they were, could not go about the city in safety and were in effect prisoners in their own houses. Others of their fellow-conspirators had already left the city, and it seems that in the first few days of April C. Trebonius departed for the province of Asia and D. Brutus set out for Cisalpine Gaul. They were perfectly entitled to do so. Both had been appointed as governors by Caesar, and all Caesar's acts and decisions had been ratified under the amnesty. They were now implementing those decisions in order to secure a position of strength at the head of provincial armies against Caesar's partisans. Little wonder that Trebonius used back roads and that Cicero was profoundly relieved to hear that Brutus had succeeded in joining the troops of his province.

On April 10 Marcus Brutus and Cassius had a meeting with Antony, at which a bargain may have been struck. Legally the two praetors were required to be in Rome, yet their position there was impossible and did them no good. Conversely Antony wanted them out of the way as their presence was an incitement to disorder and an embarrassment to himself. It is very likely that Antony promised to raise no constitutional difficulties if they absented themselves from the capital and from their duties, which public feeling was preventing them from discharging. On his motion the senate gave them dispensation from the law which forbade a praetor to be out of the city for longer than ten days. Once they were gone, he had no reason to tolerate Amatius and his quasi-terrorists any longer. The upstart, having served his purpose, could be suppressed, and public order at last fully restored.

Bargain or no, Brutus was at Lanuvium, some twenty miles south of Rome, by April 14 at the latest, and it was on the 13th that Antony acted against Amatius: the pseudo-Marius was seized and put to death without trial and his body impaled on the executioner's hook. Of Cassius's movements we hear nothing, but there is no reason to think he stayed in the city any longer than Brutus. Thus the four chief conspirators all left Rome between about April 5 and 13. This can have been no accident. They acted in concert, realizing that any chance they had ever had of swinging the course of events in their favour had gone for good. Antony was in control—not, for the moment, vindictive, but happy to see his opponents' political influence diminishing daily.

The consul had handled matters after the funeral with the same adroitness he had displayed in the crisis of March 16 and 17. His master-stroke was to bring a motion before the senate to abolish the dictatorship for ever. This was received with rapturous enthusiasm and a vote of thanks. He further consolidated the goodwill thus won by dutifully consulting the senior men of the state, the *principes viri*, before taking decisions. He was sparing in giving effect to the wishes

of Caesar as expressed in his papers, which were in his own possession. He also had the co-operation of Caesar's secretary Faberius,
and was in a very strong position to implement schemes of his own
by pretending that they were what Caesar had intended. But for
the moment he avoided even the suspicion of thus furthering his
private ends by the studious correctness and openness of his behaviour and by giving his willing assent to a motion introduced by the
consular and eminent jurist Servius Sulpicius that 'after the Ides of
March no grant of immunity from taxation, or any other benefit,
shall be officially proclaimed'. The consul was indeed showing himself a paragon of republican virtue. There was, after all, no better
way of winning over the senatorial oligarchy and consolidating his
position, while he ignored the Liberators and left them to the mercies
of public opinion.

For their part, the oligarchy had no obvious leader. Cicero, whatever his sentiments, had taken no practical part in politics since 55,
while the other Pompeian consular, Sulpicius, might better be
termed a neutral: he had prudently insured his position at the start
of the Civil War by sending his son to join Caesar. Of the Caesarian
consulars, the few apart from Antony and Lepidus who commanded
any respect were either outside Italy, or kinsmen of Caesar and his
young great-nephew, or too old and infirm to play any important
role. Nor was it any time to indulge in gratuitous discord. The vast,
newly-conquered lands of central and northern Gaul would rise
against Rome, now that their conqueror was dead: so C. Matius, a
personal friend of Caesar, gloomily prophesied to Cicero early in
April. In Spain, Pompey's younger son Sextus was still leading a far
from insignificant force in defence of a Republic which he refused to
admit had passed away, inflicting a series of minor reverses on the
Caesarian governors of the province. And in Syria, there was Q.
Caecilius Bassus, a mutineer (unwilling perhaps, but a mutineer none
the less) at the head of two legions. He had recently defeated the
force brought against him by the governor; but this would have been
of little importance if it had not been for the Parthians. By himself,
Bassus was no more than an adventurer with scant prospect of
support. Unlike Sextus Pompey, he could lay no claim to be fighting
for much more than his skin, and his men's. But the eastern frontier
of Syria was the Euphrates, and beyond the great river lay Parthia,
enemy of Rome and inevitable target of Roman attack so long as the
legionary standards taken at the disastrous battle of Carrhae remained to adorn the splendour of the Parthian king. Bassus might

turn to Parthia for help, or so distract the Roman forces in the east
that the Levantine provinces lay wide open to invasion.

To meet any or all of these threats, Rome stood in need of a tried
and capable military man. Who better than Caesar's lieutenant,
consul in office, trusted by Caesar's veterans?—provided that he
himself did not too ostentatiously parade loyalty to the dead or
unwillingness to defer to traditional attitudes. Even Cicero was won
over, mistrustful though he was. Writing to Atticus on April 9, he
says, 'I think he [Antony] takes more thought over the menus for his
banquets than planning any trouble;' and on the 16th, 'It's splendid
that Antony is approved of even by our Brutus.' Antony was, after
all, a member of the traditional governing class, and more than that,
of a distinguished noble family. It was not incredible that he should
have seen the light.

Chapter III

THE HEIR APPEARS

GAIUS OCTAVIUS WOULD have been looking forward to the end of March with pleasurable anticipation. Winter in the coastal town of Apollonia cannot have held much interest or excitement for the young man who had already followed his great-uncle the dictator to Spain on the final campaign of the civil war, and been given a place of honour beside him on the journey back to Rome. His occupations consisted of lessons from his tutor in oratory and philosophy, and of the military training appropriate for an eighteen-year-old already marked out for the highest honours—and therefore the highest commands. His diversions cannot have amounted to much more than riding, gaming, and the no doubt convivial society of his fellow junior officers; and senior officers did not fail to cultivate Caesar's relative. But by the end of March winter would be in full retreat and it would be becoming pleasant to be beside the sea, especially for one like himself whose health was far from robust.

The end of the month would also see the arrival of his great-uncle from Rome. All the preparation of his four months in this provincial town would find its point. The legions that were assembled in the region, the cavalry that he had drilled, the auxiliary troops from distant parts, the mass of supplies and money that had found their way to Apollonia, all would be welded together by the presence and personality of Julius Caesar into a fighting force able to form the nucleus of the army intended to invade Parthia, redeem the disgrace of Carrhae, and humble the power that dared to threaten the eastern borders of Rome's empire.

Towards the end of the month, in the late afternoon, a messenger arrived with a letter sent with all speed from Rome. It told the young man little beyond the bare fact that the dictator had been murdered in the senate-house. The writer was his mother. She did not know what support the murderers had, either in the senate or outside it. On the evening of March 15, when it was written, all was unclear.

The news that something of great importance had happened spread rapidly in the town. Soon a crowd had gathered, torches flaring in the dark. Octavius sent away the rabble, not without difficulty, and then told the more important members of the community what had happened. There followed a night of deliberation. Should he appeal to the Macedonian legions to avenge this treacherous murder and place himself at their head for a march on Rome? Should he take the advice of his mother to be cautious, avoid precipitate action, and come as quickly as he could to Italy to seek counsel and await developments? Or should he stay in Apollonia as the townsfolk, placing the city at his disposal and assuring him of their protection, urged him to do?

The most consummate politician that Rome ever produced chose the prudent course. Before he set sail, many of the soldiers and their officers came to offer him their services. His close friends M. Agrippa and Q. Salvidienus Rufus advised him not to spurn this support, and he commended them and asked that they should be ready when he needed them; but for the moment he intended to return to Italy as a private citizen. Taking leave of the Apollonians, he embarked in the first vessel willing to make the crossing in the direction of Brundisium, in spite of the fact that it was still the winter sailing season and such a crossing of the Adriatic in a small boat could be dangerous. But it was not as dangerous as the adventure that he was beginning. He landed safely, deliberately avoiding the usual route by the great port of Brundisium, and lodged inconspicuously for a day or two in the small town of Lupiae some thirty miles away. There he received more accurate information about the events of the 15th, and of subsequent happenings—in particular the amnesty decreed by the senate, and the reading of Caesar's will. It was now that he learnt that he had been named principal heir, and not only to Caesar's fortune. Caesar's name was his as well—a less tangible but far more potent legacy than gold. The dictator had provided, in a codicil, that if he had no natural son he wished to adopt Gaius Octavius, son of his niece Atia and her husband Gaius Octavius, 'into his name and family'.

What had prompted Caesar to single out a somewhat sickly youth, no very close relation of his, to be the recipient of his name and the bulk of his fortune? Octavian's early portraits show a lean and sensitive face set above a slender neck, of a striking beauty. The hair is short and inclined to be curly, and Suetonius tells us it was reddish brown. In later days his serene and penetrating gaze had a disquieting power which more than compensated for his shortness of stature. One can easily believe that the intensity was there from the beginning. Perhaps Caesar, famous as a judge of men, discerned in the pale and physically unimpressive lad that intelligence and that ability which were to serve a driving ambition and make him the first emperor of Rome. His father had certainly possessed both ambition and ability. It was he who had lifted the family out of its respectable obscurity. The grandfather had been a banker in the small Latin town of Velitrae (modern Velletri) twenty miles from Rome and taken no part in the political life of the great city, but his son decided to compete for office and glory and became the first member of the family to enter the senate. He confirmed his position by taking as his second wife Atia, and thus establishing an alliance with a politician who was certain to attain the highest honours a public career could offer. Early death robbed him of the consulship which Cicero assures us would have been his. If Cicero was right, C. Octavius *père* was a remarkable man. The praetorship, which he did attain, was as much as any outsider could hope for, particularly in the last years of the republic. (Cicero himself, whose origins were very similar, owed *his* consulship to a lucky combination of circumstances; but he had not married so advantageously.) It may be that the partisanship of the moment clouded Cicero's judgment, and the fame and success of the son have added lustre to the character and abilities of the father. But the ambition was there beyond doubt. It was transmitted to his son rather by heredity and environment than by example: young Gaius was only four when his father died. As stepfather he acquired L. Marcius Philippus, a wealthy and politically cautious noble, certain of his consulship, which he duly obtained in 56. Of Philippus's personality, little is known, but he kept his stepson in the public eye by getting him, at the age of eleven, to deliver a funeral oration in honour of his grandmother Julia; and Philippus's contacts with Caesar were good. Octavius was just thirteen when the civil war broke out. He could scarcely have helped admiring the great Caesar, his own blood-relative. By 46 the dictator had taken the sixteen-year-old boy under his wing. He conferred military rewards on him at the time of his African triumph, although Octavius had been too young to take part in the campaign. Then there followed service in Spain, return to Rome, winter in Apollonia —and now the murder and his adoption.

Emboldened by the news, the dictator's posthumously created son at once assumed his new name. By normal convention he became

Sipontum

SAMNIUM

Teanum Sidicinum
Cales
Casilinum
Beneventum
Suessa
Capua
Calatia
Neapolis (Naples)
Nuceria
Aenaria I.
(Ischia)
Minerva
Prom.

Venusia

Brundisium

Tarentum
Lupiae

CAMPANIA

LUCANIA

Velia

Puteoli
L.Avernus
L.
Lucrinus
Cumae
CUMAE
AREA
Baiae
Cape
Misenum

Lacinian Prom.

Vibo

Lipari
Is
Scyllaeum
Prom.
Naulochus
Mylae
Messana
Rhegium
Tyndaris
Leucopetra Prom.
Panormus
Tauromenium
Mt Etna

SICILIA

Syracusae

**S. ITALY
& SICILY**

1:4,125,000

N

0   50   100
kilometres

Malta

C. Julius Caesar Octavianus. For convenience, and to avoid ambiguity, modern historians call him Octavian(us). But it was a name that he himself never used. It signalled his adoption from another family, and that was not a fact that he wished to stress. To contemporaries, and to the historians of antiquity, he was C. Julius Caesar, or more simply Caesar. He knew already that his political future depended on being Caesar's heir. Without experience, authority, influence, or powerful friends, he looked to Caesar's name to make good the lack. How powerful an instrument it was to be he can hardly have suspected.

The new Caesar moved to Brundisium, cautiously sending ahead to make sure that the conspirators had laid no trap for him. The soldiers received him as Caesar's son, and freedmen, slaves, and friends of Caesar flocked to him. Cleopatra, hearing this, had no doubt which way the tide was running, and left Rome hastily with her own little Caesar. But Octavian still avoided any rash move. It was important to join his closest relatives, to make contact with the most trusted and influential Caesarians, above all to sound out current opinion amongst men like his stepfather who were near the centre of events—even if they avoided action and decision at this uncertain moment. So he set out, after a day or two, to the coastal resort towns of the Bay of Naples, in search of those he most needed.

The journey revealed to him quite clearly how public opinion was divided. Some of the towns were hostile to him, but the veterans from Caesar's settlements greeted him enthusiastically. The young man was polite, but non-committal, and proceeded on his way. He arrived in Naples on April 18. The next day no less an intimate of Caesar's than Balbus met him there. Balbus reported to Cicero that afternoon that Octavian was definitely going to accept the inheritance though aware that this was likely to mean trouble from Antony. On the 21st Octavian arrived to stay with his stepfather Philippus at the house next to Cicero's at Puteoli. He made a good impression on Cicero—which soon wore off, when Cicero perceived that the friendly and deferential manner of the young man went with political opinions that were anathema to him. 'His followers,' wrote Cicero to Atticus on the 22nd, 'address him as Caesar, but Philippus does not, and so neither do I; I cannot see how he can have his heart in the right place.'

There was much visiting: Hirtius and Pansa, the consuls-designate, and the ubiquitous Balbus were with Cicero as he wrote this letter. Their main interest was hardly likely to have been the witty conversation of the distinguished consular, nor even the lessons in public speaking which Cicero accused Hirtius and Pansa of making him give them. What drew them to Puteoli and Philippus's house was the presence of Caesar's heir. Decisions were going to be taken by this lad (as they thought of him) which could scarcely help affecting them all. If he persisted in claiming his inheritance, the precarious balance of forces which seemed to have established itself would be upset. The personality of the newcomer, the advice he received, the influence exerted on him or on his behalf, were all of vital importance. Their own interests—never mind Caesar's—demanded their presence.

No doubt there was a formal family council, as well as less formal and more meaningful comings and goings. Atia and Philippus did their best to dissuade Octavian from claiming the name as well as the property of Caesar. The latter he could do, and still remain a private citizen: the former entailed a public responsibility. As Caesar, he would be bound to defend the acts and memory of his father, as the dictator officially became; and how could he shirk the sacred task of exacting vengeance for a foul and treacherous murder? To lay claim to the name was to proclaim to the world that he had entered the contest for the political legacy of Caesar. At eighteen, with a hostile senate and ambiguous consuls, was that wise? But Octavian's ambition had been stirred by Caesar's judgment of him and he asserted that it would be a crime, if Caesar had thought him fit to bear his name, to think otherwise himself. 'His divine spirit,' as Velleius was to put it sixteen years after his death, 'spurned mortal advice and preferred to aim at dangerous eminence rather than at safe obscurity.' He had decided to follow his star.

There was no need to make any unnecessary fuss. The demonstrations at Apollonia, Brundisium, and along the road, had shown him where the sympathies of the soldiers lay. Brought up in an era of near-anarchy and civil war, he cannot have regarded a resort to arms as an unlikely or even wholly undesirable tactic in a political struggle. It was the last and clinching argument. Even if everything else was against him, this at least was not. For the rest, the magic of Caesar's name was best left to work by itself.

He chose to enter Rome when Antony was absent, at the end of April or the beginning of May. The consul, having piloted the state through the uncertainties of March and early April and either eliminated or removed from Rome the extremists on either side, felt free to consolidate his support among the veterans. There were still a considerable number of these in the city, awaiting settlement under plans drawn up by Caesar. Antony wanted to remove them from Rome. They were a potentially explosive element in the political situation, particularly if Caesar's heir should appear, and the fewer there were in the city the better. There was also gratitude to be won by settling them. Their interest in politics derived largely from their desire to become owners of land, and there was political capital to be made by anyone who could realize this desire. Antony therefore decided personally to lead a large body of veterans out to settlements in the fertile region of Campania. At Casilinum the splendid banner of the new colony* billowed in the wind as the consul ploughed the ceremonial furrow to mark out its boundaries. Its official name proclaimed his part as co-founder with Caesar—*Colonia Julia Antonia*. At the ancient city of Capua there was already a colony founded by the dictator, but Antony, anxious to increase his prestige, wished to establish another. He sought Cicero's advice as to whether this was legal. When Cicero replied that it was not, he had to content himself with adding new colonists to the existing foundation.

Antony was away from Rome about a month, returning in the second half of May to find the situation in the capital rather altered. His policy of compromise and conciliation was suffering the fate of all moderate policies in the presence of strong passions and men willing to exploit them. Almost immediately after he had left, at the end of April, Dolabella had taken severe measures against the cult of Caesar in the Forum. Although Antony had put the impostor Amatius to death, he had allowed the cult itself to continue. Such moderation was not for the headstrong Dolabella, whose usurpation of the consulship had so far brought him little credit. He threw down the pillar, let a contract for paving the site, and had the leaders crucified or thrown from the Tarpeian Rock. Apparently this display met with a measure of public approval, though Cicero is projecting his own feelings when he writes, 'What heroic deeds from our Dolabella! . . . It seems to me that Brutus could even put on a golden crown and walk through the Forum. Who would dare harm him at the risk of crucifixion or the Rock, particularly when the lower classes approve so enthusiastically?' Dolabella certainly succeeded in recovering a little of the credit he had lost by placing the consulship above his initial enthusiasm for the Liberators. Cicero

---

* Throughout this book 'colony' is used in its Roman sense to denote a new town (or addition to an existing town), whose inhabitants were Roman citizens. These colonies could be in Italy or overseas.

wrote fulsomely to his former son-in-law, and relayed the praises of
Antony's sick uncle, L. Julius Caesar. But if this was a blow struck
for the republicans, its effect was transitory. Brutus, with or without
a golden crown, did not dare to return to Rome, and the tone of
Cicero's letters grows increasingly pessimistic.

Much more important was the presence in Rome of Octavian. He
had made his way into the city as quietly as possible in the circumstances. Later report had it that celestial phenomena compensated
for any lack of terrestrial pomp: a great many-coloured halo surrounded the whole sun. Announcing that he proposed to accept the
adoption, Octavian set in train the legal measures necessary for
ratification. Further, he persuaded the tribune Lucius Antonius,
brother of the consul, to call a public meeting and allow him to
address it. He thus gauged for himself the state of opinion amongst
the city populace. For the moment he was careful to avoid antagoni-
zing anyone, and contented himself with promising to pay the
people the legacy left to them by Caesar. His conduct was correct and
unassuming, but consistent. Here were none of the consul's ambi-
guities of behaviour. The people saw Caesar's heir, a worthy focus
for the loyalties that Amatius had falsely exploited, willing to honour
Caesar's memory and Caesar's promises. He was of a new generation,
untainted by participation in the sordid politics of the last decade of
the free republic, and unconvinced of the desirability of a system
which offered too much scope for cynical and self-interested manipulation. Antony's behaviour so far smacked much of the republic.
He was a product of the system and his thoughts and tactics were
dictated by it. Cicero might distrust him, but he understood him as
he never understood Octavian. On the other hand the Roman people
had given Caesar their affection at least partly because he had shown
himself impatient of the feuds and sterility of traditional oligarchic
government, to which Rome seemed once more to be reverting. It
was little wonder if they saw in Octavian a man more likely than any
member of the older generation to be spiritual heir to Caesar.

Almost immediately, Octavian showed that he was in earnest. At
the games in honour of Mars, the *Ludi Martiales*, on May 12, he
attempted to implement one of the honorific decrees passed by the
senate the previous autumn, by which Caesar was entitled to have a
golden throne placed for him at the public games. The tribunes of
the people refused to allow it, but technically Octavian had the law
on his side. He did not press the point. It was enough to have made
it, and demonstrated his piety. As soon as Antony returned he sought

an interview and requested the consul to hand over Caesar's papers
and money. Antony temporized, alleging that the adoption (normally a mere formality) was not yet ratified, and that there were
difficulties in distinguishing private from public funds in Caesar's
accounts. The senate would have to order an investigation into the
matter.

Octavian remained polite. But Antony realized the altered situation very quickly—if he had not already got wind of it in Campania.
At any rate, he had come back with a considerable private bodyguard
of ex-centurions and veterans drawn from the military colonies of
that district, and he at once set about safeguarding his political
position. He had made necessary compromises in the public interest,
but that would do him little good in the face of a determined attempt
by Caesar's heir to discredit him as the leader of the Caesarian party.
He had to move decisively in one direction or the other. In terms of
practical politics, he had no choice. He was a Caesarian, or nothing.
Therefore he must reckon on the possibility of an eventual clash with
the party of Brutus and Cassius, and take steps now, while he was
still consul, to place himself in an impregnable position. It may have
been Caesar's heir who forced him to rethink his policies, but the
young man posed no solid threat. It was Caesar's enemies who
controlled, or would control in the next years, provinces and armies.
Decimus Brutus at this moment held Cisalpine Gaul, the key to
Italy. Next year Marcus Brutus and Cassius, if the senate were given
its head in allocating provinces, might obtain Cisalpine Gaul and
Illyricum. His own province was to be Macedonia, and in such a case
he would be effectively checkmated. Looking still further ahead,
Brutus and Cassius had been designated consuls for 41 by Caesar,
and by that time he himself would have relinquished any provincial
command and be no more than a private citizen—a consular certainly, but lacking the means to resist his enemies if they decided to
exterminate him politically. The decision once taken—and the trip
to Campania had given him plenty of time to reflect on the problem
—he acted with Caesarian promptness.

By May 23 it was known that he planned to deprive D. Brutus of
his province. It was normal for the senate to decide governorships,
and Antony called a meeting for June 1. But a full meeting would
almost certainly have produced a hostile vote, and it was well
understood beforehand that armed men would be on hand to deter
the opposition. Even the consul-designate Hirtius thought it would
be too dangerous to attend, and in the event the meeting was a

fiasco and Antony laid no business before it. He preferred to bring the matter before the legislative assembly of the people, where he could be sure that intimidation, along with some genuine support, would produce the required result. His brother Lucius, the tribune, prepared the ground by attacking D. Brutus at a public meeting. This assembly was called the day after the abortive meeting of the senate, the legal requirement of seventeen days' advance notice of legislation being ignored. A law was proposed, and passed, which took Cisalpine Gaul away from D. Brutus and conferred it upon Antony for six years. Thus Antony was reasonably safe from his enemies until at least the end of 39. To make provision further ahead was pointless, ascribing to the political scene a stability it did not possess. At the same or immediately subsequent assemblies other laws were passed confirming Caesar's acts and investing the consuls with full powers of decision in disputed cases, and making provision for the settlement of veterans.

On June 5 another meeting of the senate regularized the anomalous position of Brutus and Cassius by giving them special commissions to supervise the purchase and supply of corn for Rome from Asia and Sicily respectively. This gave them an official, but barely respectable, reason for absenting themselves from Italy. They were put out by this. Cicero attended a grand family council at Antium to discuss what they should do. His account of the proceedings is entertaining and revealing, both for the disintegrating sense of purpose of the Liberators and for the rarely attested influence of great Roman political ladies like Brutus's mother Servilia:

> I arrived at Antium before noon. Brutus was pleased to see me. Then before a big gathering, which included Servilia, Tertulla, and Porcia, he asked me what my advice was. Favonius was there too. I told him what I had pondered on the way, namely to accept the Asiatic corn commission. I said that his safety was now our only concern; the Republic itself depended on it. I was well started on this topic when in came Cassius. I repeated what I had just said, whereupon Cassius looking very fierce, quite the picture of a warrior, said he had no intention of going to Sicily. 'Should I have taken an insult for a favour?' 'What are you going to do then?' I said. He replied that he would go to Greece. 'What about you, Brutus?' said I. 'To Rome,' he replied, 'if you think so.' 'I don't. You won't be safe.' 'Well, if I could be safe, would you agree?' 'Naturally, and I wouldn't leave for a province either now or after your praetorship. But I wouldn't advise you to risk going to the city.' I went on to give reasons, which you can surely guess, why he would not be safe.

Much conversation followed, in which they complained, and especially Cassius, about the opportunities that had been missed, and they particularly criticized Decimus. To that I replied that it was no good crying over spilt milk, but all the same I agreed. And when I began to say what ought to have been done, nothing startling but only what everyone says, and although I missed out any reference to someone else who ought to have been dealt with and only said that they should have summoned the senate, roused the people's enthusiasm, and taken over the government completely, your lady friend cried out 'I never heard such a thing!' and I shut up. However, it seemed to me that Cassius would go (for Servilia promised to get the corn commission removed from the decree) and Brutus was soon talked out of his mad idea of going to Rome. He therefore decided to have the Games given under his name, in his absence. I thought he wanted to go to Asia direct from Antium.

To sum up, I got nothing out of my trip except the satisfaction of duty done. It would not have been right for him to have left Italy without seeing me. But friendship, and obligation apart, I was left wondering what the point of my journey was. I found the ship breaking up, or rather already wrecked. No plan, no thought, no method.

For the moment, the Liberators were finished as a political force. They had no support from army, veterans, or people. Cicero decided after the display of force at the senate meeting of June 1 that there was little point in appearing in Rome before the start of the next year. Antony seemed to be set on imposing his will on the state, and was evidently not prepared to let constitutional niceties or a respect for the freedom of speech thwart him. With Dolabella in his pocket, the senate overawed, and the veterans on his side, he appeared to have matters firmly under control. But Octavian, at first no more than a nuisance, gradually forced the consul on to the defensive. He put it about that Antony was blocking the *lex curiata*, the technical law, ratifying his adoption, alleged that Antony had converted to his own use money that rightly belonged either to himself or to the treasury, and ostentatiously started to sell up property that had come to him by Caesar's will. Not that he was seriously short of money; it is highly likely that he appropriated funds from the war-chest at Brundisium, and Caesar's friends and agents in the capital were men of substance whose credit was good. Two of them, Matius and Postumus, agreed to act for him in the provision of the public games in honour of Venus and Caesar's Victory. He was fortunate in that the priestly college which had been founded to provide them did not dare to do so. Thus he was able to ingratiate himself still further with the urban populace and at the same time gain credit for loyally respecting the institutions and memory of his adoptive father. The major games were politically important, and these, though new, were undeniably in that category. The common people of Rome had few diversions. Gladiatorial contest, beast-hunts, and racing made a welcome break in their poverty-stricken existence. It was vital to put on a good show. This was why Brutus was so anxious to persevere with his task, as urban praetor, of putting on the *Ludi Apollinares*. He hoped that he might win back the favour of the people, vainly as it turned out. What good-will his games, held between July 7 and 13, may have generated was very quickly forgotten when Octavian staged the *Ludi Victoriae Caesaris* from July 20 to 30. At these, Octavian made another attempt to set up the golden throne and wreath for Caesar in the theatre, and for a second time it was vetoed, by Antony himself. The crowd resented the veto and gave Octavian generous applause, affording fresh evidence for sympathies they had already made clear at Brutus's games, sympathies which were over-whelmingly reinforced when the heir paid Caesar's legacy of seventy-five denarii a head during the festival, a sum equivalent to just over half a year's pay for a legionary soldier. The legacy, how-ever, was a mundane matter beside the comet.

The comet appeared during the days of Octavian's games. For seven days it blazed in the evening sky to the north, filling the popu-lace with awe and wonder. They said it was the star and spirit of Caesar, received into the heavens and into the company of the gods. In a superstitious age, it was a token that was portentous and un-deniable. The favour of heaven and of the dead man shone upon his heir, the one man in Rome who strove to uphold his memory and prevent the Roman people being robbed of the benefits he had bestowed upon them. And what clearer sign could there be that Caesar was in truth one of the gods, or at least worthy to dwell with them on high? Octavian made sure that the sign would not be for-gotten by placing upon the forehead of his new father's statue a star whose uppermost ray was a flame. Nor did it escape notice that the month of the portent was the month of Caesar's birth, whose name had been changed for that reason from the ancient Quintilis to July; and that this was the first July since the passing of the decree.

Fortune, or the gods, favoured Octavian. How effectively, Antony's actions reveal. Outplayed as a Caesarian, he veered back again to the other side. Perhaps, if he were able to heal the divisions in the state, his young rival would have no grounds for attacking him.

Of external menaces, the Gauls that Matius, and not only Matius, had feared in the days after Caesar's assassination, had shown no signs of revolt; the Syrian troubles were delegated to Dolabella and were in any case too remote to matter at the moment; there remained Sextus Pompey, successful and popular in Spain. With him the consul had opened a dialogue through Lepidus, now governing Provence and Nearer Spain, and negotiations were in train. Sextus, though he professed to be defending the true republican cause, had barely known the republic, and that when he was not of an age to participate in its struggles. He was willing to accept the right to return home granted him by Caesar; but he insisted on compensation for his father's property which had been sold under the spear at public auction. Also, as the son of a great man, he demanded office and prestige. Antony was ready to meet these terms, but communications with Spain were slow and it was not until well on in the autumn that agreement was finally reached: the sentence of exile on Sextus was revoked, 50,000 denarii compensation voted, and the command of the fleet in the western Mediterranean conferred upon him.

The consul went further. Brutus and Cassius had not left Italy, probably because Servilia's efforts to get the corn commission removed from the senate's decree had been successful. Almost certainly in the second half of July, Antony persuaded the senate to grant the two praetors far more generous terms of exile: the governorships of Crete and Cyrene—unimportant provinces, and lacking legions, but not a humiliation. For good measure, the new decree permitted them to appoint extra staff-officers and granted them supernumerary quaestors. In pursuit of this new policy of reconciliation, Antony spoke in such moderate terms to a public meeting held during Octavian's games that when report of it reached Cicero he immediately turned back from the voyage he had already started to make to Greece. Rumours circulated that Antony would give up his Gallic provinces, allow the Liberators to return to Rome, and respect the authority of the senate.

The senate was summoned for August 1. Antony was very soon made aware of the impossibility of his own position. Piso, taking advantage of the consul's changed mood, delivered an attack on his conduct of affairs. Piso was a respected moderate, and his status as Caesar's father-in-law added weight to his words. No one dared to support him, which is curious. A consular of Piso's standing and caution did not take such dramatic action on a private and quixotic impulse. His Epicurean beliefs, Philhellenic tastes, and independent political position suggest a pragmatist, a man likely to know what he was playing for. Is it fanciful to see the influence of Octavian? The young man could hardly have persuaded Piso to join his party, or even to lend him assistance in a piece of political jockeying: Piso had once offered to mediate between Caesar and Pompey. What Octavian may have done is to convince Piso that Antony was a menace, that his true intentions were to dominate the state, and his moves towards a rapprochement were merely deception. If this is so, it marks the beginning of Octavian's policy of using non-Caesarian elements to destroy the Caesarian leader. As to Piso's charges against Antony, we do not know what they were; perhaps little more than a complaint about the irregularity of Antony's mode of government in the past two months. Anything would serve Octavian's purpose, so long as it prevented Antony from effecting a reconciliation with the republicans.

This it did. Antony immediately published a consular edict against Brutus and Cassius. He threatened them with force for resigning their judicial functions and attempting to justify themselves in an earlier edict of their own. He also wrote to them personally, in the same vein, insulting and menacing. Their answer, dated August 4, survives. It is written in a tone of pained surprise. 'We are amazed,' they say, 'that you are so little able to control your animosity that you reproach us with the death of Caesar.' But they hold their freedom dearer than the friendship of Antony, and they conclude with a warning to Antony to beware of his own limitations and to remember, not how long Caesar lived, but how short a time he played the monarch. It was plain that what hopes there had been for a reconciliation were irretrievably shattered. Brutus thought there was nothing to be gained by staying any longer in Italy, made his way south with a few ships along the coast from Naples, and had left Italian waters before the end of the month. Cassius stayed longer, believing that Cicero's forthcoming intervention might alter the position again in their favour.

Chapter IV

THE CRUSADE AGAINST ANTONY

AS BRUTUS went south he met Cicero at Velia, returning with all speed to Rome. He was able to give him news of Piso's speech and congratulate him on his change of heart. He heard how a southerly gale had blown Cicero's ship back to Leucopetra on the toe of Italy, so that he was still there when the news of the political thaw of the last days of July arrived. Abruptly, Cicero had changed his mind about going to Greece. He hated exile from the political arena, and some had said that it was cowardice that was taking him abroad. Here was a chance to vindicate himself and help lead the republic back to better things. He was delighted about Piso's speech. At last someone had said the things he would like to have had the courage to say himself.

Cicero timed his journey back so as to be able to attend the meeting of the senate that Antony had called for September 1. Tired from travelling, and learning that the business was routine, he decided not to appear after all. Antony, who was well aware of Cicero's antipathy to him, took exception to this absence as though it were a slight on himself. He indulged in ill-tempered and injudicious threats that he would send workmen to reduce the orator's house to rubble, and absented himself from the next day's sitting. But Cicero did appear at this. He followed up Piso's attack of a month before with the first of that great series of speeches against Antony which he christened the Philippics in memory of Demosthenes's onslaughts on the enemy of Greek freedom. By comparison with its later fellows, the first Philippic is mild. But the criticism of Antony is biting: the consul had misused Caesar's notes and memoranda, perverted the dictator's laws, ignored a tribunician veto, granted the coveted citizenship wholesale, and squandered the monies in the Temple of Ops. Cicero goes on, in uninhibited republican fashion, to pour scorn on two laws which Antony had promulgated but not yet carried; both were designed to diminish senatorial control of the judicial machinery of the state, which played a very important part in the game of republican politics.

Here was opposition indeed—outspoken, weighty, and damaging. Cicero had taken no effective part in politics since his famous 'palinode' of 56 B.C. But his tongue had lost none of its power and he must have relished saying what he really thought in public for the first time for a dozen years. Antony was furious. Piso's attack and the coolly dignified pronouncements of Brutus and Cassius had been a serious setback to his policy of conciliation. But he had persevered, since there was nothing to be gained from trying to outbid Octavian on his own ground. What he could do was to adhere, more or less, to republican practices: defer to the senate in its traditional areas of competence, make a show of consulting with the leading men, and avoid the open display of armed force. In this way he might prevent Octavian from finding allies, paradoxically, where he ought least have been able to find them—among the ranks of the traditionalists. He would show himself as good a constitutionalist as they. But he could not pretend that the events of May and June had never happened. A politician lives with his past. Nor could he suddenly abandon the interests that supported the Caesarian party. And so Cicero had two fronts on which to attack: Antony's recent unconstitutional behaviour, and his current anti-senatorial measures.

Antony retired to his villa at Tibur, that had once belonged to Pompey's father-in-law, to plan his counter-attack. The position was not good, for Cicero, unlike Piso, had not stood alone. There had followed him P. Servilius Isauricus, whose motives may be deduced: son of a respected and aged father, he had chosen, in 49, to align himself with Caesar, in spite of the fact that his family connections were rather with the party of Pompey and Cato. He was rewarded (or bribed) with the consulship of 48, and had subsequently made a success of governing Asia. From this province he had very recently returned. Married to one of the daughters of Servilia, he was thus related to Brutus, Cassius, and Lepidus. Furthermore, he was senior to Antony as a Caesarian consular and belonged to a more powerful and extended political family. Servilius might accept Antony as a rival, never as a superior. Plainly Servilius hoped to emerge as the leader of a group which might reconcile the interests of Caesarians and others, or at least exploit the advantages of a middle position. The pattern of free politics as it had been known two decades ago was beginning to emerge again.

Antony decided therefore to abandon his constitutional posture and attack his enemies within the senate with all the power he could muster. Neither Piso, nor Cicero, nor Servilius, dared to appear in the senate on September 19 to hear him (as Cicero put it to Cassius) 'not speak, but, as usual, spew up his words'. The senate met, inappropriately enough, in the Temple of Concord, behind closed doors, with Antony's bodyguard much in evidence. Antony set about Cicero to good purpose: in *his* consulate Cicero had packed the approach to the Capitol with armed slaves, put citizens to death without trial, and refused burial to the body of Antony's own step-father; afterwards he had engineered the murder of Clodius, precipitated the civil war by estranging Caesar and Pompey, and crowned his achievements by inciting the Liberators to stab to death their benefactor the great Caesar.

Cicero felt himself to be in physical danger. He wrote to Plancus in Further Gaul, protesting his concern for Plancus's interests but excusing his inactivity: 'no one of liberal opinions can be safe in the senate where intimidation by the sword is quite condoned; nor is it consistent with my public esteem to give my counsel there, where it is not senators who are best placed to hear me, but men with weapons in their hands.' He withdrew to his study to write philosophy and compose the 'divine Philippic', the famous Second, which was his answer to Antony's speech of September 19. It was never delivered, nor intended to be, but was circulated as a political pamphlet under the form of a speech. Cicero did not dare to publish it until in his view the free constitution had been restored. This was synonymous with the removal, or withdrawal, of Antony from metropolitan politics, and meant that it did not see the light until, at the earliest, the end of November. For all practical purposes, Cicero had withdrawn from the fray.

Meanwhile relations between Antony and Octavian had been deteriorating fast. In pursuit of his Caesarian claims Antony had set up in the Forum on the speakers' platform a statue of Caesar with the inscription TO A MOST WORTHY PARENT. The wording referred to the title 'Parent of his country' conferred on Caesar by the senate in the previous year. It was obviously an attempt to neutralize Octavian's propaganda which must have relied heavily on his adoptive paternity. On October 2 one of the tribunes, T. Cannutius, no friend of Antony, brought the consul before a public meeting. His questions to Antony were sharp and malevolent, and elicited a tirade against the Liberators which ended by accusing Cicero of being responsible both for their actions and those of Cannutius. A little while before, some of the centurions, the professional officers of the army, had come to Antony to protest about the growing coolness between him and Octavian and the folly of a breach between two men who both professed to be upholding the memory and policies of Caesar. Antony allowed himself to be persuaded and a reconciliation of sorts was staged before the Capitoline Temple in front of the soldiery. Neither man had his heart in it, however, and a day or two after Cannutius's meeting a major scandal broke. Some members of Antony's bodyguard were arrested in his house. Under questioning they confessed that Octavian had suborned them to assassinate Antony. Octavian indignantly denied the charge, claiming that the whole affair had been elaborately staged to incriminate him, and that Antony dead was far less protection to him against his father's murderers than Antony alive. He hurried unarmed to the consul's house, made a great show of anger, appealed even to his political enemies. The people thought that Antony had concocted the plot, but the better and more intelligent citizens, according to Cicero, were able to persuade themselves of Octavian's guilt. True or false, it was an evil omen, and when Antony set out on October 9 for Brundisium to meet the legions which he had summoned some time ago from Macedonia, the danger of civil war, or at least the armed suppression of civil liberties, seemed very near.

Antony stood in need of legions, not so much to overawe the opposition in Rome as to safeguard himself against the Liberators. D. Brutus had found only two legions in Cisalpine Gaul in April. He had since raised more and blooded them in a campaign against the Alpine tribes. In the east, all was uncertain, though for the moment there was no apparent threat. Trebonius in Asia was too distant to cause concern, and had few troops. M. Brutus was staying quietly in Athens. Cassius was en route for Cyrenaica, or so it was believed. It was the west which was most in Antony's mind: Lepidus in Provence was not entirely trustworthy, and Plancus in Further Gaul still less so. Even Pollio in Spain, though by personal loyalty a Caesarian, had an honesty and an independence of mind that might take him in what Antony considered the wrong direction. A determined seizure of Cisalpine Gaul, his legal province, with four of the choice legions that Caesar had mustered in Macedonia, would hearten Lepidus and Plancus, provide a military concentration in the Gallic provinces that could not be matched elsewhere, and completely dominate Italy.

It may be that when Antony set out for Brundisium, he did not intend to move into his province until the new year, when Decimus's term would be near expiry. In the meantime, it would do no harm to have his legions ready at hand near the capital. But whatever his intentions may have been, his actions seemed to speak all too clearly. Cicero, writing to his friend Cornificius, governor of Africa, a day or two later, says simply: 'On October 9 he left for Brundisium to meet the Macedonian legions, which he intended to win over by cash bounties and bring to Rome to subjugate us.' The parallel with Sulla in 88 was too close to be comfortable: a consul, threatened by his enemies in Rome, appealing to the legions to defend what were essentially his private interests. Certainly Octavian thought so. He countered by sending agents to distribute money among the soldiers in camp at Brundisium and tamper with their loyalty to their lawful commander. But he could hardly expect to corrupt the whole of the consul's very considerable army. If even one legion stayed faithful to its oath, that was four or five thousand men. He decided to meet force with force. He could at least find enough volunteers among the discharged settlers to make sure that Antony could not squash him like a mosquito on the wall. He would show the people of Rome, and of Italy, that he was in earnest as Caesar's champion, and theirs. He had made Antony so unpopular in Rome that even a small and militarily insignificant force might call forth a massive demonstration of popular support and convince the consul of the folly of trying to suppress him by force.

Octavian had acquired, or borrowed, large sums of money in the previous six months. What the source of them was can only be guessed. The enemies of Antony, then and later, drew a vivid picture of the debauched and unscrupulous consul squandering for his own corrupt and selfish purposes the seven hundred million sesterces which had been in the Temple of Ops at the dictator's death, and denying to Caesar's heir his legitimate inheritance. All Octavian's assets, so Appian informs us, together with the fortunes of his mother and his stepfather, went to pay Caesar's legacies to the people. Cicero is a more reliable witness. Giving Cornificius the news of the plot to kill Antony, he says that the public thought that Antony invented it so as to have a reason for getting at Octavian's funds—and this was after Octavian had paid the legacies. It is not impossible that Antony did in fact pay Octavian something out of the state reserves. The property the young man sold undoubtedly realized a useful sum. But the strength of his financial position, as shown by subsequent events, reflects the resources he could draw upon. Apart from the personal wealth of non-senators like Oppius, who had helped put up the money for the games, and the millionaire

Balbus, who had been the first Caesarian of importance to meet him in April, there were amongst Caesar's freedmen many who must have prospered and become rich enough to contribute to their new patron's fund. His co-heirs Q. Pedius and L. Pinarius, also nephews or great-nephews of Caesar, are said to have waived their claims on the estate in favour of their young kinsman. There may be some truth in this, at any rate in the case of Pedius: this obscure man was later appointed to the consulship.

Certainly Octavian was not short of cash, or his next move would have been impossible. He set out on a tour of the veteran colonies of Campania, determined on the flagrantly illegal course of raising a private army. He was accompanied by five intimate friends, amongst them Agrippa and a certain Maecenas, and followed by a train of carts containing money and equipment. He was lavish with his promises, and more to the point, with his money. By the end of the month he had raised 3,000 men from the district round Capua (where the newly founded colonies of Calatia and Casilinum consisted of Caesar's old Seventh and Eighth legions), and proposed to go inland into Samnium in search of more volunteers. His money was very tempting. He paid 500 denarii on the spot—more than two years' ordinary pay—and promised 2,000 in the event of success in the forthcoming struggle.

Meanwhile things had not been going well for Antony. At Suessa Aurunca, en route for Brundisium, he put to death some soldiers who were being held under arrest—probably the men accused of planning to assassinate him. This episode cannot have enhanced the consul's public image, and when he arrived at Brundisium to find the legions restive he was angry. Octavian's agents had done their work well. The soldiers demanded to know why Antony had let Caesar's murderers get away scot-free. They shouted him down when he tried to win them round, and refused to accept a bounty of 100 denarii a head. No doubt Octavian's agents had let it be known what *his* rates were. Antony refused to be drawn into an auction, proclaiming principle rather than admitting lack of means. Instead, he gambled on restoring discipline by a dose of traditional severity. He ordered the officers to supply the names of the most turbulent, and put to death a proportion selected by lot. He did not dare to provoke a full-scale mutiny by applying the full rigour of decimation. Even so, he was only partly successful. Order was restored, but at the price of anger and resentment. Then came the news of Octavian's activities and the lavish scale of his bounties in

Campania. Antony countered by repeating his former offer, and dismissing some of the officers. Plainly, to delay in camp under these circumstances was to invite more trouble. Even though the last of the four legions from Macedonia was still on its way across the Adriatic, Antony decided not to wait for it. Action and a sense of purpose was what his men needed. He sent the three legions that had arrived directly north along the coast, with orders to wait for him at Ariminum near the borders of the Cisalpine province. He himself took the legion called the *Larks*, which he had re-formed from its discharged veterans, and started off with Caesarian speed for Rome, pausing only to exact financial contributions from the unfortunate towns along the way.

Antony left Brundisium before the end of October, for Octavian knew of his march on November 2 or 3. Apart from raising his own forces, the young man laid siege to Cicero—who was at Puteoli—in earnest. He wrote to him from Capua on November 1, requesting a secret interview somewhere near by. It was childish, in Cicero's view, to expect that it could remain secret, and he would have nothing to do with it. But Octavian was persistent. He sent a personal friend, Caecina of Volaterrae, with the news that Antony was coming, marching his legion under colours. He asked Cicero's advice as to whether he should try to block Antony's route at Capua, or take his 3,000 veterans to Rome, or go and join the three legions marching north along the Adriatic coast in the hope that they would defect to him. It was an agonizing decision for him to take. The more conventionally military the struggle became, the more the advantage swung back to the experienced Antony. Cicero advised him to make for Rome, because of his support there, and Octavian concurred. But if he were to occupy Rome he must keep up some sort of constitutional façade. He could only offset his military inferiority by political superiority. He bombarded Cicero with letters, sometimes two in a day, begging him to do his bit, save the republic a second time (a reference to Cicero's finest hour, when he suppressed the conspiracy of Catiline), and anyway return to Rome at once. He sent no less an emissary than Oppius to profess his concern for the welfare of the tyrannicides. Cicero mistrusted the youth and his intentions, and played for time, though he gave Octavian a better chance of success than did some of his contemporaries. He was sceptical of the lad's hopes of having a meeting of the senate called. And if he did, who would come? But there was no doubt of his popularity in the towns of Italy. There were tremendous demonstrations of enthusiasm

when he passed through Cales and Teanum—so much so that
Cicero was induced to change his mind and start for Rome, instead
of staying prudently out of the way. His longing to participate in the
imminent confrontation was getting the better of his caution, and he
was beginning to convince himself that Octavian was not beyond
redemption.

That Octavian should seek Cicero as an ally is not surprising. He
was driven on by ambition. Nothing less than a position equal to his
adoptive father's would content him, and to attain it he sought help
where he could, untroubled by conscience or principle. Cicero,
admittedly, rejoiced over the Ides of March (even if he complained
that the job had been left unfinished). That need not be an obstacle.
The shifting coalitions of Roman politics, dictated by expediency
and personal obligation, looked to the future not to the past. They
had no long-term aims. They were formed to capture momentary
advantage for their members, not to change the nature of the state or
its government or implement great programmes of social and
economic reform. Caesar's skeleton could remain firmly in its cup-
board. The fact was that each of them could give the other what he
wanted. Cicero had spoken out against Antony but, for all his
eloquence and reputation, was but a head without a body. Octavian,
on the other hand, had the backing of thousands of veterans and
tens of thousands of humble citizens, but this potentially formidable
political strength was wasted without a champion in the inner circles
of government—at any rate so long as the forms of the republic
lasted. No doubt he could count on the loyalty of a fair number of
lowly and insignificant senators, Caesar's appointees, men without
influence or authority. But he needed more, and in Cicero he might
obtain it: devastating eloquence, tireless pleading, the purest
republican sentiments, all issuing from the lips of a senior consular
who had ever put the interests of the state above his own. Cicero's
proclaimed beliefs were certainly irreconcilable with Octavian's
aims; but for the moment the two men had a common enemy, and in
a world where personalities counted for more than programmes, that
was the important thing.

It is more surprising that Cicero should have been willing to
contemplate alliance with Octavian, but he had always longed to be
the mentor of the powerful. In earlier days he had flattered himself
that he had Pompey's ear. He made a point of being friendly and
agreeable to all, even to Caesar. Now, perhaps, his chance had come
at last. Octavian was little more than a boy, shrewd certainly, and

fortunate in a great name, but lacking powerful allies and political experience. It was not beyond all possibility that—in the right hands —he might become a good citizen. What he needed was good advice, republican connections, and a modicum of public recognition. Even so, his heritage was dangerous, and Cicero waited for a decisive turn of events before deciding to support him. On November 12 he wrote to Atticus in Rome, from his house at his native Arpinum: '. . . I agree with your advice to go one step at a time—though I had thought otherwise. Nor am I swayed by what Philippus and Marcellus do. Their position is different; and if it isn't, it still looks as though it is. But although that young man's got plenty of spirit, he carries too little weight. . . .' This Marcellus was C. Claudius Marcellus, husband of Octavian's sister Octavia, and therefore bound to him as closely as was Philippus. As consul in the crisis of 50, he had placed a drawn sword in the hand of Pompey, but had soon discerned the better cause and, like Philippus, stayed neutral in the war. Cicero had curtly dismissed them little more than a month before. Briefing Cassius on the parlous state of the republic, he mentioned (apart from Servilius, Piso, and himself) only three consulars who were worth considering: L. Cotta, hopelessly despondent; L. Julius Caesar, sick; and Ser. Sulpicius, out of Rome; Cassius must pardon him if he does not count the others as consulars. The open adherence of Marcellus and Philippus to Octavian was to be expected, and shed little lustre on his cause. It was certainly not a reason for Cicero to do likewise.

Cicero's doubts about Octavian's real intentions were not allayed by further news from Rome. Octavian arrived there at the head of his veterans about November 10, and camped at the Temple of Mars some two miles outside the city. Cannutius the tribune again obliged by calling, as was his right, a public meeting and producing Octavian to speak. The new Caesar's speech was inflammatory. He swore by his hopes of rising to his father's honours, and stretched out his right hand to his father's statue—there were two on the Rostra, depicting Caesar as saviour of Rome. He defended himself, brought charges against Antony, and praised the men who had chosen of their own free will to help him protect the city. His one firm hope lay in making Antony so unpopular in Rome that it would be impossible for him to hold the city in the face of a hostile populace. Otherwise, he depended on desertion and disloyalty amongst Antony's troops.

But the plan misfired. Octavian had not been quite honest with the veterans. They had understood that he was mobilizing them to defend Caesar's acts against the tyrannicides. Antony they knew to be a loyal Caesarian and a fine officer who could fight and drink and take his pleasures with the best of them, and they had presumed that he and Octavian had essentially the same aims. The revelation that it was Antony, the consul, who was the enemy, was unpleasant. Things were indeed not what they seemed to be. The least intelligent of them must have realized that Octavian, in pitting himself against the consul, had not a shadow of legality on his side. He was a revolutionary, without office or authority. However, their respect for Caesar's heir prevented any wholesale or dramatic reversal of loyalties. 'Some of them,' said Appian, 'asked if they could return to their homes to get their weapons and equipment, since they could not manage with those that were not their own; others hinted at the truth. Caesar was at a loss, as things had turned out not at all as he had expected, but hoping to prevail upon them by persuasion rather than by force, he accepted their excuses and sent some to get their weapons and others simply to their homes. He concealed his disappointment, praised the gathering, gave them further bounties, and promised to reward them on a still more generous scale—always treating them, not as soldiers, but as his father's friends for emergencies. By saying this he got only one thousand, or according to others three thousand, to stay with him out of the ten thousand.'

All hope of resisting Antony gone for the moment, Octavian withdrew with his supporters and the rump of his private army to Arretium. Etruria had yielded a fine crop of discontented settlers, runaway slaves, brigands, and debtors twenty years before when Catiline had raised revolt against the established order. There was a good chance that it might do so again: the lot of the peasantry of Italy had scarcely been improved since 63 by the insane political strife that had finally erupted into civil war, and by the subsequent confiscations, sales, and foundations of new veteran colonies, which all disrupted the economic patterns of the life of the countryside.

A few days later, Antony arrived in Rome with his *Larks*, happy at last in the knowledge that he had a clear-cut situation to handle. No sophistries could conceal the fact that Octavian had flagrantly and audaciously flouted the law of the state. He was in open rebellion, in pursuit of nothing but the enhancement of his own status. Antony called a meeting of the senate for November 24, confident that even his enemies could scarcely refuse to condemn Octavian and give him authority to suppress this second Catiline. His consular edicts declared that he would consider any senator who did not attend as a traitor to him and to Rome, and hurled the familiar accusations of political invective against his youthful opponent: unnatural vice, country-town origins, and forebears who were manual workers.

But once again the intervention of the soldiery transformed everything. Eight months after Caesar's murder, it seemed to be all over with his heir, who had played high and lost. He was reprieved by desertions. The news that the Martian legion had declared for Octavian and had turned west to meet him reached Antony on the 24th. He immediately postponed the meeting of the senate and hurried to confront the deserters at Alba Fucens. They greeted him with a hail of missiles from the walls and refused to negotiate. Hastily he took measures to prevent matters worsening. To the remaining legions he sent an additional bounty of 500 denarii, and himself made all speed to cover the fifty miles back to Rome. He was there by the 28th, and summoned the senate to meet the same evening. The unheard-of hour betrayed his urgency. He did not risk waiting even until the next morning. Perhaps he had already heard advance rumours of the blow that was to fall. It was plainly his intention to declare Octavian an enemy of the state, and he barred from the meeting three tribunes who might have dared to veto such a motion: Cannutius, D. Carfulenus, and L. Cassius, the brother of the Liberator (so much for family loyalties in this complex political situation!). The meeting was well attended, though Cicero, perhaps because he was already compromised, did not appear. A consular was ready with a prepared motion condemning Octavian, but the matter was never raised. At the opening of the sitting Antony heard that another legion, the Fourth, had deserted him for Octavian.

He decided not to stay any longer in Rome. It would be folly under the circumstances to attempt to see the year out as consul in the capital. Since Dolabella had set out for Syria a month previously, Antony would be bound to take the field in person against Octavian. Because of the desertions the rival armies were nearly equal in strength. He would need every soldier he could muster. In his absence, the agents of Octavian could again swing the city against him and persuade an uncertain and disunited senate to withdraw their support from him. Far better to avoid armed conflict with Octavian and certain unpopularity with the common people. Cisalpine Gaul was the fortress he had prepared for himself by the legislation of June. He would go to his province immediately, order D. Brutus to hand over to him, and await events. He would then have five veteran legions—three of his own and two belonging to Decimus—plus Decimus's recruits: a substantial enough army to deter any attack. The legal basis for such action was incontestable, and from this position of strength he could surely undermine his opponent who had put himself so clearly in the wrong. As to Decimus, he should be willing enough to hand over to his constitutional superior and help Antony eradicate the presumptuous heir of the hated dictator.

Antony therefore hastily pushed through some very necessary business, the allotment of provinces for the next year to those who were currently praetors. Strangely, the operation of the lot favoured the consul's staunchest supporters. His brother Gaius (whom Cicero said was 'between his brothers in age, but a rival of both in wickedness') obtained Macedonia, and C. Calvisius Sabinus, one of the two men who had attempted to defend Caesar on the Ides, happened to draw Africa, a province he had already governed for the dictator and where he had excellent connections. The consul also took a vote on a thanksgiving to be decreed for Lepidus. This kind of honour was normally innocuous routine, but Antony found it important enough to bring up at this critical moment. It was vital to ensure that Lepidus remained on his side, for if the governor of Provence and Nearer Spain, with his powerful forces, abandoned him, his plan of retiring to Cisalpine Gaul was gravely harmed. He must show Lepidus that even in the hour of crisis he was mindful of his friend's glory and public acclaim. Lepidus was a man who liked the outward show of power.

Business concluded, Antony left for Tibur, cloaked as for war. There he rejoined the bulk of his own forces and made his final preparations for going north. He enrolled a number of veterans who had come in to join him, and administered the customary oath of loyalty to himself as commander, not only to them, but also to the *Larks*. While he was thus occupied, a great body of senators, wealthy commoners, and less influential but still solid citizens made the journey out from Rome to assure him of their support. Appian says they went so far as to take the same oath as the soldiers. The propertied classes were rallying to the defence of the existing order. They feared the revolutionary adventurer who appealed to a magic name and to the hopelessness and misery of the urban proletariat. The last thing they wanted was a civil war. Antony's expedient of avoiding immediate conflict and withdrawing to a position of safety where he had Italy under lock and key until Octavian's folly and presumption reaped their own reward seemed to them a satisfactory solution of the crisis. They wished to make it plain to the consul that he could count upon men of substance and importance in the coming months. 'And so,' says Appian, 'he got a splendid send-off for Ariminum.'

Chapter V

WAR IN THE NORTH

UNFORTUNATELY FOR Antony, Decimus Brutus did not share his appreciation of the situation. Letters do not survive, but it is certain that he kept in constant touch with Marcus Brutus and Cassius—at any rate up to the time of Cassius's departure from Italy about the end of September. Throughout the summer and early autumn they had no doubt whom they had to fear. Even after the alleged attempt on Antony's life and his hasty departure for Brundisium in the first days of October, the ill-feeling between the Caesarian rivals cannot have seemed a matter of any great importance. If it came to open conflict, the consul would have the senate and the army behind him, and the views of the urban mob would be irrelevant. What the murderers had to fear was the erosion of their positions of power, of which Decimus's governorship was the chief; then political annihilation; finally abrogation of the amnesty of March 17, condemnation in the courts, and exile or death. It was not for this that they had slain Caesar. So Decimus soon busied himself with entirely legal but hardly disinterested activity. He raised several legions of new recruits from amongst the tough and newly enfranchised natives of the region beyond the Po, trained them, and blooded them in battle towards the end of the summer against the Alpine tribes, 'not so much,' he says to Cicero, 'desiring to win the victorious general's salutation of *Imperator* as wishing to give some satisfaction to the soldiers and ensure their loyalty to our cause; which I think I succeeded in doing; for I gave them a taste of both my generosity and my determination'.

This of course was long after the legislation of June 2 by which Cisalpine Gaul became Antony's province. Whether Decimus intended right from the beginning to refuse to hand over his command to Antony, or whether he raised his new forces as an insurance in case some sort of armed struggle should break out for other reasons or in other places, is quite unknown. The only certain fact about his intentions is that before Antony's return to Rome in November

Decimus was in touch with sympathizers in the capital, among them the consul-designate Pansa and Cicero. Cicero approved of his sentiments, but the guarded phraseology of a correspondence liable to interception cloaked the full extent of his determination. At any rate Cicero thought it necessary to write to him on December 9 as though he might give in: 'If that creature gets control of your province . . . I see no hope of salvation left. Wherefore I pray and beseech you, as do the senate and people of Rome, that you may liberate the state for ever from slavery to a monarch, that your actions may end as they began.'

Decimus stood in no need of these exhortations. Even before this letter came, he had been ordered by Antony to hand over the province, and refused. A copy of his edict affirming his intentions reached Rome just before a meeting of the senate called for December 20 by the new tribunes of the people. These officials had entered office on December 10, in accordance with the elections held before Caesar's death. This had given Cicero and others, who saw in Octavian a useful ally but were unsure of his good faith, a chance to test his protestations of good-will—or at least absence of ill-will—towards his father's murderers. One of the tribunes-designate was Casca, and it would have been a simple matter for Octavian to whip up such a pitch of feeling against him that he could not enter office. He did not do so. He was playing for bigger fish than Casca. It suited him for the moment to pose as one who would never let personal vindictiveness triumph over the true interests of the state. What he understood to be the true interests of the state would become clear in time. Meanwhile he was happy to let Cicero leap to his defence against the slanders of Antony with the Third Philippic, delivered at this meeting of the senate. The business before the house was nominally non-committal: measures to ensure the safety of members at the debate the new consuls Hirtius and Pansa would hold as soon as they entered office on January 1. But by the senate's rules of procedure it was in order for a speaker to bring up any topic he liked before giving his answer to the formal question. Cicero had not intended to be present, but changed his mind when he heard about Decimus's edict, and quite justifiably used the occasion for a major political speech. He threw all his considerable powers of persuasion behind the illegal cause, praising Decimus for refusing to hand over his province and his army, Octavian for protecting the state from the gravest perils, and the legions for defending the authority of the senate and the liberty of the Roman people—not that either quality had been much in evidence at the time of the legions' mutiny. He stopped short of a formal proposal that Antony be declared a public enemy, contenting himself with the observation that his actions proved him to be one; and he invited Plancus in Further Gaul and all other provincial governors to follow Decimus's example and not surrender their commands until the senate had made a fresh allotment of the provinces so hastily distributed by Antony at the night sitting of November 28.

There can have been little accurate information available in Rome about the situation in the north when Cicero spoke. He alleged that Antony was leading 'the shreds of an army . . . one legion, and that of doubtful loyalty' and waiting for his brother Lucius to bring up reinforcements. In fact things were far otherwise. There were no more defections, and thus no reason to believe that Antony did not lead the *Larks* and the newly enrolled veterans to a successful meeting with the other two legions, the Second and the Thirty-fifth, at Ariminum. As for Lucius, he may well have laid down his tribunate before December 10 in order to recruit a few more veterans for his brother, a job for which he had unimpeachable qualifications, having been chairman of a special board appointed earlier in the year to distribute public land to veterans and needy citizens. But it was optimistic of Cicero to suppose that these extra troops were of any great moment to Antony. The province as a whole was sympathetic to the consul—or recognized *force majeure* when it saw it. Town after town opened its gates to Antony, who shrewdly did not proceed directly against Decimus. Decimus for his part withdrew with his army southwards through the province until he came to Mutina (the modern Modena). There he decided to make a stand, and force Antony to besiege him. His plan was to prepare for a long siege and give his friends in Rome time to swing the senate against his opponent and mobilize the forces of the state for his relief. To stand and fight was risky, for he was outnumbered in veteran troops, and they were the only sort that counted in a serious battle. Flight was the third course open to him, and that, as yet, was unthinkable. For the moment, he must play for time and conserve his forces while the senate decided which of them to outlaw—for one they surely must, once Antony actually engaged in hostilities against him.

Meanwhile, in Rome, the new consuls entered office: Aulus Hirtius and Gaius Vibius Pansa. Caesarians both, Cicero had been alternately hopeful and suspicious of them in the past nine months. Like himself, they were men from country towns of Italy, lacking

senatorial ancestry and noble connections, who had won the highest
office by personal ability. Pansa had entered politics before the civil
war, as one of the tribunes for 51, Hirtius only under the dictatorship. How they would behave in the present crisis was quite uncertain. Pansa was son-in-law to one of Caesar's generals, Q. Fufius
Calenus, a consular of Antonian sympathies and not at a loss for
words to defend them; but that did not mean that Pansa shared his
views. Hirtius was innocent of any such ties.

They called the senate at once. Pansa presided. To the surprise of
all, he asked Calenus, who as a consular was very junior, to speak
first. Calenus urged moderation and proposed that an embassy be
sent to negotiate with Antony. This is remarkable. On constitutional
grounds Antony's position was unshakeable. His command had been
conferred on him by the sovereign vote of the people, and had not
been abrogated or declared invalid for technical reasons. On the
other hand, neither Decimus nor Octavian had any excuse in law for
defying the consul's authority. It is obvious what it was that inhibited
Calenus from launching a full-scale attack on the rebels: the army
of Octavian and the sympathies of the urban plebs. After Antony's
flight—as his opponents represented it—from Rome, Octavian had
marched his veterans to Alba to join the legions which had deserted.
He sent messages to the senate, assuring it of his loyalty and good-
will, and proceeded to build up his strength by further recruiting.
By January 1 he had five legions in all, some archers, and the
cavalry and elephants of Antony that he had cut out on their march
northward and persuaded to join him. With this considerable force
Octavian had started to move in the direction of Cisalpine Gaul,
confident that the senate would have to acknowledge the logic of
necessity.

Hence the reasonableness of Calenus, and on the other side the
confidence and the withering broadsides of Cicero. At the meeting of
December 20 Cicero had publicly committed himself to a policy
which he had already been privately pursuing—and not only in his
contacts with Octavian. He had written to Plancus in Further Gaul,
to Q. Cornificius in Africa, and to C. Asinius Pollio in Spain, as well
as to Decimus himself, offering discreet encouragement and unex-
ceptionable sentiments, nothing so crude or dangerous as open
exhortation to resist the consul. The success of his policy depended
on the loyalty of the provincial governors and their armies. He had to
convince them that they should obey the wishes of the senate, even if
those wishes lacked strict legal force. As he put it to Decimus: 'The

feeling of the senate ought to be considered sufficient authorization, when authorization proper is prevented by fear.' Now that the new year had come, and with it consuls, the senate was again an effective constitutional organ. Cicero was bound to press for a policy of no compromise, and obtain the approval of his fellow-senators for the course that he was already following. The Fifth Philippic is a powerful speech. Cicero praises Decimus Brutus, Octavian, and the legions for their treasonable actions; attacks Antony bitterly and proposes that he be declared an enemy of the state; makes a bid for the support of Lepidus, asking the senate to erect a gilded equestrian statue of him and vote him a triumph; and moves that Octavian be legitimized in his *de facto* command, and admitted to the senate with the right of speaking from the praetorian benches and of standing for the senior magistracies twelve years before the minimum age prescribed by the law. Cicero did not hesitate to compare the young man so providentially sent to save the state from the tyrannical designs of Antony with Alexander the Great and with Scipio Africanus, the conqueror of Hannibal. Finally, he moved that the troops of Octavian, both the re-enlisted veterans and the serving soldiers who had deserted Antony, should be rewarded in suitable fashion with money, exemptions from service, and grants of land. Thus the state was to take over from Octavian the responsibility for paying the soldiers the price of their sedition. Whether their loyalties could be so easily transferred remained to be seen.

Cicero's view seemed likely to prevail, but Pansa was unwilling to take a vote and let the debate go on into the third day. Piso pointed out that it was not the custom to condemn a man unheard, nor decent that one who was consul yesterday should be an outlaw today, but finally the tribune Salvius interposed his veto on the proceedings. A Ciceronian claque outside the senate-house tried to whip up public feeling against Salvius and invited him into the forum to defend his actions. This he was fully prepared to do—in the hope of putting the Antonian case forcibly to the people and influencing the course of the senate's deliberations when they were resumed. His opponents took fright and a compromise was arranged. Debate on the question of Antony and the envoys that one party wished sent to him was put off until the next day, and a vote was taken simply on the various honours to be conferred. Certain additions and modifications were made to Cicero's proposals. Philippus proposed a gilt statue to Octavian; Servilius that he be allowed to stand for the consulship ten years early; the author of the motion that he be called to speak in the

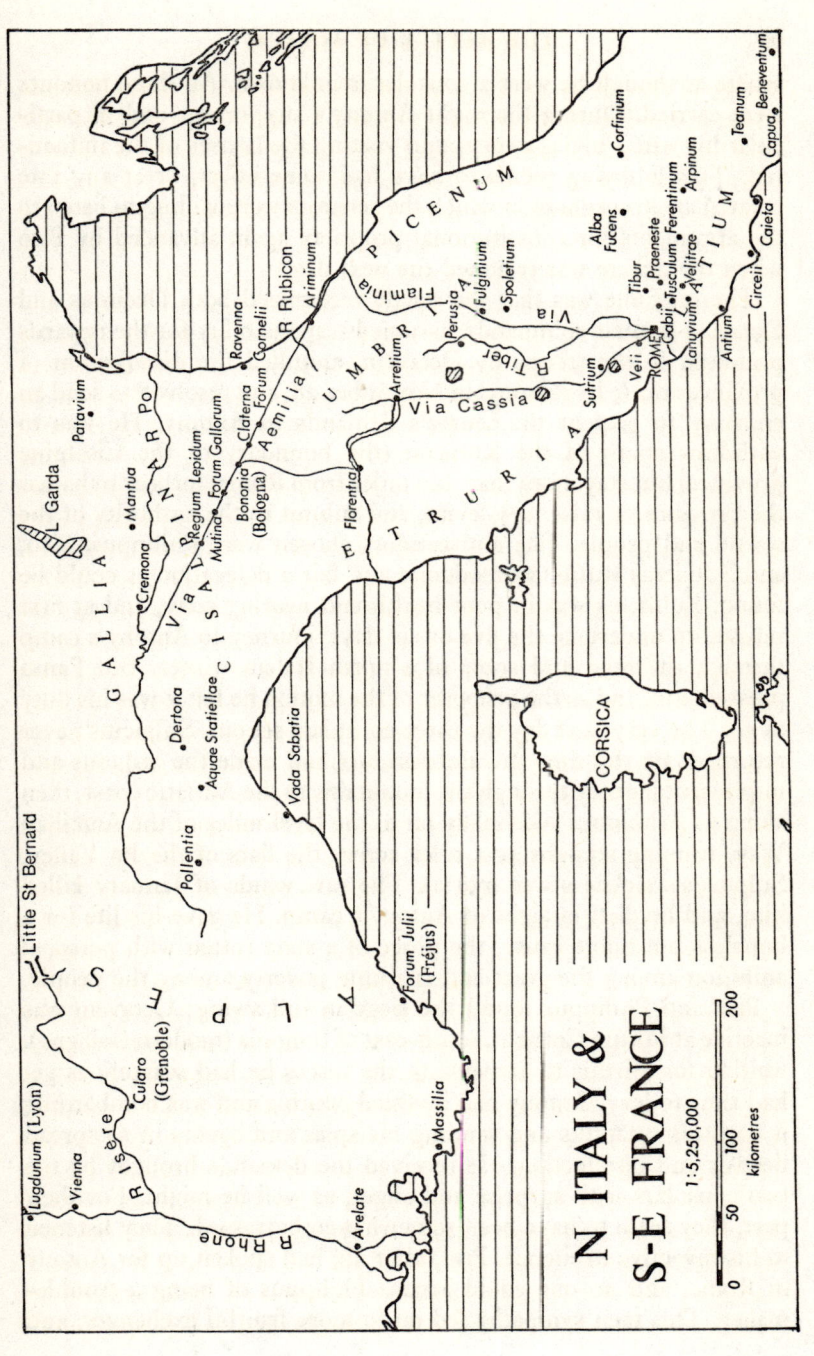

N ITALY &
S-E FRANCE

1:5,250,000

0 50   100   200
kilometres

Beneventum
Capua
Teanum
Caieta
Corfinium
Circeii
Alba
Fucens
Ferentinum
Arpinum
Tibur
Praeneste
Antium
Tusculum
Gabii
Lanuvium
Velitrae
Fulginium
Spoletum
ROME
Perusia
Veii
Sutrium
Via Flaminia
Via Cassia
R Tiber
Arretium
PICENUM
Ariminum
R Rubicon
Ravenna
Forum Cornelii
Florentia
Aemilia
Bononia
(Bologna)
Mutina
Forum Gallorum
Regium Lepidum
Claterna
ETRURIA
UMBRIA
LATIUM
CORSICA
R Po
Via
Cremona
Mantua
Patavium
L Garda
GALLIA
CISALPINA
Via Aemilia
Dertona
Aquae Statiellae
Vada Sabatia
Pollentia
Forum Julii
(Fréjus)
ALPES
Little St Bernard
Lugdunum (Lyon)
Vienna
Cularo
(Grenoble)
R Isère
Massilia
Arelate
R Rhone

senate as though he were a consular is unknown. All these honours were carried. During the night Antony's supporters, and in particular his wife Fulvia, went round visiting the houses of the influential. This lobbying seems to have had some effect, or at any rate created an atmosphere in which the senators were willing to listen to the arguments for constitutional propriety again advanced by Piso when the debate was resumed the next day.

The outcome was that the senate recognized both Decimus and Octavian in their commands, assumed responsibility for the rewards promised to the troops by Octavian, annulled the distribution of provinces made by Antony on November 28, and resolved to send an embassy to present the senate's demands to Antony. He was to withdraw south of the Rubicon (the boundary of the Cisalpine province) but stay more than 200 miles from Rome, forbear to harass the province or raise new levies, and submit to the authority of the senate and people. The ambassadors chosen were Philippus, Piso, and Sulpicius Rufus: as moderate and fair a delegation as could be found. Sulpicius was in poor health and nearing sixty, and at first refused to undertake the five or six days' journey to Antony's camp through the mud and snow of a north Italian winter. But Pansa pressed him, and as the proposer of the motion he felt it was his duty to go. The very next day the three consulars set out. Sulpicius never returned. By the time the ambassadors had made the arduous and unpleasant journey through the mountains to the Adriatic coast, then along to Ariminum and finally on to the level miles of the Aemilian Way, running straight as a ruler across the flats of the Po Valley, Sulpicius's sickness was mortal. The raw winds of January killed him, and he died in sight of Antony's camp. He gave his life for a hopeless but noble cause, the peace of a state rotten with personal ambition among the great and crushing poverty among the people.

Piso and Philippus found the siege in full swing; Octavian was inactive at Forum Cornelii, south-east of Bononia (modern Bologna), waiting for Hirtius to arrive with the forces he had scarcely as yet had time to levy. Antony had invested Mutina and was bombarding it with his catapults and sending his spies and agents in to spread despair and disaffection. He received the demands brought by the two consulars with surprise and anger, as well he might. For their part, they seem to have been somewhat embarrassed. They listened to his invective in silence. Piso, after all, had spoken up for Antony in Rome, and no one could accuse Philippus of being a trouble-maker. This tacit sympathy led on to more fruitful exchanges, and the three men were able to discuss in some detail Antony's terms for laying down his command. But for the moment Antony was giving nothing away. He refused to let the envoys deliver any message to Decimus, nor did he relax his siege operations for an instant. Hirtius would soon be on hand to take the offensive against him when the weather and the deliberations of the senate permitted. He must defeat Decimus before he was engaged on another front.

Piso and Philippus, returning to Rome, communicated the news of the death of their colleague and the terms proposed by Antony to a meeting of the senate held on February 2. Antony, they said, was willing to abandon his province, but only if he were given Further Gaul, with six legions, for five years. This period of time, as he stated, was to allow for M. Brutus and Cassius to hold their consulships and proconsulships, and lay these down, before he found himself without the protection of an army and the legal right to command it. Of Octavian, no word. But Antony would cease to be Octavian's enemy if the senate agreed to his terms. It was as consul, not as Antony, that he had opposed the young man's seditious ambitions. Let him turn, if he wished, against the new representatives of constitutional authority, and against his father's murderers. More significant is Antony's acknowledgement of Brutus's and Cassius's claims to the consulships of 41. Antony, evidently, was still prepared to observe the spirit of the amnesty of March 17. The news cannot yet have reached him that they had both taken the law into their own hands and were preparing in the east for an armed struggle—unless rumours to this effect were about and Antony wanted to show that he was ready to come to an understanding in order to avoid war. Antony's second main condition for withdrawing was that all the legislation of his consulship should be confirmed. This was very important if he was to retain the gratitude of the veterans whose land-holdings depended on his enactments.

Cicero was full of righteous fury when he heard these terms. The envoys had had no authority to enter into negotiations or bring back such outrageous demands. He wanted to declare a state of war and pronounce Antony a public enemy, but once again more temperate views prevailed. On the motion of Antony's uncle L. Julius Caesar, a good republican, the senate decreed that the situation be declared a 'state of emergency' not a 'war'. Thus there was no need to proclaim Antony an enemy. It further passed the so-called 'final decree' exhorting the consuls to 'see to it that the state took no harm'—innocuous words, conferring no extraordinary powers, but only employed in times of grave emergency; their moral force was considerable. The senate, then, had rejected Antony's requests, but further negotiation was not completely ruled out. Antony had sent back to Rome, at the same time as Philippus and Piso, a senator, L. Varius Cotyla, who took notes in the debate. Cicero wished to prevent him from returning to Mutina, but was overruled. Cicero was not finding it easy to drag the state into the war he so much desired.

Then came news which heartened the extremists. First, a despatch from Hirtius. He had captured Claterna, on the Aemilian Way, from Antony's most advanced troops. However, the weather was not yet right for any sort of extended operation, and for the moment he and Octavian preferred to remain quiet. And not only for military reasons. Both men had more to gain from a compromise than from a conflict with Antony. The second piece of news was an official letter from M. Brutus to the consuls. The contents were sensational: Brutus, spending the earlier part of the winter quietly in Athens, had gained the support of many young Romans who were pursuing their studies there, and of men of more importance, notably Q. Hortensius Hortalus, the governor of Macedonia and a relative of his. He acquired funds and cavalry, treasonably handed over to him by junior magistrates and subordinate officers. Early in January Gaius Antonius, the consul's brother, had arrived from Brundisium to take over Macedonia in accordance with the arrangements of November 28. Hortensius, anticipating the wishes of the senate, refused to hand over to him and instead placed the province under the command of Brutus. C. Antonius took command of the one legion still left on the west coast out of the six originally gathered there by Caesar, but Brutus with superior forces soon shut him up in Apollonia. Finally, the three legions in Illyricum, to the north, had also come over to Brutus. It would be interesting to know why. Perhaps they had fought for Pompey at Pharsalus. At any rate their commander was P. Vatinius, a staunch Caesarian who had had to suffer the invective of Cicero and the jibes of Catullus as the price of his advancement. Vatinius is hardly likely to have engineered the desertion of his men to the Republican side. Thus Brutus had taken over the forces of three provinces, Achaea (Greece), Macedonia, and Illyricum, without striking a blow, and had penned Antony's brother up in a hopeless position.

The third piece of news was equally sensational, but lacked confirmation. Cassius, it was rumoured, had been as successful in the east as Brutus had been in Greece. The rumours were persistent and, as it turned out some weeks later, true. Cassius had gained possession of Syria. Both Cassius and Dolabella had left Italy about the same time the previous autumn, but Cassius of course had let it be understood that he was going to his legitimate province, Cyrene. Dolabella proceeded without undue haste to Syria, by way of Greece and Asia, suspecting nothing. Had he not thrown in his lot with the conspirators and joined them on the Capitol that fateful day? Meanwhile the purposeful Cassius anticipated him, turning aside from unimportant Cyrene to make a bid for the loyalties of the Syrian armies. He had served as quaestor in Syria in 53 and later as proquaestor had won some successes against the marauding Parthians. He had also commanded the Syrian squadron in Pompey's navy at the time of Pharsalus. His credit was good in Syria. The gamble came off, better perhaps than he could have hoped. He arrived to find the lawful forces of Syria and neighbouring Bithynia, under the command of the Caesarians L. Staius Murcus and Q. Marcius Crispus, besieging the last remnant of the Pompeian forces in the east outside the town of Apamea. All seven legions, besiegers and besieged alike, went over to him, and very shortly afterwards the governor of Egypt, A. Allienus, brought his four legions north to join Cassius's army.

None of this was known for certain in Rome when Brutus's account of his doings in Macedonia was delivered to Pansa. The consul immediately convoked the senate and read the despatch. Calenus protested against the illegality of Brutus's conduct; but Cicero's policies appeared to be having the ultimate justification of success and the senate carried his proposal to legitimize Brutus in his command.

Then came news that forced even Calenus to support the party of Brutus and Cassius. Dolabella, arriving in the province of Asia with his one legion en route for Syria, and learning that C. Trebonius, the governor and tyrannicide, was at Smyrna, sent one of his staff ahead to greet him. He followed himself with his troops. Each was unsure of the attitude of the other. Trebonius would not admit the troops to the city, but was prepared to grant a polite audience to Dolabella. We can only guess at the mutual accusations of disloyalty that must have been the cause of the horrific sequel. Dolabella made a feint at leading his troops away in the direction of Ephesus, laid an ambush for Trebonius's scouts who were keeping an eye on him, and returned to make a surprise night attack on Smyrna. Trebonius was captured and imprisoned on charges of mismanagement of public monies. His quaestor M. Appuleius, returning to Rome with the revenues of the province, had handed them over to Brutus in Greece. If Dolabella had been sincere, he should now have sent Trebonius back under escort to Rome to stand trial—and, of course, be acquitted. But if Cicero could invoke patriotism and the higher legality in defence of actions that were constitutionally illegal, so could others. Dolabella, like D. Brutus, M. Brutus, Cassius, and Octavian, took the law into his own hands, and put Trebonius to death. Cicero alleged that he tortured him for two days; according to Appian, the soldiers mutilated the body and rolled the severed head of the proconsul along the pavements of Smyrna as though it were a football.

Whatever the truth about this ghastly episode, Dolabella could not be acquitted of brutal and bloodthirsty behaviour. Execution of one's peers was not a sport commonly practised by Roman senators, except under the gravest provocation. The same precipitate enthusiasm and lack of mental balance that had made Dolabella act so strangely at the time of Caesar's murder had this time put him beyond the pale. The senate unanimously adopted Calenus's motion that Dolabella be declared a public enemy and his estates confiscated. There remained the question of who was to prosecute the war against him. The consuls were fully occupied in Italy, likewise M. Brutus at Apollonia; while L. Tillius Cimber, the governor of Bithynia, lacked both legions (which were besieging Apamea) and the personal standing desirable to offset his part in the stabbing of Caesar. There were two other possibilities: an extraordinary command specially created and entrusted to a consular not at present holding any office; or the recognition of Cassius, whose usurpation of Syria was still only a rumour. For the first alternative, P. Servilius Isauricus was an obvious and suitable choice. He was nominated, and was not unwilling. But he did not dare to accept and by so doing invite the enmity of the extreme Republicans and the jealousy of others. The second alternative, the appointment of Cassius, was proposed by Cicero, who pinned his faith on the accuracy of the rumours and his own knowledge of the situation and the men involved. His motion in the Eleventh Philippic is an uncannily accurate prediction of what actually happened, conferring on Cassius the command of the forces of Syria, Egypt, and Bithynia, and entrusting him with a general mandate to proceed against Dolabella. But he had overstepped the mark this time. The senate had heard arguments of this sort too often: 'This [divine] legality then was what Cassius obeyed, when he set out for Syria—not his own province, according to the written law, but when that law was obliterated, indeed his own by the law of nature.' Pansa attacked Cicero fiercely, and in the end the operations against Dolabella were entrusted to the two consuls, with the provision that they could appoint deputies until they were able to take charge in person.

All this while, through February and into March, Hirtius and Octavian remained at Claterna and Forum Cornelii, inactive while Antony starved out Mutina. Antony was in constant touch with Piso and with Calenus, in whose house Fulvia and his son were staying; and letters were also passing between him and Hirtius and Octavian. A last attempt at negotiation was made after the check to Cicero's extremist policies over Cassius. Piso and Calenus hinted that Antony might be more amenable than the senate thought, that he might be willing to withdraw from Mutina, that he had some unsuspected weakness. So a delegation was chosen to go to him: Piso, Calenus, Cicero, P. Servilius, and L. Caesar—three moderates of varying shades of opinion, a committed enemy, and a committed friend. But Cicero decided he had been tricked by false hints into a compromising position, and withdrew. Servilius did the same, and the embassy, fatally sabotaged, never set out. It may have been on receipt of this news that Hirtius and Octavian started to move up the Aemilian Way, and took Bononia. A few days later, on March 19 or 20, Pansa left Rome with four legions of new recruits to join them, and the war had begun in earnest.

It was a war entirely of the senate's making, one might almost say entirely of Cicero's making. Without his personal prestige and oratorical abilities, the mass of unknown senators who must have supported his views would have been overruled by the weight of moderate opinion amongst the influential consulars. With some of the common people Cicero was personally unpopular. He admits how he was afraid to take a trip into the country around Rome on the festival of the Terminalia on February 23, even though he proposed to return the same day. Yet in the city he felt no hesitation in addressing public meetings and giving voice to the same sentiments as he professed in the senate.

Not for the first time in the history of Rome, there was an alliance between the urban plebs and the property-owning classes against the rural peasantry. The property owners were represented by the senate, the peasants by the veterans. The veterans were in themselves a symptom of the malaise of Italy. The country poor saw the wealth of the local landowners and of the great landed families of the Roman senatorial order, and compared it with their own miserable huts and their daily struggle to earn a living on the land. The gulf in living standards and in way of life was enormous. Many of them enlisted in the armies of the republic, preferring the chance of gain to the certainty of agricultural drudgery. Their pay was low, less than a tenth of what a smart young man about town might pay to rent a flat in Rome. Caesar doubled it—an index of the pittance it had been. What they hoped for was booty, a slender hope now that the wars of the state were mostly against uncultured mountaineers and trousered northerners; and if not booty, at least a decent reward for years of service. Being peasants, they wanted land. They lacked the training to set up as craftsmen in the cities. But where was the land to come from? Ultimately, when the state had exhausted by distribution the vast reserves of public land it had acquired in previous centuries, it could only come from the estates of the landed. But even this public land, if it was any good, was farmed by men who leased it or squatted on it. These tended to be the wealthy, who possessed the means to stock and improve it. Thus any distribution even of public land was unpopular with the upper classes. Conversely, it was the most successful members of these upper classes, the generals of the Late Republic, who found themselves committed to finding allotments of land for their faithful armies—since the state took no responsibility for any sort of pension scheme for a standing army that the constitution did not acknowledge to exist. Thus the great generals came into conflict with large numbers of their own class. In the end, this provoked civil war, by creating armies that owed their loyalty not to a state too big, too diverse, and too fragmented by conflicting interests to command it, but to their generals. The power-hungry, ambitious, and status-seeking Roman oligarchy brought its own destruction by exploiting a genuine social injustice which in the end shaped the political conflict.

The veterans, with rare exceptions, did not want to fight each other, and in the next few years often avoided doing so. But civil war and rival leaders offered prospects of wealth and promotion that were hard to resist. The veterans had everything to gain from an auction for their services. But however high their bounties might go, in the end they would be discharged, in the end they wanted their peasant smallholdings. Hence Cicero's unpopularity in the country: he had dared to attack the wishes and interests of the veterans. Not because they were a threat to the rights of landed property, but because they hated Marcus Brutus and opposed his command in Macedonia. In reality, the two reasons were identical: for Caesar had behaved like a tyrant because he was impatient with a system which took no account of the economic needs of the great mass of the people it was supposed to govern. The senate and the party of Cicero was prepared to give to the veterans the current scale of rewards—when it needed their support. Octavian's men had nothing to complain of, nor would any of Antony's who claimed the price of desertion. But this was clearly a short-term expedient, contrary to the principles of those who made these promises. The senate had shown its true attitude on these questions when it had adopted at the January debate a proposal of L. Caesar that the agrarian legislation of Antony's consulship be annulled. Antony, on the other hand, had included in the terms communicated through Piso and Philippus a request that land actually assigned under his law should not be taken back. He had also asked that a judicial law which helped to correct the upper-class bias of the courts should be exempt from repeal.

The urban plebs, however, had quite different interests. They lived under appalling conditions, crowded into multi-storey apartment blocks that were liable to collapse and fire and lacked sewerage or water-supply. Their main preoccupation was with the supply and cost of grain, their staple food. For this reason there had been a series of measures over the past ninety years, aiming to pacify, conciliate, or bribe the urban population by controlling the price of grain. The final step had been taken by P. Clodius, who as tribune in 58 had introduced completely free distributions of grain to the citizens resident in the capital. Urban rents were also very high, four times those prevailing in other parts of the country. In 48 there had been bloodshed before Caesar had been forced to agree to a measure cancelling all rents, up to a reasonable limit, for a year. What made life bearable for the city dwellers was the climate, which permitted a largely outdoor life for most of the year, and the entertainments and largesse distributed to them by the senatorial class. These included both public games provided by magistrates as part of their official duties out of their own pockets, and private disbursements of food and money made by interested parties to clients, fellow-tribesmen, and any others whose political support they could claim or expect. A spectacular example was the meal which Julius Caesar gave to the whole population of Rome after his Spanish triumph. He thought the caterers had been stingy, and four days later repeated it on a more generous scale. It was no wonder that the people of Rome regarded him as their patron. And when his young heir showed himself a worthy successor by paying Caesar's legacy to them—about three months' wages for a labouring man—and by staging ten days' games, there could be little question of where the people's loyalties would lie.

The city populace had no interest in a war, except to protect their lives and dwellings. A substantial proportion of them were not Italians at all, but freedmen, freed slaves, of Greek or Oriental extraction, sharp-witted, often craft-trained, and possessing a better education than the native working man. These monopolized the trades and workshop industries of Rome. Their prosperity depended on peaceful conditions and on the affluence of the upper classes, their main customers. The great households and luxurious standard of living of senators and wealthy businessmen generated a constant demand for goods and services, of quite a different order from the modest necessities of the ordinary man. These freedmen, too, were tied to the upper classes by more than economic facts. The bond between a freedman and his former master was a particularly close one. The patron helped the freedman to establish himself, and in return could call upon him for his vote, his services, and even his money.

Thus the alliance between Caesar's heir and the senate rested on a more solid basis than a common hostility to Antony. Even so, Cicero would have been unable to bring about the war without the compliance of Octavian. It is ironical that one of Cicero's grounds for backing out of the embassy to negotiate with Antony was that Hirtius and Octavian did not know of the proposal. Yet both commanders had been in touch with Antony themselves, as soon as they had heard of it. Confident in the underlying strength of his position, Octavian was willing for the moment to obey the senate. If Antony negotiated, so much the better: he would not win very favourable terms from a senate that contained Cicero. If he did not negotiate, he stood a poor chance against the combined forces of the republicans. Either way, Octavian's chief rival for the leadership of the Caesarian party was likely to suffer a reverse. And so, when Cicero and Servilius withdrew and caused the collapse of the embassy, Octavian was ready to co-operate with the consuls and move against Antony.

Antony's forces fell back from Bononia, without attempting to contest the town. They took up a position south-east of Mutina, between Mutina and the village of Forum Gallorum on the Aemilian

Way. Thus the besieging forces and those which faced the republicans were united and there was no possibility of the besiegers being taken by surprise after an outflanking movement. Decimus Brutus's situation was becoming desperate. He had been under siege for almost three months, and could not hold out much longer. But Hirtius was unwilling to attack without Pansa and his four legions. The forces on the two sides were roughly equal: Antony had six legions, three at least of them veteran, and had been notably reinforced by the praetorian cohort, 1,000 picked men, which Lepidus had sent from Provence under M. Junius Silanus when he heard of the siege. Lepidus, true to his character, did not commit himself: he preferred to be the servant of events, not their master, and he threw the onus of deciding which side to join upon Silanus. If Silanus was shown by events to have chosen wrongly, he could be labelled a deserter. On the other side, Hirtius and Octavian had four legions, all veteran, though two were below strength, and Decimus three or more, but weakened by starvation.

When Hirtius heard that Pansa was on the way, he sent a senior officer, Ser. Sulpicius Galba, to tell him of the urgency of the situation and speed his march. As it was, Pansa had been forced to take the more mountainous route through Arezzo and Florence by the Cassian Way, since P. Ventidius was in Picenum, astride the Flaminian Way, with three part-veteran legions which he had been recruiting on Antony's behalf. Antony, too, got wind of Pansa's impending arrival and formed a bold plan to destroy his new recruits before they could be stiffened with seasoned men. Galba's letter to Cicero tells most of the story:

In camp
April 15

On April 14 I was with Pansa (who was expected to reach Hirtius's camp that day) because I had been sent on a hundred miles to meet him and hasten his arrival. On that day Antony led out two legions, the Second and Thirty-fifth, and the two praetorian cohorts, one his, the other Silanus's, and some of his re-enlisted men. He came to meet us because he thought we had only four legions of recruits. But that night, to give us greater protection as we made for camp, Hirtius had sent the Martian legion, which I generally commanded, and two praetorian cohorts to us. When Antony's cavalry appeared, it was impossible to restrain either the Martian legion or the praetorian cohorts; we had no choice but to follow them, since we could not hold them back. Antony was holding his forces at Forum Gallorum and wanted to conceal the fact that he had legions; he only showed his cavalry and light-armed troops. When Pansa saw that the legion was pressing on against his wishes, he ordered two legions of recruits to follow him. After we had crossed some difficult ground, marshy and wooded, we formed a line of twelve cohorts [there were ten cohorts to a legion]. The two recruit legions had not yet come up. Suddenly Antony brought his troops out of the village, formed them up, and engaged immediately. The battle was so fierce at first, that neither side could have fought any harder; although the right wing, where I was with eight cohorts of the Martian legion, at its first onslaught drove back Antony's Thirty-fifth more than half a mile from its original position. And so when his cavalry tried to outflank my wing, I began to withdraw and use my Moorish light-armed against them, to stop them taking us in rear. Meanwhile I saw that I was between Antonian forces, and Antony himself was a little way behind me. Immediately I spurred my horse in the direction of the legion of recruits which was coming from our camp, and threw my shield away. The Antonians followed me; our troops wanted to loose a volley of javelins. By some chance I was saved, being quickly recognized by our side. On the Aemilian Way itself, where Octavian's praetorian cohort was, the battle was long. The left wing, which was weaker, having only two cohorts of the Martian legion, and its praetorian cohort, began to retreat, because they were being ouflanked by the cavalry, in which Antony is very strong. When all our formations had withdrawn, I began to retreat last of all towards our camp. Antony, considering himself to have won, thought he could take the camp, but when he reached it he lost a number of men there without result.

Hirtius, hearing what had happened, took twenty veteran cohorts and met Antony as he was returning to his camp. He destroyed all Antony's forces, and routed him on the very spot where the battle had taken place, at Forum Gallorum. Antony and his cavalry got back to Mutina about ten o'clock at night. Hirtius went back to the camp from which Pansa had set out, where he had left two legions which were attacked by Antony. Thus Antony has lost the greater part of his veteran troops; unfortunately it was not possible for this to happen without some losses in our praetorian cohorts and the Martian legion. Two eagles and sixty standards of Antony's were captured: a fine achievement.

Galba does not mention one of the most important facts about the battle: Pansa was seriously wounded, and had to be carried back to Bononia. Galba may not have known of this when he wrote the letter, and in any case its full significance only became apparent a week later. Nor does Galba comment on what was a commonplace for one who had served with Caesar in Gaul and lived through the war with Pompey: the grim purposefulness with which the veterans fought, enhanced on this occasion by real animosity. It was the centurions of the Martian legion who had suffered execution at Brundisium in October, and there were scores to settle with Antony and the legions that had remained loyal to him. Appian describes the locking together of the lines, each unable to dislodge the other, the economy and accuracy of the swordwork, the wounds, the slaughter, and the absence of any human sound save groans. 'Anyone who fell was immediately carried away and another came up to take his place. They had no need of encouragement or exhortation. Experience made each his own general. When they were tired, they drew back a little from each other to take breath, as though it were a sporting contest, and then grappled with each other again. The new recruits who had come up were amazed at the silence and good order with which all this was done.' There is no more vivid description of the terrible efficiency of the trained Roman legion in pitched battle. As to the recruits, the veterans told them to keep out of it—and that in spite of the fact that they were outnumbered without them.

The news of Pansa's defeat reached Rome first, and for some thirty-six hours there was panic. Rumours, engineered by Antonians, swept the town that Cicero planned a coup, and the tribune Appuleius actually held a public meeting to allay these suspicions. Hours later, when Hirtius's success became known, an enormous crowd accompanied Cicero to the Capitol in thanksgiving for the victory. It was a glorious moment for the champion of the republic. It only remained to release Decimus Brutus from siege and corner Antony between the armies of Lepidus and Plancus in Gaul and Hirtius and Octavian in the valley of the Po. Plancus, though he had at first pleaded for negotiation with Antony, had sent a letter which, arriving a fortnight previously, professed his obedience to the wishes of the senate. Lepidus was a more doubtful quantity, but if all went well his nice sense of his own advantage ought to bring him over to the winning side. The very next day, April 21, while the senate was debating the official report of the three generals, and the honours to be conferred as a result of the victory, the second battle of Mutina took place.

Antony, though seriously weakened by his losses, was not without hope. He was on the point of capturing the town. Should he succeed, suitable generosity might persuade Decimus's troops to come over to him. And there was Ventidius. Publius Ventidius was one of the more remarkable characters of this revolutionary epoch. Born in Picenum, he had been captured as a child in the war that the Italians had had to wage against Rome to obtain the Roman citizenship, and had been led in the triumph of Pompey's father on December 27, 89 B.C. His family, of the local aristocracy, had been persecuted by the son a few years later. So it is hardly surprising to find Ventidius in the service of Caesar. He had been at some stage in charge of engineering and supply, which gave his enemies the chance to label him a 'muleteer'. He and Antony must have served alongside each other in Gaul, and the friendship evidently persisted. When Antony left Rome at the end of November, Ventidius, now praetor-designate, had gone to Campania to play Octavian at his own game—and with some success. The veterans knew him as a seasoned and capable officer, a true Caesarian; whereas Octavian, in spite of his name, remained, as yet, nothing but a name. Ventidius was able to raise enough men from the old Caesarian legions to call them by their Caesarian numbers again, and make them up to strength in his own homeland of Picenum, a notable recruiting-ground for the armies of Rome. Ventidius, having assumed the rank of praetor with the new year, was at last on his way north. Why he delayed so long is unknown. Perhaps he was reluctant to attack an army which contained the 'missing halves' of his own Seventh and Eighth legions—for it was from the veterans of these legions that Octavian also had recruited.

Hirtius and Octavian therefore, fearing Ventidius's arrival, attempted to liberate Mutina by outflanking Antony's camp to the south-east of the town and breaking through on the north, where he was weakest. Antony tried to stop them with his cavalry—his great strength in this arm being due to the fact that the cavalry which had previously been enticed away by Octavian had deserted a second time—but was unsuccessful. He had no choice but to engage with his legionaries, and the battle took place right amongst his lines. Hirtius was killed in the fighting around Antony's tent when Antony's Fifth Legion succeeded in driving back Hirtius's Fourth. Octavian displayed notable courage in the fight for Hirtius's body, and was later credited with having actually carried the legionary eagle for some time when its bearer was severely wounded. He recovered the body, but was unable to retain possession of Antony's camp. The garrison within Mutina made a sally under Pontius Aquila—the tribune who had failed to rise to his feet as Caesar passed—but Aquila was killed and the siege had still not been raised. On balance, the second battle was a victory for Antony. The enemy had lost a consul, a senior officer, and a good part of the Fourth legion.

Antony, however, now decided to withdraw—a manoeuvre erroneously represented by his enemies as a flight. It was an astute and unexpected move, and threw his opponents off balance. He judged that with his weakened forces he could not both take Mutina and hold off Octavian. It was more important to preserve his strength and place his faith in political developments and in the armies and generals of the west. His intelligence service was surely good enough to have told him that Pansa was far too badly hurt to resume command. That left Decimus and Octavian as the two senior commanders, and the essential absurdity of an effective alliance between Caesar's murderer and Caesar's heir was obvious. Nor did he despair of the provinces of the west. Their governors, Lepidus, Pollio, and Plancus, were all in correspondence with him. Better to remove himself, avoid armed conflict and the bitterness engendered by it, and let events take their course.

Chapter VI

THE GENERALS AGAINST THE STATE

THE NEWS of the second battle of Mutina arrived in Rome on April 26. The senate was summoned forthwith, Antony and his followers at last declared public enemies, and a fifty days' thanksgiving, unparalleled even for victories over foreign foes, decreed. Lavish honours were awarded, but not in the right quarter. While Decimus Brutus was granted a triumph, and his soldiers the same rewards as those already promised to Octavian's, Octavian himself was all but ignored. The crisis was over, and the young man could now be taken down a peg. Cicero, indeed, proposed that he be granted an ovation (a kind of second-grade triumph); but as he also proposed that April 26 be permanently named in the calendar after Decimus, since the day on which the good news arrived happened also to be Decimus's birthday, the ovation was made to seem very small beer. It was probably not voted, in any case.

On the same day it was learnt that Pansa had died of his wound the day after the second battle. The question immediately arose: who was to pursue Antony? And who should take over responsibility for dealing with Dolabella? Hitherto the two Caesarian consuls had prevented the senate from assenting too blindly and enthusiastically to the extreme policies urged by Cicero and made feasible by the successes of Marcus Brutus and Cassius. They had ensured a fair hearing for the supporters of Antony and done their best to prevent wholesale condonation of illegal seizures of power. But now the old Pompeians felt no check. Already before the battles at Mutina, M. Brutus had taken Apollonia. He held C. Antonius under open arrest in his camp, but did not act harshly towards him or strip him of his rank (Cicero reproached him for this; but it was this streak of generosity and nobility in Brutus that made other men follow and respect him). Antony's flight from Mutina and the deaths of Hirtius and Pansa left the Pompeians alone in the field—or so it seemed for the moment. So the task of pursuing Antony, and the command of the forces of Octavian and the consuls, was entrusted to D. Brutus.

From the east, official despatches had at last been received which corroborated the rumours of Cassius's activities: he had indeed taken over the armies of Syria, Egypt, and Bithynia. On Servilius's motion, he was officially charged with the conduct of the war against Dolabella. For this purpose, he received a supreme command in the eastern provinces. For good measure, and for no very evident purpose Sextus Pompey, who was now at Massilia, was made admiral of the Roman fleet. Finally the senate decreed a public funeral for the two consuls, and the erection of a statue to Pontius Aquila.

Meanwhile, in the north, things were not turning out according to the sanguine expectations of Cicero. Decimus Brutus was quite unable to pursue Antony at once. He had no cavalry and no baggage animals—doubtless eaten during the siege. He was unaware that Hirtius and Pontius Aquila had fallen. Octavian had taken over command of Pansa's legions as well as those of Hirtius and his own, but Decimus wanted to meet and sound him out before placing any trust in him. So one day passed. On the next day an urgent message reached him to visit Pansa at Bononia. Decimus set off, only to be met on the road by the tidings of Pansa's death and turned back to his own 'pitiful force' as he described it. Antony now had two days' start on him, and increased his lead daily. On April 29 Decimus was still at Regium Lepidum, a mere seventeen miles from Mutina.

Octavian refused absolutely to co-operate with him, on the grounds that his soldiers would not obey an order to join the forces of Caesar's murderer. Nor did he make any attempt to stop Ventidius and his three legions from safely crossing the Apennines to the south of him and marching north along the Italian riviera coast to effect a junction with Antony in the region of Genoa. These decisions Octavian took before he knew anything of the decrees passed by the senate when it heard of Antony's flight. His reasons are unrecorded, but apparent. At the most practical level, his veterans had been cut about in two battles; even with the dubious reinforcement of Pansa's recruits he would be lucky to stop the experienced Ventidius with three good legions. The political calculation yielded the same answer. Lepidus's sympathies were generally known to lie with Antony, even if Cicero managed to persuade himself that he might be induced by honours and exhortations to oppose him. The conjunction of Lepidus, Ventidius, and Antony was thus to be expected. The three Spanish legions, isolated by geography and commanded by an honest man who was Antony's friend and hated the evils of civil war, were unlikely to make a decisive intervention. Plancus was more doubtful, closer to

D. Brutus and the senate. But he had the reputation of a time-server.

On the other hand in the east lay M. Brutus and Cassius, the architects of his father's death, with seventeen legions. The hopes and sympathies of the senate were with them. A clash between them and the Caesarian armies of the west was highly likely, and from such a conflict he could hardly stand dispassionately aloof. His piety towards the dead Caesar, his proclaimed intention of taking vengeance on the murderers, and his determination to show himself worthy of his adoption had won the veterans to him in the first place. To take the republican, neo-Pompeian side at this moment, or in a future civil war, was contrary to all logic and emotion. He must stand in the end with Caesar's men and Caesar's generals. How right he was, he learnt when he heard of the decrees of the senate. Having served his purpose, he was evidently to be discarded with an honourable mention. Cicero never admitted the authorship of the famous and untranslatable pun which expressed this policy so neatly: *laudandum, ornandum, tollendum.** The fact remained that it was *ben trovato*.

Meanwhile Ventidius slipped across the mountains and met Antony with his 5,000 cavalry and the skeleton of three legions at Vada Sabatia, about thirty miles west of Genoa on the coast. On his way from Mutina Antony had liberated slaves employed on the farms, and with these and local recruits he scraped together another legion under the command of a local notable, one P. Bagiennus. Decimus followed him by way of Dertona and Aquae Statiellae. When he was some thirty miles north of Vada he heard that Antony's troops had refused to follow him across the Maritime Alps into Provence and insisted on going by way of Pollentia at the head of the Po valley. Decimus was thus almost across Antony's line of march and he sent five cohorts on with all speed to Pollentia. They arrived there just an hour before L. Trebellius with some of Antony's cavalry; but it was all a clever feint. By the time Decimus himself with the bulk of his force reached Pollentia, Antony was safely out of range of pursuit, marching his weary troops along the precipitous coastal route where the autostrada now runs between Italy and France. Lepidus's lieutenant Q. Terentius Culleo, so far from making any attempt to stop Antony, actually joined him.

Antony reached Forum Julii (modern Fréjus) in Lepidus's province on May 15 and encamped on the eastern bank of the Argenteum, the small river which flows into the sea at that point. Ventidius

---

* 'He must be praised, honoured, and extolled;' the last word also means, equally commonly, 'removed'.

followed him two days later. Lepidus brought his army up to face
the invaders, having previously taken the precaution of letting his
men demonstrate their desire for peace: it was enough that two
consuls and many good citizens had died. The sentiments of both
armies were identical, and Lepidus did nothing to stop fraternization.
A potent factor was the presence in his army of Caesar's famous
Tenth legion, which had fought alongside the Fifth, Seventh, Eighth,
and Ninth now encamped opposite. It took exactly a fortnight for the
inevitable to happen. Lepidus's troops were loyal to the Caesarian
cause, not to Lepidus, and the idea of a fight to decide between two
Caesarian commanders when there were other available enemies was
absurd. The commanders themselves were in constant communication. On May 29 the men of the Tenth legion, which had once been
commanded by Antony himself and had made no secret of its
Antonian sympathies in the past month, arranged for the gates to be
opened to their old commander and a vast throng of soldiers accompanied him to Lepidus's tent, in the darkness before dawn. Lepidus
maintained the show to the end, leaping out of bed in his night
attire and embracing Antony in the cause of peace. One officer in the
camp of Lepidus protested against the smooth and treacherous
volte-face of his superior, so damningly documented in the fine-
sounding letters he wrote to Cicero and the senate protesting his
patriotism: Juventius Laterensis, a man of principle, fell on his
sword, preferring death to disobedience to the government in Rome.
Lepidus himself was duly declared an enemy of the state.

There still remained Plancus and Pollio. Plancus had put off as
long as possible the moment when he would have to intervene in the
war of Mutina, and declare himself on one side or the other. He had
weighty reasons for delay: the slowness of communications with
Rome, the unreliability of his army, and the necessity of making sure
of the local Gallic tribes. His letters are full of the most admirable
sentiments, couched in elegant Latin, but utterly ambiguous in the
context of civil war. Like Pollio, he was very much Caesar's man
and came from outside the circle of the senatorial nobility. Unlike
Pollio, he lacked firm principle. There was no telling how he would
act, except that he would avoid any difficult decisions. He disliked
Lepidus's shifty character, and distrusted him. Decimus Brutus was
to be his colleague in the consulship next year. Therefore he began
with the best of intentions, once the spring was fairly on him and he
could reasonably expect the Alpine passes to be open. It may have
been no more than a coincidence that the siege of Mutina was so far

advanced that a decision was almost bound to be reached before he could arrive.

With his four legions and about 5,000 cavalry, he crossed the Rhône somewhere south of Vienna (modern Vienne) on April 26. He was not sure whether Lepidus would let him pass; but if he was blocked, he had no intention of forcing the issue. A day or two later he heard that the siege had been raised and that Antony had fled. An urgent exchange of messages with Lepidus followed, the two men were reconciled, and Laterensis brought Lepidus's word of honour that he would make war on Antony if he could not keep him out of his province; he also requested Plancus to join him. Plancus, still mistrustful, asked for a hostage of Lepidus's good faith, and a Greek freedman, Apella, was sent to him. Meanwhile he crossed the Isère, on May 12. He already knew that D. Brutus would come over the Alps by one of the St. Bernard passes, and intended at first to wait for him. But Lepidus's messages were insistent, and on May 18 he started on his way down the left bank of the Rhône to join Lepidus at Forum Voconi, leaving his pontoon bridge in place so that Decimus would not be delayed by having to make another. But almost at once he met a courier: Lepidus could manage by himself, and Plancus was, after all, to wait at the Isère. Plancus was willing to put the most favourable interpretation on this sudden change of heart. Lepidus, he thought, was anxious to keep for himself the glory of defeating Antony. Nevertheless, his plan was still to press on and hold himself in readiness near at hand in case Lepidus should meet with a reverse; he could do this without diminishing the credit of this 'insignificant man' if he were successful. But there came also a letter from Laterensis which revealed the treacherous purpose which lay behind Lepidus's strange request and besought Plancus not to fail the republic. Plancus therefore pressed on. He had got to within forty miles of Fréjus when he heard that Antony and Lepidus had united their forces and started to move against him. Twenty miles only separated the armies when Plancus withdrew, as fast as he decently could. Lepidus had seven legions, Ventidius three, Antony one and the elements of more. Plancus could not possibly hope to do anything against them, even if that had been his inclination.

He recrossed the Isère on June 4, broke up his bridge, and decided to march up the river to Cularo (modern Grenoble) and there await Decimus. However, the latter had no special cause to hurry, once Antony had given him the slip. In particular, he needed troops if Lepidus turned traitor as feared. He therefore raised three new

legions, bringing his total to ten, impressive in number but in little
else. He made vain attempts to extract the Martian and Fourth
legions, or what remained of them, from Octavian. He carried on a
constant correspondence with Cicero, for as consul-designate, let
alone one of the chief actors in the current drama, he was intimately
concerned with the political manoeuvring going on in Rome. Short
of money, forced to feed the legions out of his own pocket, he crossed
the Alps only because he had no choice. He eventually joined
Plancus at Cularo some time in the second half of June. There the
two armies lay, too weak to challenge Antony and Lepidus, until
Plancus had had time to take stock of the situation and arrange things
for himself.

Octavian had been ordered by the senate to hand over his best
troops to Decimus and co-operate with him against Antony. Only
his additional forces could alter the military balance the other side of
the Alps. Yet he refused to do anything. Plancus communicated
with him. He observed that Octavian promised one thing and did
another. But it did not escape him that it was to Octavian that
Antony owed his life, his army, and his alliance with Lepidus. No
reproaches, therefore, in Plancus's correspondence, but praise of the
young man's character, and recollections of friendship with Caesar.
Meanwhile the remaining governor of the west, Pollio, arrived in
Provence with two legions. He had not heard the news of Mutina
until the end of May; and when he did, he grieved for the desolation
of Italy. But he had received no order from the senate to go to the
help of Decimus, as Plancus and Lepidus had, and in any case he
could not have passed through Provence against Lepidus's wishes.
He might indeed have mediated, as the friend of Antony and a true
lover of freedom. Now the moment was past. In July, the choice
between Antony and the senate was no choice. Six years before, in a
similar situation, he had decided for Caesar. This time, the logic of
his military position confirmed his natural wish to join Antony.
Pollio was also on good terms with Plancus, and long before the
summer was out Antony, Lepidus, Pollio, and Plancus stood together.
Plancus took his legions with him, leaving Decimus in an uncomfortable position—with troops certainly, but quite unable to challenge
the united Antonians. Decimus's one hope of safety lay in Macedonia with his namesake Marcus, but the direct route back over the
Alps and across the plain of Northern Italy was held by his enemy
Octavian. He decided to swing round north of the Alps, but his
army soon deserted him. Struggling on, a fugitive in a strange land

where the power of Rome was a mere shadow to the south, he was, some said, captured and put to death by a local chieftain. Others believed that Antony's agents tracked him down at the house of this man, who had given him shelter, and there murdered him.

Thus died the second of Caesar's murderers. Octavian was, at least indirectly, the agent of Decimus's death by his masterly inactivity throughout the late spring and summer. Hirtius and Pansa had died so opportunely for him that it was alleged that he had connived at the death of the one and engineered the poisoning of the other. The republic was left temporarily headless, and the archaic complexities of the constitution ensured that nothing could quickly be done to remedy this situation. There was no force in Italy that could bring the young man to heel, nor anyone able to command such a force and retain its loyalty. New levies would be useless, re-enlisted men untrustworthy and inclined to join Octavian or even Antony. And so decisions were taken in Rome that bore no reference to reality. Octavian, since he could not be disciplined, must be treated as the ally of the senate; and if an ally of the senate, one willing to defer to it, to admit his junior status, to bow to republican precedent and usage.

The senate first ordered him to transfer his best legions, the Fourth and Martian, to Decimus Brutus. Having already refused the same request from Decimus himself, he saw no reason to change his mind or to suppose that the legions would be any more willing than they had been at that time to forsake him. Then the senate attempted to implement the promises to the veterans originally made by Octavian and subsequently confirmed in the name of the state in order to retain their services and weaken their dangerous attachment to Caesar's heir. A commission of ten was appointed to pay the rewards to the veterans. Octavian was not made a member of it. This was a blatant manoeuvre to undermine Octavian's patronage, not concealed nor justified by the parallel omission of Decimus, already in pursuit of Antony. The commission was instructed to deal directly with the soldiers, but the legionaries would have none of this and refused to hear the commission except through their commanding officer. They were equally angry because the senate was attempting to whittle down what it had promised. Half the money was to be paid at once, the other half only on completion of the campaign against Antony under the command of D. Brutus. The senate also tried to economize on land-allotments by excluding veterans who had served with Antony.

Such tactlessness in dealing with the soldiers was folly. Certainly the public treasury was in a grossly depleted state. No revenues had come in from the rich provinces of Asia and Syria, for the quaestors who should have brought them had defected to M. Brutus. Pansa had raised five new legions for the war of Mutina, which all had to be armed and paid, as did Octavian's private army. The vast reserve of seven hundred million sesterces which had been in the Temple of Ops at Caesar's death had all gone, whether legitimately disbursed or fraudently embezzled we shall never know. During the siege of Mutina the senate had been forced to impose a war-tax of 4 per cent on all capital, and a special roof-tile tax on all property owned by members of the senatorial order. In the circumstances, the offer of 2,500 denarii per man, instead of the promised 5,000, was probably the utmost the impoverished treasury could afford. But there was no need to annoy the soldiers by trying to cut out Octavian, and thus ensure that they would think that the sum had been reduced for purely political reasons. More than ever, they regarded Octavian as their patron and protector, and the war against Antony as an engine for their own destruction. They swore that they would never fight against any legion that had been Caesar's.

This inept attempt to undermine the loyalty of the veterans to Octavian only confirmed the essential strength of his position. The veretans followed him because he bore Caesar's name, because he wished to take vengeance on Caesar's murderers, and because he promised to adhere to, or improve upon, Caesar's policies towards his soldiers. He need fear no rival in Italy. Meanwhile the consulship was vacant, the government needed an army, and he was willing to wait. The price of his co-operation was soon evident in the capital, and afforded much scope for political intrigue.

If Octavian were to be allowed to stand for (and presumably win) the consulship, he would need a colleague of prudence, distinction, and experience to guide him—and restrain him. Cicero himself was an obvious candidate, as the chief architect of the policy of winning Caesar's heir for the Republic. But there were others equally eminent and less fanatically opposed to negotiation with the enemies of the state, notably Cicero's chief rival, the capable and reasonable P. Servilius. It may be significant that Servilius's daughter was betrothed to Octavian in the summer (or earlier). When Cicero got wind of such plans, he denounced them vigorously in the senate, alleging criminal plotting and the dissemination of inaccurate information, and naming Octavian's relatives as their authors. Where the nefarious wickedness of these designs lay is not apparent from Cicero's complaint to M. Brutus; we can only infer that it was in the threatened check to his own ambitions. The prospect of a second consulship for one of the consulars brought out the worst in the body that claimed the right to manage the affairs of Rome. Such an honour had not been won since the second century, at least not without the threat of armed force or the name of Caesar. Bound by the traditional outlook of republican politics, the senate was incapable of appreciating the true nature of the crisis that was upon it. By its failure to agree upon candidates, its failure to set in motion the machinery for replacing the consuls, its failure to realize the necessity for negotiating with Antony and Lepidus, and its failure to conciliate the veterans, it showed itself unfit to govern. Infighting for personal prestige had no relevance to the problems of Italy.

The only positive measure taken by the senate was to summon M. Brutus from Macedonia. He had six legions, perhaps more by this time. They were a match for Octavian's eight, four of which were Pansa's new levies. But Brutus refused to come. He feared both alternatives open to Octavian. If the immoderate praises and fulsome solicitations which Cicero addressed to the young man succeeded in retaining him on the side of the Republic, Brutus could scarcely feel happy. Cicero was incautious enough to ask Octavian, in a letter, to be indulgent to the Liberators. Brutus heard of this through Atticus and furiously reproached Cicero for having led the state into war against one would-be despot only to exchange him for another; there was no difference, Brutus declared, between Cicero and Salvidienus—an insult indeed, for Salvidienus, though one of Octavian's ablest and most valued supporters, was not even a senator; and Cicero's language, he said, was that of a slave before a monarch. Brutus did not delude himself about Octavian's character or motives. If he were bought by the consulship or extravagant honours, it was naïve to suppose he would forgo the command of his legions. Italy was no place for Brutus. The army of Macedonia might have chosen him in preference to a C. Antonius or a Vatinius; but could he be so sure of them when there was a Caesar in the other camp?

On the other hand, if the senate refused to acquiesce in Octavian's attempt to win power and prestige by blackmail, it would drive him into an alliance with Antony and Lepidus. Friends they might not be at the moment, but where interests coincided, that was no obstacle. The feelings of the soldiers, the presence of Caesar's veterans in both armies, were a still more powerful reason for alliance. And if that should happen, what hope for Brutus and his six poor legions? Cicero besought him to come: all Italy would run to join him the moment he set foot on Italian soil. But Brutus did not share Cicero's optimistic delusions about his popularity in Italy. It was he, not Cicero, who had been forced by public opinion to skulk in the towns of Latium the previous year, not daring to show his face in the city whose magistrate he was. Nor did Brutus share Cicero's almost paranoid hatred of Antony and his brothers. His kind treatment of C. Antonius—though in the end he had to put him under guard for tampering with the loyalty of his troops—demonstrated his willingness to reach some sort of compromise. He also protested to Cicero that it was unnecessarily harsh of the senate to have declared Lepidus a public enemy. Lepidus was his brother-in-law, Lepidus's children, exiled and disinherited by this decree, were his nephews and nieces. On the other side, Mark Antony in the negotiations of January had recognized the claim of Brutus and Cassius to the consulship of 41; and in the previous year he had made it easy for them to leave Italy without great loss of face, when they had objected to the original idea of giving them a mere corn-commission. The breach was great, but it was not beyond all hope of healing.

What Brutus wanted was a free republic, one in which no single man wielded disproportionate power. For that, he had murdered Caesar. Antony, to him, was a far less dangerous menace than the young usurper of the name and the ambitions of Caesar. Yet the policies of the senate, over which he had no control, were driving the possibility of compromise with Antony ever further away. Every constitutional step worsened the situation: the ratification of himself as legal governor of Macedonia and Greece; the outlawing first of Antony, then of Lepidus; the ratification of Cassius's command in the east. And the more hostile the senate was to Antony, the more it needed the support of its anomalous ally Octavian. But Brutus himself was devoid of constructive ideas, not perhaps surprisingly for one who had thought that to strike down Caesar would be to restore the ideal Republic. He saw how dangerous Octavian was, but all he could do was to exhort Cicero to bestir himself: the people, he said, needed leaders to withstand the machinations of the wicked. Brutus, like Cicero, perhaps even like Antony, was operating with the political terminology and the political concepts of a system that had already failed because it was out of touch with reality. The people of Rome and of Italy were ripe for leaders—but not the leaders Brutus meant, not the pillars of the senatorial oligarchy.

Thus Brutus remained, disobediently pursuing his own activities in Macedonia, while the other Brutus trudged through the Alpine passes to his ineffectual union with Plancus, and the Caesarian generals of the west closed their ranks against the resurgent Pompeians. Octavian meanwhile let boredom and frustration mount among his troops as they sweltered in the summer heat of the flat-lands of the Po. He had no fear that they would turn against him, for they had a common adversary. It was the senate which had attempted to reduce the rewards that had been solemnly promised to the men. It was the senate which denied to their general honours that he had surely earned by his signal services to the state. And so it was against the senate that the wrath of the men finally erupted.

In July a delegation of 400 centurions appeared in the senate to demand the consulate for Octavian and the promised rewards for themselves. When the senate refused, one of the delegation made a brief and threatening answer. Throwing back his military cloak, he pointed to his sword and said, 'If you do not make him consul, this will.' And so it did. Octavian marched his eight legions south to the Rubicon. There he divided his forces, going ahead with picked men by forced marches while the remainder followed more slowly behind. Indecision paralysed the government in Rome. A delegation went out to meet Octavian with last-minute concessions, then two legions which had been summoned from Africa after Mutina arrived and gave rise to hopes of eleventh-hour resistance. There was one of Pansa's newly recruited legions still in the neighbourhood, owing its loyalty, it was hoped, to none but the legitimate authorities. A proclamation went out that all who were of military age should stand to arms. But these hopes were no sooner raised than dashed. Octavian sure of his popularity in the city, advanced close to Rome, just beyond the Quirinal hill, and sent messages to the people that they were to have no fear. Resistance collapsed. The three legions went over to him, only one of their commanders seeing fit to take his own life. Senators and notables proceeded out to pay their respects to the bloodless victor as he approached the city with nothing but a body-guard. Cicero lay low, reluctant to greet 'the youth who had been sent by divine providence to save the state'. When he emerged, Octavian observed acidly that Cicero appeared to be the last of his friends to greet him.

The constitutional and personal difficulties that had for so long prevented the election of new consuls suddenly vanished. Octavian maintained the fiction of legitimate election by removing himself outside the city walls, since one who held the power of military command was not entitled to enter the city without laying it down. As colleague, he passed over the discredited, status-seeking consulars, amongst them his relations Philippus and Marcellus, and allowed his obscure cousin Q. Pedius to be elected—doubtless as a reward for services rendered. There was no danger that Pedius would attempt to pursue an independent policy. On August 19, five weeks before his twentieth birthday, Octavian entered the city as consul. It was said that twelve vultures appeared in the sky, the same sign that had been granted to the founder of Rome.

Octavian persuaded the people to pass the long-delayed law ratifying his adoption, blocked by his enemies for so long. Through Pedius he passed a law setting up a special court to try the murderers of the man he could now legally call his father. Friends or flatterers showed their devotion to him by prosecuting the absent criminals. The circumstances allowed of no doubt about the verdict, though one brave man cast his vote for acquittal. Octavian also seized the treasury and paid his men the 2,500 denarii they had been voted on Cicero's motion long before, but had angrily rejected. From Octavian it was sufficient, and they were ready to follow him north again to resolve the question of Antony.

He may already have been in correspondence with Antony and Lepidus, though letters can scarcely have been necessary either to explain or obfuscate his intentions. His refusal to pursue Antony or aid Decimus spoke clearly enough. He had done nothing in the meantime that indicated any change of heart. So it was no surprise to the people of Rome to learn that the consul Pedius, soon after Octavian's departure, had managed to convince the senate that Antony and Lepidus were not, after all, the enemies of the state. The ground was prepared for a reconciliation between the rival Caesarian leaders—on a firmer basis than the sham reconciliation of October 44. Then Antony had been consul, Octavian a private and seditious citizen. Now, Octavian was consul, Antony proconsul at the head of a powerful army. Then Brutus was attending philosophy lectures in Athens, Cassius sailing the Mediterranean en route, so it was believed, for his lawful province of Cyrene. Now, they were the overlords of all Rome's territories east of the Adriatic and their joint armies numbered seventeen legions—a formidable force, but not as formidable as the united armies of Italy and the west. By themselves,

Antony and Brutus might have come to some arrangement, but the presence of Caesar's heir made this unthinkable. Antony could decide either to eradicate the Liberators or to resist Octavian. The first course was drastic, the second hazardous and unprofitable— hazardous because many of his men might desert him, unprofitable because an armed struggle would leave the weakened victor a prey to the Liberators.

Lepidus appears to have acted as the intermediary, and to have owed his importance to this fact, since he had no discernible personal following. There was no personal rancour between Lepidus and Octavian. The events of the previous October and November were known to him only by report. Until the end of May and his defection from the cause of the Republic, he had had official reason to be in communication with Octavian. There was no hurry over the negotiations. It was late in October or early in November before the decisive meeting of the three men took place, on a small island in the river Lavino near Bononia. Elaborate precautions were taken. Antony and Octavian each brought five legions up to opposite sides of the river and proceeded with a bodyguard of 300 to the bridges leading to the islet. Lepidus went ahead, searched the islet, and waved his cloak as a signal that all was clear. The other two then joined him and they sat in full view of their troops, Octavian in the middle as consul. They deliberated for two days, then announced to the cheering troops their concord and their decisions.

The form in which they chose to cloak their seizure of despotic power was a new invention—in fact a joint dictatorship, in name a combination of republican precedents. They were to become a Triumvirate for the Ordering of the State (*Tresviri Reipublicae Constituendae*) with consular power for five years. Octavian agreed to resign his recently acquired consulate—the glory of having held it being sufficient—and allow Antony's partisan Ventidius the reward of his loyalty. In terms of power, the consulate became again a meaningless office, as it had been under the dictatorship of Caesar. But those who did not aspire to be the masters of the world still coveted it as a visible token of their worth and a gauge by which they could be seen to have equalled or surpassed their ancestors. The triumvirs allotted the consulships as far ahead as 40, demonstrating clearly the predominance of Antonians among their most senior and important supporters. Lepidus himself, as the most insignificant of the three, had his vanity flattered by a second consulship. Of the others, Pollio, L. Antonius, and perhaps Plancus could be reckoned

Antony's men. P. Servilius, prospective father-in-law of Octavian, was deprived of that honour, since the alliance of Antony and Octavian was felt to require the cementing of a marriage-tie. Octavian was betrothed to Clodia, Antony's stepdaughter. Servilius was compensated with the consulship of 41, his Caesarian past and present standing making him too important to be passed over. But he could hardly be described as an unambiguous partisan of Octavian. The last of the six was Cn. Domitius Calvinus, consul in 53, intended by Caesar to be his Master of Horse, and like Servilius a member of the republican nobility. History has preserved no record of his allegiance at this time. Cicero's silence, and this second consulship, may indicate that he had worked for Octavian; and certainly he was later on Octavian's side.

The arrangements made for the control of the provinces also reflected Octavian's comparative weakness. While Lepidus retained Provence and Nearer Spain, adding to it Pollio's province of Further Spain, and Antony claimed Cisalpine and Further Gaul, Octavian had to be content with the unimportant and still troubled provinces of Africa, Sicily, and Sardinia and Corsica. In Africa, Q. Cornificius, governor of the Old province, was still loyal to the senate and embroiled in a war with T. Sextius, the Caesarian governor of the New province. As for the islands, they were subject to the depredations of Sextus Pompey, who had once again taken to the high seas after his brief period of accommodation with the Caesarians. All three men were to govern their provinces by deputies. Lepidus was to remain as consul in Rome, while Antony and Octavian were to undertake the war now declared against the outlaws Brutus and Cassius.

So much, though high-handed, was tolerable. The remainder was not. The triumvirs were utterly dependent on their veterans—one could almost say that the veterans made the triumvirate. It was necessary to make generous provision for them, to induce them to do their work well and without flinching in the coming struggle with their fellow-citizens. No more public land remained to be divided —Antony's allocations had used the last of it. So eighteen of the wealthiest cities of Italy were marked down to become colonies for the veterans when victory was theirs. (Not that wealth alone was the criterion; some districts of Italy had been notably more patriotic than others in the war of Mutina.) Cicero, in a philosophical treatise written earlier that year, had delivered an impassioned tirade in defence of the rights of private property. It was prophetic. By the

edict of the triumvirs the finest land in the country was to be taken
from its possessors and distributed to the rough peasants whose
ancestors had made Rome great and who were at last scenting their
reward. This civil war was in reality a war of poor against rich,
disguised beneath the devious turns of personal rivalry and political
phraseology, its true nature unrealized by its participants. Rhegium
and Vibo in the far south, Venusia in the rolling country of Apulia,
Beneventum, Nuceria, and ancient Capua in Campania, and Ariminum beside the Adriatic were some of these unfortunate cities which
were to be treated as though they were the prizes of war. Italy was
indeed a land divided against itself.

Finally, there was one thing not announced to the troops: the list
of the proscribed. This was a matter of personalities, not of policy,
once the triumvirs had agreed in principle to clear their enemies
from the country. A man who was proscribed could flee to exile.
Otherwise he faced almost certain death, with a price on his head.
His property was confiscated and became the property of the state.
Thus proscription served two purposes, to eliminate political opposition and to replenish the treasury. In this case, the latter was the
paramount motive. Octavian had emptied the treasury in August.
The legions must be fed and paid, and Italy and the western
provinces provided only a quarter of the normal revenues of the
empire. Proscriptions had to make good the balance that Brutus and
Cassius now enjoyed; between one and three hundred senators were
proscribed, and many more of the wealthy businessmen and land-
owners up and down Italy. It is possible to detect the settling of
certain old scores, in particular the sacrifice of Cicero to Antony.
Antony for his part allowed the proscription of his uncle L. Caesar,
Lepidus that of his brother Paullus. These are the famous examples
of the cruelty of the triumvirs; but Cicero could have escaped, as the
other two in fact did.

Their compact made and their policies agreed, the triumvirs
journeyed to Rome. Octavian entered first, then on successive days
Antony and Lepidus, each with his praetorian cohort and one legion.
A tribune, P. Titius, immediately proposed a law conferring upon
the three the powers they had appropriated to themselves. It was
passed forthwith, without regard for constitutional formalities. Thus
the triumvirate came into being on November 27, with a faint show
of legality. Pedius died, according to Appian from the fatigue
induced by attending to the publication of an advance list of some of
the proscribed and at the same time endeavouring to prevent a state

of general panic. In his place the triumvirs appointed one of Caesar's marshals, C. Carrinas, a man lacking all claim to political distinction or influence. He was of Umbrian or Etruscan origin, and his father had been one of Marius's generals in that earlier civil war, when Sulla had triumphed bloodily over those very interests which Octavian now represented. It was not unfitting that Carrinas should preside over proscriptions which recalled those of Sulla.

Chapter VII

THE END OF THE REPUBLIC

THE FORMATION of the Triumvirate marked the end of senatorial government in Rome. Even a Brutus could not ignore the evidence. Antony and Octavian had each defied the senate, and survived. Whatever might be the outcome of the forthcoming struggle against Brutus and Cassius, the ancestral form of government could not go on unmodified. The state was in the throes of a revolution whose causes were deeper than the reckless ambition of a few, and there could be no going back. The assassins' daggers had brought no release from tyranny, only renewed despotism; and with it, the horrors of civil war. Whichever side triumphed, the towns of Italy would be the losers, for the soldiers of the Liberators would hardly be content with less than had been promised to the soldiers of the triumvirs.

For the moment, the surface patterns of the revolution were clear. On the one side, Caesar's heir and Caesar's generals; on the other, Caesar's murderers; their battle cries, Vengeance and Freedom—both irrelevant, both obscuring behind the traditional moral vocabulary the question really at issue: were all Italy and the Mediterranean lands to be governed by a small inbred clique of ancient and wealthy families who regarded the holding of office as more important than the manner of its exercise, or was government to become at least partly accountable to and shared by the businessmen, traders, bankers, local gentry, artisans, and peasant smallholders of Italy? That this was the question was not apparent at the time, and in this form it would have been unintelligible to the participants. Personalities were the stuff of Roman politics, not theories or programmes. Hence the clear-cut distinction between Caesarians and Pompeians, regardless of the fact that it was Pompey's career which had opened in unconstitutional violence while Caesar's had been blameless (relatively speaking) before his consulship. What mattered was that Pompey had ended by embracing the senatorial oligarchy, Caesar by defying it.

The present struggle, then, appeared as a re-enactment of the other, and Octavian and Antony were now perfectly in harmony. Octavian contributed the powerful magic of Caesar's name and guaranteed the authenticity of the desire for vengeance on Caesar's murderers, Antony was of proven military ability and had experience of organization and administration at the highest level. So long as their objective remained and their adversaries menaced them equally, their alliance, based on mutual advantage, would remain unshaken. The proscriptions served as a further bond. Each of the triumvirs shared in the odium produced by the decree, whatever guesses might be made about which of them was responsible for any particular name on the list.

The effect of the proscriptions, the first and most detested work of the triumvirate, was not as dreadful as later accounts would have us believe. It has been remarked that the ancient stories about the proscriptions 'went a long way towards compensating the lack of prose fiction among the Romans'. In the pages of Appian appear tales of heroism, treachery, good fortune and retribution; men saved by disguising themselves as charcoal-burners, hiding in sewers, travelling brazenly in daylight, being recognized by their former centurions; wives who wrapped their husbands up as laundry, hired ships for their escape, or bought their pardon by offering themselves to Antony's lust. It is evident that a good number of the proscribed made their escape—indeed it was in the triumvirs' interest that they should. The head of one of the proscribed carried a reward of 25,000 denarii if brought in by a free man, 10,000 if brought in by a slave. The most celebrated killing was that of Cicero, and that was caused by his own inability to make up his mind. He had put to sea in a small boat, but becoming seasick, put in to shore again at Caieta, where he had a villa. In this he incautiously lay low. Inevitably, a party of soldiers came searching for him, and although he got away from the house, carried in a litter by some slaves, he was soon overtaken in a wood. He accepted death bravely, true to his philosophic ideals. Pollio later passed a fair verdict, condoning the last fifteen months of the orator's life: 'Since no mortal is perfect, we must judge a man by the ends to which he has chiefly devoted his life and intellect.'

The proscriptions served one of their two purposes well, as they could hardly help doing, given the willingness of the soldiery to hunt down men whom they were given to understand were accomplices, in thought if not in deed, to the murder of Caesar. They cleared

Italy of those who were known to dissent from the triumvirs, and must have forced many more who were not proscribed, but feared they might be, to join the others in their flight. The pattern of Caesar's clemency was too risky for lesser men to imitate at this stage. It was also too unproductive. But the second purpose, to raise much-needed money, was only partially accomplished. Certainly, the brief terror elicited declarations of loyalty like the statue erected by the citizens of Saticula in Samniun which can hardly have been convincing without a donation. On the other hand, much of the wealth of the proscribed was in the form of property, and what was not was easy to conceal or send out of the country. This property had to be converted into cash before it could be of real use to the triumvirs. Rome once again experienced the depressing spectacle of great estates put up for auction and purchased at knock-down prices by successful upstarts, foreign freedmen, and inglorious hangers-on of the triumphant faction. Public confidence was non-existent, money in short supply. Land was a dangerous investment when veterans were soon to be settled, and certain to be re-confiscated if Brutus and Cassius should win. Partisans of the triumvirs with a taste for speculation were the only possible customers. As a result, the sales did not bring in as much as was anticipated. Appian says the deficit was 200 million denarii.

The inevitable consequence was further taxation. Owners of house-property had to contribute a year's rent from leased premises and half a year's rent from those they occupied themselves. Land-owners paid half their annual income. Those who had over 100,000 denarii were compelled to lend 2 per cent of their capital at interest, certainly low, to the state. Owners of slaves had to pay 25 denarii per slave. Even wealthy women, traditionally exempt from such measures, were made to pay. Soldiers were billeted without payment all over the country. The civil war was indeed starting to correct the uneven distribution of the wealth of Italy.

As if to confer divine blessing on this process, the New Year brought the deification of Julius Caesar. Plancus and Lepidus celebrated triumphs in the last days of December, ostensibly over the barbarians of Gaul. But both had allowed brothers to be proscribed, and it was of this 'victory' that their soldiers sang (*De germanis, non de Gallis, duo triumphant consules*). The consulship of this ironically yoked pair opened with the passing of various honours appropriate to the new god. The tribune Rufrenus, who had been one of the Antonian agitators in the camp of Lepidus at Forum Julii, continued his services to the cause by proposing that Caesar's statue be set up in all the municipalities of Italy. The real beneficiary was Octavian. His official nomenclature now described him as 'son of the God Julius'. His colleagues did the best they could in this superhuman line by causing the coinage of the state to bear their portraits, an honour hitherto aspired to in his lifetime by no Roman save Caesar. In the Greek east it denoted kingship. The aged Etruscan seer who, the previous year, had divined the return of monarchy to Rome, had spoken true.

Before turning to deal with Brutus and Cassius, the triumvirs made a brief attempt to defeat Sextus Pompey. After the collapse of the republican armies towards the end of the previous summer, Sextus had put to sea with his fleet and descended on Sicily. He was of course proscribed, but this did nothing to stop him first gaining a foothold at Lilybaeum in the west and then seizing the whole island from its governor A. Pompeius Bithynicus, whose political sympathies were elastic enough to allow him to be reconciled to Sextus. The reconciliation was effected by two of the proscribed, who had fled in considerable numbers to join Sextus. Thus Sextus, in the early months of 42, stood in undisputed command of Sicily, menacing the coast of Italy and offering welcome refuge to the enemies of the triumvirs. His fleet was powerful, commanded by Greek freedmen of proven experience and seamanship. His land forces were sufficient to hold the island, and he consolidated his grip on it by establishing at Syracuse and Panormus settlements of the Spaniards who had supported him so well in Spain and had now accompanied him to Sicily. But he was not dependent simply on Greeks and Spaniards. He had Roman staff officers who had followed him from Spain, like his quaestor L. Appuleius Decianus, and his claim to represent the Republic became daily more credible as the refugees from the proscriptions and volunteers from the eighteen designated towns made their way across to him. Furthermore, where Octavian was merely an adopted son of Caesar, and posthumously adopted at that, Sextus himself was a son of Pompey's flesh and blood. Between him and Octavian there could never be peace.

Salvidienus was despatched to dispose of Sextus, early in the summer of 42. Sextus sailed out with a sizeable fleet and met Salvidienus at the northern entrance to the straits of Messina, off Cape Scyllaeum. Salvidienus's ships were large and clumsy, designed for boarding operations, and in the short steep irregular chop produced by the violent current were quite outmanoeuvred by the lighter and more practised Pompeian vessels. The latter, however, lacked the means to destroy their wallowing enemies and Salvidienus was able to withdraw to the port of Balarus where he repaired his damaged fleet. Octavian now arrived, after travelling overland, and thought it expedient to promise to the inhabitants of neighbouring Vibo and Rhegium that their towns would be removed from the list of those marked down for the veterans. But he was unable to take the offensive against Sextus, for he received an urgent summons from Antony, who was at Brundisium and required his assistance in ferrying the army across the Adriatic for the encounter with the Liberators.

While Cicero's policies had collapsed and the last vestiges of senatorial authority been swept aside by Octavian's coup and the triumvirate, fortune had continued to favour Brutus and Cassius. Cassius's first opponent was Dolabella, who did not linger in Asia after his glorious exploit against Trebonius at Smyrna, but raised a second legion and proceeded by way of Cilicia to Syria. Apart from the two legions, he had a few Rhodian ships and the hope of some Lycian transport vessels. With these he faced the eleven legions and the fleet of Cassius. Rational calculation was never Dolabella's strong suit. It was lunacy to suppose that he could succeed—though perhaps he was counting on Allienus's four legions which had already deserted. Lentulus Spinther, Trebonius's quaestor, defeated the 'governor' Dolabella left in Asia and harried his ships from behind, the towns of Syria were not enthusiastic about admitting him, and the Rhodians, whose navy was renowned, sent him only a token force. He took refuge in the seaport of Laodicea, but the inhabitants were spared the horrors of a prolonged blockade. Cassius bribed the commanders of the guard to open the gates to him, whereupon Dolabella committed suicide by ordering a slave to cut off his head. This occurred about the end of July. Cassius gave a foretaste of the treatment he was later to mete out by demanding the enormous sum of 1,500 talents from Tarsus for admitting Dolabella and relenting only when freeborn citizens were being sold into slavery to raise the money. He next considered moving against Egypt, since he had heard that Cleopatra was about to send help to Antony and Octavian; but Brutus informed him that their enemies were crossing the Adriatic, and towards the end of the year the two men met in Smyrna to confer.

Brutus, for his part, had been as energetic and successful in the preceding months as Cassius. He had waited at Dyrrhachium through April, anxious for the news from Mutina. Then in May he marched south to Apollonia, and took the Via Egnatia that climbed up through the Albanian mountains and skirted the shores of Lake Ohrid to emerge in the plains of the lower Vardar valley—that land route from Italy to Macedonia and the Hellespont for which no power before or after Rome has had a use. Pursued by letters from Cicero exhorting him to come to the aid of the republic, he preferred to trust his own judgment of Octavian, calling him Octavius and, contemptuously, 'your Caesar'. Salvation, in Brutus's view, lay in the resources of the east, not in heaping praise and honour where it could do little good. Young Marcus Cicero, the orator's son, who had been one of the first to join him in Athens, brought him a force of cavalry. At Abdera he held a review of his army, now numbering seven or eight legions, and then crossed over into Asia, where he received the expected affirmations of loyalty from the cities and dynasts of the region. The men of Pergamum offered the generous sum of 200 talents in the hope of buying their way out of further contributions to finance a civil war that barely affected them. King Deiotarus of Galatia, who sent troops, was more sincere: he had once been forced to plead for mercy before Caesar.

Asia thus secured, Brutus turned to the immediate task of protecting what was likely to be his rear and also his chief supply line in any conflict with a Caesarian army that came across from Italy. Thrace was a difficult and mountainous region, ruled by difficult and treacherous princes. It was important to convince them that there was no profit in joining his enemies. He demonstrated the proposition by making an expedition against a refractory tribe and secured a success that was convincing enough for his troops to salute him as *Imperator*. Brutus was glad to have the salutation, cheaply though it was often earned. It immediately replaced the title of proconsul on the coins he struck. Octavian, Antony, Lepidus, Plancus, and Decimus Brutus all had it. In the struggle to win over neutrals and confirm waverers, it was not enough to invoke patriotism and high ideals. To be a credible leader, one needed to display military ability; the soldiers saw no future in following a general who was incompetent, however laudable his motives and noble his character.

His campaign over and his new troops satisfactorily blooded, Brutus was back at the Hellespont before the beginning of September. There he learnt how Octavian had marched on Rome, extorted the consulship, and secured the judicial condemnation of Caesar's murderers. The news confirmed his gloomiest predictions. The last hopes of compromise had vanished. He crossed into Asia and devoted his energies to persuading the cities which had been so gratifyingly eager to make promises earlier in the year to translate their promises into cash. Three months later came the news that the triumvirate had been formed.

It was now that he met Cassius at Smyrna for a council of war. An invasion of Italy was out of the question, given the season of the year and the strength of their enemies. Brutus favoured an immediate move into Macedonia, but Cassius argued that it was more important to consolidate troops and resources where they were strong. Above all, they needed money, and they acted brutally to obtain it. Even loyal and inoffensive allies were savagely treated. The wretched cities of Asia Minor had barely recovered from the incursion of Mithridates, a generation before, and the frightful indemnities demanded of them afterwards by Rome. This did not prevent the Liberators requiring that they pay in the space of two years the tribute that they would normally have paid in ten. There were also richer victims to hand. The wealth of the independent communities of Lycia and Rhodes was still untouched, and both had supplied ships to Dolabella. What matter if these had been mere token forces, sent in ignorance of the political upheaval then in progress? Brutus gave the erring Lycians a taste of the Roman whip, while Cassius turned against Rhodes.

When the Rhodians refused to co-operate, alleging lack of instructions from the senate, Cassius set about reducing them by force. He defeated them at sea and invested the city by land. The Rhodians resisted bravely, but treachery (or wise counsels) prevailed. Cassius was secretly admitted to the city, with a select band of soldiers, and overawed resistance. He punished the leaders by death or banishment and turned to his real task of raising money. Appian's account of Cassius's attack on Rhodes would have us believe that the Rhodians were friendly to Octavian and Antony. But the Rhodians had always pursued an independent policy, as far as they could. Their crime at the present moment was to want to be neutral, to avoid committing themselves until matters were a little clearer. Unfortunately, they paid the price of being too wealthy and too weak to do this. Cassius needed money and ships, and the Rhodians had both. If he did not get them his enemies might. So he, the tyrant-slayer, was forced to attack an innocent and noble city, the home of his former tutor and one of Rome's oldest allies. Victory achieved, he plundered the temples and the public treasury, extorted all the gold and silver he could from the citizens, and underlined the irony of it all by turning some of the silver into coins bearing the effigy of the goddess Freedom.

Cassius also left a colony of Romans to ensure the loyalty of the island. This must have consisted largely of old soldiers who were more use on what amounted to garrison duty than on field service. But why did Cassius go to the trouble of establishing a colony in full legal form? The answer lies in the fact that Rhodes was not an isolated case. Brutus and Cassius and their lieutenants founded several other colonies at the same time in other parts of the eastern Mediterranean. Their uses were not simply, or even chiefly, military. The soldiers lost nothing by the restoration of the republic and the end, the same interests as those for whose loyalties Octavian and Antony had been competing. The Liberators had to ensure that these soldiers lost nothing by the restoration of the republic and the removal of the man from whom they expected their rewards. Caesar had already founded colonies of veterans in the eastern provinces. It was vital for Brutus and Cassius to show that they were patrons as effective as anyone on the other side, and that Caesar's heirs had no monopoly of founding new cities for the benefit of those who served them. Hence colonies were founded in Macedonia by Q. Hortensius and in Cyrenaica by P. Cosconius, acting under the authority of Brutus and Cassius respectively. The coinages issued to mark these foundations were a tangible sign of the authority, legitimacy, and effectiveness of the supreme commands held by the two men, as were the more widely circulated silver issues bearing symbols and legends redolent of the powers claimed and the ideals professed by the overlords of the eastern provinces.

While the Liberators belied their name east of the Aegean, the triumvirs had shipped their army across from Brundisium. The port was blockaded by L. Staius Murcus who had originally been stationed by Cassius at Taenarum, the southern promontory of the Peloponnese, to stop Cleopatra and a fleet from joining Octavian and Antony at Brundisium. The queen was caught by a storm and her ships wrecked on the African coast, leaving Murcus free to harry the triumvirs. Antony was reduced to waiting for strong westerly winds to enable his transport ships to evade Murcus's squadron. Octavian's arrival, after the abortive attempt to defeat Sextus, strengthened his side sufficiently for the main body of the army and the two commanders to cross unchallenged. Sextus was conspicuous by his absence. His fleet, with that of Murcus, could have made this crossing too dangerous to attempt. Not for the first time, Sextus showed himself unwilling to help others when his own position was secure. But after the Caesarians had gained the Macedonian coast, their communications were cut. Cn. Domitius Ahenobarbus, in command of the bulk of the fleet of Brutus and Cassius, came to reinforce Murcus and the pair of them effectively dominated the Adriatic. There could be no retreat for the Caesarian army.

Octavian remained at Dyrrhachium, ill, while Antony saw the army over the mountains and into the fertile land of Macedonia. Once his army stood at the head of the Gulf of Salonika, he had denied Greece to his enemies and eliminated the chance of being outflanked to the south. He sent ahead C. Norbanus and the trusty L. Decidius Saxa to hold the route along the coast. They took up a position not far from Philippi and awaited the forces of the Liberators, which had mustered at Sardis in the summer and crossed the Hellespont in August or September. Brutus and Cassius were in no hurry to engage. On the other hand, they had to stop the Caesarian army from passing across into Asia. The longer they could leave this blocking operation, the better chance they had of prolonging the campaign into the winter without committing themselves to a decisive battle, while the Caesarians wasted away, unable to advance, cut off by sea, and depending for their commissariat on the scanty resources of Greece and Macedonia.

The campaign of Philippi opened well for the Liberators. Circumventing Norbanus and Saxa, they put to flight an outlying garrison, and came back to a strong position astride the Via Egnatia. Brutus took the right flank, protected by the mountains, Cassius the left, resting against a marsh. Provided their army remained loyal— for there were amongst it men who had served with Caesar—there was no way in which they could be defeated except by a straight fight. In ancient warfare, it took two to make a battle. One side might offer, but if the other refused and its position were good, no result could be achieved. 1,500 denarii a head, and the promise of more, took care of the men's loyalty. For the rest, Brutus and Cassius methodically strengthened their joint lines, while Antony brought his army up and encamped opposite them. Sallies and counter-sallies took place, but for some time Antony was unable to force an engagement. Then he started to work through the marsh to outflank Cassius to the south and brought on the first, indecisive, battle on October 23. Brutus on the right was triumphantly successful, breaking through and capturing Octavian's camp. In spite of his illness Octavian had judged that he could not afford to miss a victory, and had come up to take his share of the command. But there was no sign of him in his camp. It was said that he took refuge in a marsh when Brutus's men were pillaging his camp. On the other wing, fortune was reversed. Cassius's camp was overrun by Antony's men, and believing that Brutus too had been defeated, he fell on his sword.

His death, for the Liberators, was a tragedy. Cassius was the general of the pair, for all his intense and brooding nature and lack of the approachability and transparent honesty that Brutus possessed. His unnecessary suicide engendered a loss of confidence in the Republican camp, though the strategic situation had not been altered by the battle and still favoured Brutus. Officers and men started to become impatient. A waiting game is hard to play. The more unreliable of the princelings and their soldiery started to filter away, judging that they no longer needed an insurance policy. The Caesarians taunted their enemies with cowardice and made it more difficult for Brutus to hold his men in check. Finally, he gave way when he least needed to. Every day that passed increased the supply problems of the Caesarians, and Antony had been forced to despatch a legion to Greece to obtain essential provisions. Furthermore, Ahenobarbus and Murcus in the Ionian sea caught and destroyed the fleet of Domitius Calvinus as he was transporting two urgently needed legions to reinforce the Caesarian army at Philippi.

The second battle took place about three weeks after the first. It was hard and murderously fought before the Republicans yielded. Brutus himself committed suicide, ushering out the republic that his ancestor had ushered in. Not a few followed his example. Among the fallen were many representatives of the great families whose names were synonymous with the history of Rome. Pharsalus had been the same. No one could accuse the Roman oligarchy of being unwilling to fight and die for its interests, and its passing was made easier by the toll the civil wars exacted from its members. Those that survived and did not wish to perpetuate their exile with Sextus or with the fleets of Ahenobarbus and Murcus preferred, if they were spared, to transfer their allegiance to Antony rather than to Octavian. Antony at least was one of their own class. Later propaganda reported that after the battle the republican officers, brought before the victorious commanders, saluted Antony as *Imperator* but cast abuse at Octavian: a fiction, but one containing that particle of truth necessary to all propaganda.

For the other ranks on the defeated side, things were easier. In such a civil war, soldiers could hardly lose—at any rate in the long run. An amnesty offered by the victors was accepted immediately by the vast majority. The troops of Deiotarus, deserted at the correct moment by their general Amyntas, chancellor to the old king, returned home. The only part of the Republican forces able to carry on the struggle elsewhere was the fleet, and that portion of it in Aegean waters made its way to join Ahenobarbus and Murcus. The victory of the triumvirs was complete. There remained only Sextus and the Republican admirals, the latter reduced in practice to the status of pirates, the former disparagingly but less accurately termed one.

Chapter VIII

PERUSIA

THE DEFEAT of Brutus and Cassius removed the chief cause of the alliance of Octavian and Antony. However, there was as yet no reason for the alliance to crumble. There remained tasks which arose naturally from the present situation, the consequences of the course of action they had embarked upon at the momentous conference of the previous autumn. The recalled veterans and the men who had served out their time, both from the twenty-eight legions which had fought to avenge Caesar at Philippi, and from the others which had remained in Italy and the west to ensure security, must now at last be permitted to reap the promised rewards of their loyalty. They could be put off no longer. That meant two things: the provision of money to pay their discharge bounties, and the allocation of land in Italy. Both were likely to entail unpopularity. More rewarding, perhaps, might be the final snuffing out of the Republican flame. Again, this task divided itself naturally in two: one part was the pursuit of those few Republican notables who had taken refuge in various parts of the eastern provinces, together with the reduction or conversion of those client-kings of Rome who had been unwise enough to support Brutus and Cassius; the other was the prosecution of the war against Sextus Pompey. A third matter, not so pressing at the moment but ultimately unavoidable, was the security of the eastern borders of the empire. Since Crassus's defeat by the Parthians at Carrhae in 53, Rome had been racked by almost continuous civil strife. Successive Roman commanders in Syria had been able to do no more than beat off Parthian raids, and it was very fortunate that the Parthian monarchs, whether from choice or necessity, were unable to take advantage of Rome's internal troubles.

There is no record of any quarrel between Antony and Octavian over the division of these tasks. The ordering of the eastern provinces entailed the possibility of a major war against Parthia, and this alone was enough to ensure that it was Antony who went east. The glory of Philippi was his, visible proof of his acknowledged ability as a general. And besides, Antony had connections in the east. He had served under Gabinius in Syria in 57–55, and in 55 had been sent on a special mission to restore Ptolemy Auletes, Cleopatra's father, to the throne of Egypt. He had also had occasion during these years to fight alongside Antipater, commander of the Judaean forces and father of Herod who now coveted the throne of Judaea. Such personal contacts were of the greatest importance in procuring arrangements favourable to Rome in the petty kingdoms along the eastern borders. Octavian entirely lacked these contacts. His precocious and meteoric rise was not without its disadvantages. To him therefore fell the job of settling the veterans—appropriately enough. It was his solicitude for their interests that had elevated him successively to a special command, a consulship, and his present eminence. With this, for geographical reasons, went the conduct of the war against Sextus. As for Lepidus, his loyalty was suspect, his following negligible, and his importance minimal. Antony and Octavian preferred not to trust him with serious matters. A fresh distribution of the western provinces was made, to his detriment. He lost Spain to Octavian, most of whose original portion was now in the hands of Sextus, and Provence to Antony, who needed compensation for Cisalpine Gaul which at last became part of Italy. In addition Octavian took Numidia, and Antony Africa, pending the satisfactory proof of his loyalty by Lepidus. These arrangements were recorded in writing and sealed, a pointless precaution since there was no higher authority to whom appeal could be made. The alliance depended on mutual trust.

Antony departed to Greece to pass the winter; Octavian, still in poor health, made the journey back to Italy. The winter travelling nearly killed him, and for some time he lay so ill at Brundisium that rumours swept Rome that he was dead. Meanwhile L. Antonius, the triumvir's brother, inaugurated his consulship by celebrating a triumph (for a victory over some Alpine tribes) on January 1. His colleague was P. Servilius, who, equivocal as ever, managed to stay neutral in the dramatic events of this year. If his past loyalties are anything to go by—and that is more than doubtful—he was Antony's man rather than Octavian's. Much more important than Servilius was Fulvia, Antony's wife and mother-in-law of the young Caesar. The propaganda later put out by the enemies of Antony alleged that the consuls of 41 were L. Antonius and Fulvia. Physically attractive and politically ambitious, Fulvia had been previously married to two of the most important and independent of the younger politicians of the fifties. After Clodius's death in a wayside brawl she had become the wife of C. Scribonius Curio, the tribune reputedly bought by Caesar for an enormous sum in 50. Widowed a second time by Curio's death in Africa in the first year of the civil war, she married Antony two or three years later. There was more to her than attractiveness: she was an heiress, she was almost certainly descended from the celebrated Fulvii of Tusculum, and she had remarkable determination and strength of character—Velleius says that 'she had nothing womanly about her except her body'. Her choice of husbands shows clearly enough her ambition, and her powers of judgment.

When he reached Rome, Octavian found himself the centre of a bitter dispute. Deputations from the eighteen towns (sixteen if Vibo and Rhegium were exempted) which had been selected as sites for veteran colonies protested that the hardship should be spread equally over all Italy, or at least that lots should be cast and that those who gave the land should be paid for it. The veterans were impatient for their land, and there was no money to buy it. Appian says the Italians 'flocked to Rome, young and old, women and children, to the Forum and to the sanctuaries, lamenting and protesting that they had done no wrong, but, although they were Italians, were being driven from land, hearth, and home like a conquered people. The Romans grieved with them and joined in their tears, particularly when they realized that the war had not been undertaken in defence of the state but amongst themselves for a change in the form of their government; and that the rewards of victory were given, and the colonies founded, so that democracy should never again raise its head, for the colonies were composed of mercenaries ready to do whatever their rulers might wish.'

It was clearly impossible to satisfy both parties. Octavian attempted for a while to steer some sort of middle course, perhaps in the hope that Antony would raise enough money sufficiently quickly in Asia to enable at least some of the land to be acquired by purchase. He seized temple treasures on the pretext that he needed them for the war against Sextus and put up for auction the property of the last of the proscribed and of those who had fled or lost their lives at Philippi. But this produced little, and the veterans, conscious of their own power, knowing that the masters of Rome owed everything to them, would not be put off for long by half-measures. Up to this point Octavian had had the co-operation of L. Antonius and Fulvia, though they were not motivated by the same reasons as himself. They wished to delay the foundation of the veteran colonies until

Antony himself should return to Italy, so that Octavian should not alone profit from the glory and good-will to be obtained among the soldiers. When it became apparent that the veterans would not wait, they asked that Octavian choose from amongst Antony's friends those who were to perform the official act of settlement of Antony's legions. They forced Octavian's hand by addressing the veterans and begging them not to allow the victor of Philippi to be deprived of his share of credit. Manius, Antony's private agent in Italy, and Lucius even went so far as to produce Fulvia and Antony's children before the soldiers. Such was Antony's standing that Octavian did not dare refuse the request—though, if one may judge by the sequel, he probably wanted to.

Octavian's position was bad. For the first time since his bid for political power, he could not call upon armed men under the pretext of avenging Caesar. There was no clear enemy—except Sextus, and he could hardly be blamed for this social crisis. Antony, the victor of Philippi, was not a credible target. The chief adversary, if such he could be called at this stage, was Lucius—and he was the legitimate consul, between whose authority and that of a triumvir with consular power there was little apparent difference. What difference there was rested on personal standing rather than on constitutional enactment. Lucius, unwilling to be overawed by the youthful Caesar, representing in the popular eye the more powerful triumvir and possessing a considerable hold on the Roman people because of his activities as a tribune in 44, was no mean opponent. And this was not all. There was open friction between Octavian and the Antonian commanders. Q. Fufius Calenus in Provence refused to deliver over to Octavian two legions, replacements for two of Octavian's that Antony had taken with him after Philippi. Pollio, in Cisalpine Gaul, impeded Salvidienus, who was marching by the normal overland route to take possession of Spain for Octavian—though why Pollio did so is not at all clear. Perhaps it grated on him that a man who was not even a senator, whose rise epitomized what the revolutionary party of Octavian stood for, should be sent to govern a great proconsular province, one which, furthermore, he himself had so recently governed.

Worst of all, Octavian took the chief blame for the misery of the expropriated, the dislocation of agriculture, and the chaotic economic conditions. For the unhappiness of the times we have the personal testimony of Virgil and Horace. Virgil himself was one of the dispossessed when Pollio made allotments to Antonian veterans around

Cremona and Mantua. Horace, a survivor of Philippi, and by his own confession no fighting man, was sure that the anger of the gods must lie heavy on a people so soaked in the gore of civil war. The themes of dispossession, disgust with the senselessness and brutality of the present strife, and longing to escape to another world of childlike peace and magic, are prominent in the poetry that both men wrote between 41 and 38. Even wolves and lions, Horace says bitterly, spare their own kind.

Some of the veterans took matters into their own hands and forcibly seized the lands to which they considered themselves entitled. Others menaced Octavian himself, surrounding him angrily in the theatre, and killing a centurion who took his part when he was late for an assembly. The soldiery at this time reached a pitch of insubordination never surpassed in the history of Rome. Appian's analysis is one of his classic paragraphs:

> The cause of their reluctance to accept authority was that the generals, as usually happens in a civil war, were not chosen by constitutional means, and their armies were not enrolled from the military registers according to the ancient custom, nor for the benefit of their country; neither did they serve the state, but only those who had enlisted them, and then not by the compulsion of the laws, but by private promises; and they were used against the enemies of private individuals, not of the public weal, and against their fellow-citizens and equals, not foreigners. All these things slackened military discipline. The soldiers thought that they were not so much on military service as helping of their own kindness and free-will commanders who stood in need of them for their own personal ends. Desertion, formerly an unpardonable crime to the Romans, was at that time actually rewarded, and it was practised both by whole armies and by some eminent individuals, since they considered it was not desertion to change like for like. For all parties were alike, and none of them could be distinguished as genuinely patriotic; the common claim of the leaders that they were all striving for the good of their country made men less reluctant to desert, since they could serve their country on any side. The generals understood this well, and tolerated such conduct, knowing that their authority over their men rested not on law, but on bounties.

Finally, there were the external enemies—not of Rome, but of the triumvirs: Sextus, Murcus and Ahenobarbus, ringing Italy with their fleets. Sextus had profited by the campaign of Philippi to consolidate his position. Adventurers, political refugees, and dispossessed landholders fled to him. He was strong enough to menace the whole southern and western coasts of Italy, even as far as Ostia, the port of Rome. His control of the sea and of Sicily itself gravely impaired the supply of corn to Rome, which had become in the last hundred years almost totally dependent on imported grain to feed the swollen population. Ahenobarbus and Murcus were still at large in the Adriatic and Ionian seas. Although Murcus very soon decided to take his two legions and eighty ships to join Sextus, and sent for the remainder of his forces from his base on the island of Cephallenia, Ahenobarbus continued to harry the eastern coasts and make life uncomfortable for the citizens of the seaport towns. However, Sextus's interruption of the grain supply was the more serious matter. It hurt the urban population, amongst whom Octavian had never lost his popularity and on whom he might otherwise have been able to rely in the present crisis.

Octavian's enemies now judged that the time had come to resolve the clash of authority between consul and triumvir. Lucius could count on the support of the civilian population of all Italy. In addition, Pollio in the Po valley and Plancus at Beneventum were engaged in making land settlements to Antonian veterans and could quickly reconstitute legions. Calenus, governor of the Gallic provinces, had the able Ventidius as his associate and the formidable total of eleven legions at his disposal. He was already across Salvidienus's route to Spain and could be relied upon not to fail Antony in a crisis. As for Octavian, his only solid backing lay in his own veterans and the four legions he had in camp at Capua—and Salvidienus's six legions, if the Antonians allowed them to return to Italy. Now, if ever, was the moment to put the upstart pseudo-Caesar back in his place, when for the first time in his career he was neither popular nor militarily strong. The weapon he had used so often, the promise of spectacular rewards, was now blunted in his hand.

It seems unlikely that Lucius intended to provoke a war. None the less, he had to be strong enough to threaten one if his challenge were to succeed, and to start one if it did not. With the backing of Fulvia and Manius, he began to take the side of the dispossessed, who flocked with petitions to any man who might have influence and particularly to himself as consul. He accused Octavian of exceeding his authority, and their disagreements became increasingly serious. At the same time he attempted to show he was not unsympathetic to the veterans by taking Antony's children and ostentatiously following Octavian as he led out the last of the colonists. When Octavian sent a troop of cavalry to the south, ostensibly against Sextus,

Lucius claimed that this was an attempt to intimidate him, and raised a bodyguard from the Antonian colonies. He was able to draw support from his brother's veterans in this way because it was alleged that Octavian was discriminating against them by dividing unequally the proceeds of the sales of the property of the proscribed, and by trying to settle his own men who had not fought at Philippi alongside those who had.

The officers of the army—that is, the centurions—viewed this bitterness and new threat of bloodshed with alarm. They arranged a conference at Teanum, where Octavian and Lucius agreed to put right the various grievances. Calenus was to hand over the two legions owed to Octavian, and, with Pollio, allow Salvidienus to go on his way unhindered, and Lucius was to dismiss his bodyguard; on the other hand Octavian promised to give Antony's veterans an equal share of the money derived from confiscated property, to settle only men who had fought at Philippi, and not to interfere with Lucius's consular authority. Further, neither Octavian nor Antony should have the right of conscription in Italy. This was a highly significant provision; for Rome had never, in theory, abandoned the principle that her armies should be composed of her own citizens. In fact, the exigencies of the civil wars had led to the principle being frequently broken: Caesar in Gaul, the Pompeians in Africa, and Brutus in Macedonia had all raised legions containing men who did not possess Roman citizenship when they were enlisted. Rome's present troubles had arisen largely because the institutions of a city-state—one of which was the citizen army—had not been adapted to the needs of an empire. So the men who negotiated this agreement were striking, in all probability unwittingly, at one of the root causes of these troubles. Slowly, events were starting to bring their own remedies.

The agreement turned out to be abortive. None of the provisions were obeyed, except that Pollio let Salvidienus pass and Lucius dismissed his bodyguard. Evidently neither principal was sincere in wishing for a reconciliation. Lucius still refused to trust Octavian. Antony himself gave no clear instructions, but this was scarcely surprising in the circumstances. It must have been difficult to make out from the self-justifying letters written to him by Lucius, Lepidus, Octavian and Fulvia—not to mention lesser notables—exactly what was happening or whose interests were truly at stake; and the difficulty was compounded by the two months or so that it took for a letter to get to Asia Minor and back. Octavian divorced Antony's stepdaughter Clodia, sending her back to Fulvia still a virgin. This was a repudiation of her mother Fulvia, rather than of Antony. Antony contented himself with giving instructions in a letter that his adherents should take up arms if his 'standing' (*dignitas*) were threatened. He left to those on the spot the onus of deciding how this vague phrase—which Caesar had used to start a civil war—should be interpreted.

Lucius remained in the town of Praeneste, twenty miles from Rome. He paid his recruits, and proclaimed his loyalty to his absent brother's interests, by striking coins which bore on one side Antony's portrait and titles, on the other the personification of PIETAS accompanied by the storks that are still the symbols of devotion. The officers who had mediated the agreement made a vain attempt to arbitrate, with the support of the leading senators. The Antonians countered with allegations that Octavian was undermining and defrauding Antony, and assuming powers in excess of his mandate. It was not till an embassy from two colonized legions of Caesar's veterans, who had served under Antony, added their voices to the plea for negotiation that Lucius, Fulvia and Manius agreed to submit their case to a tribunal. Gabii, half-way between Rome and Praeneste, was chosen for the hearing, and the decision was to be made in accordance with the pacts of Philippi, as recorded in writing. Again, lack of mutual trust destroyed any chance of agreement. The mounted advance parties of the two sides came to blows, and Lucius flatly refused to have anything else to do with a negotiated settlement. Both men made preparations for war, issuing polemical edicts the while.

When the agents of the two sides travelled the country, it became plain that Lucius had the support of the vast majority of citizens. Octavian made a last bid for the sympathies of the upper classes by addressing the senate and the wealthier section of the Roman community, and a final deputation visited Lucius at Praeneste. Manius read them Antony's instructions and, when they asked if anybody had in fact attacked his standing, prevaricated until they departed. Appian hints that the letter may have been fictitious; but if Manius had wished to manufacture false authority for a war, he would surely have done it in more convincing terms. The letter, then, was genuine; and Antony ignorant of or unable to prevent the activities of his wife, brother, and agent. Lucius judged that it was in the interests of his brother and of Italy to eliminate the man who had been responsible for disrupting the compromise reached after the murder of Caesar and for plunging the commonwealth into the wars of Mutina and Philippi. He saw clearly enough the ambition of Octavian and the dangerously non-senatorial nature of his most trusted following. Such a man was unlikely to rest content with the limited periods of primacy sanctioned by the customs of their ancestors.

The course of the war cannot be clearly made out from the ancient accounts. There were sporadic outbreaks of fighting up and down the country, and a major disturbance in Campania. Most of the leading men joined Lucius, but Lepidus stayed loyal to his triumviral colleague and was entrusted with two legions and the defence of Rome. Lucius, after quelling disaffection among two legions of his at Alba Fucens by the well-tried methods of a bounty and large promises, tricked Lepidus and entered Rome. Lepidus fled, his troops went over to Lucius, and the consul made a speech to the people. He promised vengeance on Octavian and Lepidus, and said that his brother would voluntarily resign his unlawful and tyrannical office and accept instead the ancient dignity and authority of the consulship. True or not, this promise was rapturously received by the citizens. This was a saviour with a difference.

Lucius then marched to meet Octavian, collecting fresh levies from the Antonian colonies. His strategy seems to have been to prevent Salvidienus, who had been recalled by Octavian, from making a junction with Octavian's own forces. Salvidienus came south with Pollio and Ventidius shadowing him; he was in grave danger of being trapped and annihilated by vastly superior forces. He was saved by Agrippa (who here emerges into the light of history for the first time since the Campanian recruiting tour of 44), and by the uncertainty of the Antonian generals. Agrippa seized Sutrium, a strong town north of Rome. There was an engagement at Veii, in the same area. Lucius could not ignore the threat to his flank and rear, and turned aside to attack Agrippa. But Salvidienus was then behind him. So Lucius, caught in his turn between forces that in combination outnumbered his own, decided to draw away to the north and join up with Ventidius and Pollio. These, in the meantime, had not dared to attack Salvidienus's army—not because they were afraid of the outcome, but because they had no idea what Antony's wishes were. Their uncertainty on this vital point was increased by reports circulated by one M. Barbatius, who had been serving with Antony as quaestor but had been sent home after some disagreement with his commander. Barbatius put it about that Antony was greatly distressed by the turn events had taken and regarded war against Octavian as war against their joint rule.

Lucius, harassed by Salvidienus and Agrippa as he made his way north early in the winter through the hills of the upper Tiber valley, decided not to cross the Apennines but to wait instead for the others to join him. He therefore turned aside to Perusia (modern Perugia) which was strongly fortified, and encamped outside it. Octavian, arriving with a third army to add to those of his two generals, forced Lucius to take refuge in the town, threw up a seven-mile circuit of ditch and palisade, cut the town off from the river, summoned reinforcements, and sent troops forward to check the advance of the other Antonians. Lucius despatched Manius to Pollio and Ventidius requesting their urgent assistance, and countered with siege works of his own: he did not have the provisions to withstand a long siege. On receipt of his message, and of others from Fulvia, Pollio and Ventidius started to advance to his relief, but Octavian and Agrippa went to meet them with sufficient forces to block them. Jealous of each other, still ignorant of Antony's intentions, and with their armies not yet united, they deemed discretion the better part and withdrew to Ariminum and Ravenna. Meanwhile Plancus, coming up from the south after destroying one of Octavian's legions which was on the march to Rome, took up a position at Spoletium, thirty miles away to the south-east. Octavian stationed a force to prevent him coming any closer, then hastened back to prosecute the siege.

Lucius grew short of food. He made an ineffectual attempt to break out. In Rome, public opinion was solidly against the war; the food shortage there was exacerbated by requisitions for military rations. In Perusia, the besieged invoked the name of Mark Antony, inscribing it on their lead sling-bullets in token of their devotion to him. The Caesarian soldiers answered with coarse messages to Fulvia, Octavian with an equally obscene but, as befitted his station, much more polished epigram. The Antonian generals consulted. They decided not to allow Lucius to perish beneath their eyes, and again moved on Perusia, this time united. Things were critical for Octavian, who was now in a similar position to Antony at Mutina. He sent Salvidienus and Agrippa, with the strongest forces he could spare, to meet the Antonians, who avoided battle and took up a strong position at Fulginium, half-way between Perusia and Spoletium. Pollio and Ventidius were for going on and fighting, Plancus (characteristically) for waiting. Their watch-fires blazing in the night could be seen from Perusia, but the hope they offered to the beleaguered army was illusory. Plancus had his way, in the absence of instructions from Antony, and the Antonians withdrew again. Those in Perusia did them the credit of believing that they had been destroyed.

The only chance left to Lucius and his hungry army was to fight their way out. They made a night assault on the circumvallation. The fighting raged until dawn all round the circuit, but when morning came the Caesarian lines were still intact. The siege went on. Food was so short that slaves were entirely deprived of rations, nor would Lucius let them escape in case the enemy discovered the desperate situation. For the same reason he refused to burn the bodies of the dead, lest the oily smoke be seen, and buried them in long trenches. The soldiers, at the end of their endurance, pleaded with Lucius to make one last attempt to break out. Death in battle was preferable to death by starvation and cold. So they prepared equipment for filling the ditch and assaulting the rampart, and sallied out under Lucius at first light. But the bravery and spirit of the Antonians was of no avail. Their wooden towers for scaling the rampart were too few, their physical strength too wasted, and the advantage of the besiegers too great. In their desperation they came near to success, but finally they were thrown back, the stripped bodies of their dead comrades flung insultingly upon them.

Capitulation was now inevitable unless outside help came. Lucius hung on for some days longer; but morale was sinking lower among his men, desertions of soldiers and even officers were becoming more frequent, and the civilian population was in distress. Negotiations were opened. Octavian, as was prudent, was inclined to be merciful. In a civil war, mercy paid dividends, and gratitude, if not synonymous with loyalty, went a long way towards ensuring it. If one can believe his autobiography, it was a spontaneous demonstration by Octavian's soldiers that secured an unconditional pardon for Lucius's veterans. He pardoned Lucius and the men of station who were with him, but the town council he put to death—except for one man who had been a juror in Rome at the trial of the murderers of Caesar and had been a model of zealous enthusiasm for the cause. The rest were not important enough to be worth winning over; and besides, it was necessary to *encourager les autres* in the towns of Italy. Republicanism was a dangerous disease. Perusia itself, an ancient and important city of the Etruscans, was destined for pillage by the soldiery. It was saved from this depressing fate by a notable of the town, said to be mentally unstable, who set fire to his own house. A high wind was blowing, and in a short while he had a funeral pyre worthy of an Etruscan king. The god Vulcan alone could control the flames. His temple survived while the rest of the town was entirely consumed.

So perished Perusia, and with it the threat to Caesar's heir. The Antonians dispersed: Pollio, sincere in his hatred of civil war but mistrustful of Octavian, withdrew to the Veneto with seven legions and prepared to defend himself; Plancus took ship with Fulvia to Greece; Julia, the mother of the Antonii, in company with many prominent supporters of her sons, took refuge with Sextus. Octavian marched to Campania, and suppressed the outbreak of resistance led by the aristocrat Ti. Claudius Nero, a courageous and cultivated man. Nero little suspected, as he fled with his young wife Livia and their infant son along unfrequented tracks to the sea and Sextus, that Livia would become his present persecutor's wife, and little Tiberius, fifty-four years later, emperor of Rome. Nor can the equally aristocratic Ahenobarbus, the last of the Republicans, roaming the Adriatic with his formidable fleet, have had any idea that his great-grandson, bearing his and Nero's names, would be the last of the dynasty that their chief enemy had yet to found.

Chapter IX

PEACE RESTORED

PERUSIA FELL in January or February of the year 40. Some fifteen months had passed since Antony and Octavian had parted to set about their respective tasks after the victory of Philippi. Antony was energetic, but only when it was necessary. He had received the surrender of a group of prominent Republicans on the island of Thasos, then, leaving Octavian to make the journey across to the Adriatic coast, he himself travelled south to Athens, where he spent the rest of the winter. His pleasures were those of a cultivated man, as was fitting in this once powerful but still honoured university town. He made gifts to the city, listened to literary conversation, attended games and religious ceremonies, and delighted in complimentary addresses. It is not recorded what the Athenians did with the statues they had set up to Brutus and Cassius two winters previously, but the base of Brutus's with part of its inscription, survives to this day. Such things were the necessary signs of loyalty to the master of the moment, prudent political gambits in the Hellenistic game of inflated compliments. Antony was mollified by yet grander honours voted by the Athenians, although he was not impressed by the efforts of their neighbours the Megarians. Invited to inspect their senate-house, 'It is small,' he commented, 'but rotten.'

In the spring he left L. Marcius Censorinus in charge of Macedonia, and crossed to Asia. Deputations from the cities and kingdoms of the region assembled at Ephesus to meet him and plead for lenient treatment. A great show was laid on for the benefit of the conqueror. Women dressed as Bacchanals, and men and boys as satyrs conducted him into the city. He was hailed as the new Dionysus, the Beneficent, the Bringer of Joy, and everywhere could be heard the music and seen the ivy-wreath and the garlanded beribboned staff that belonged to the god and his devotees. Antony was pleased. It was no new thing for Roman governors and generals in these eastern provinces, long used to rule by god-monarchs, to be accorded epithets and honours that made the old Roman distinctions of triumph, thanksgiving, or statue, seem very small beer. But to be acclaimed as Dionysus, this was indeed something that went beyond the hackneyed vocabulary of high-flown praise, something to set against the claim of his youthful colleague to be the son of a god. There was another advantage, too. Where Julius Caesar, regarded as a divinity, was somewhat colourless, there could be no mistaking the character of Dionysus. He was the god of ecstatic release, dark and powerful, destructive perhaps if thwarted, but capable of bringing an end to earthly misery, and the promise of a fuller and happier existence.

For the moment, however, it was the punitive streak in Dionysus's nature that prevailed. Antony explained that he wished to be merciful and that he fully understood that the cities of Asia had supported Brutus and Cassius because they were coerced by them, but he and Octavian had the task of finding discharge bounties for 170,000 men and more. He would therefore pardon them and spare their lands and citizens. In gratitude for this magnanimity they would contribute to him no more than they had contributed to Brutus and Cassius, namely the taxes of ten years; but since the triumvirs were pressed for time, this sum must be paid in one year. The protest from the cities, already squeezed brutally by the Republicans, was tremendous, and Antony was forced to remit one year's taxes and permit a second year for payment. To those Republicans who had taken sanctuary in the precinct of Diana he granted pardon, as was politic—the murderers of Caesar always excepted.

From Ephesus he proceeded south and east, deposing or confirming the petty dynasts of the area, granting special assistance to the Lycians and the Rhodians on account of their maltreatment at the hands of Brutus and Cassius, and liberating those citizens of Tarsus who had been sold into slavery to meet the exactions of Cassius. In Cappadocia, he settled a dispute over the succession by yielding to the beautiful, seductive Glaphyra, mother of one of the contenders. More famous, but emotionally little more serious, was his encounter at Tarsus with the queen of Egypt. The true importance of the meeting, at that moment, was political. Egypt was vital to Antony. It was by far the wealthiest, most fertile, and most easily defended of all the kingdoms that lay within Rome's orbit. He could, of course, take it by force—though even Caesar had learnt how difficult that could be. But his major task, in the years immediately ahead, was to

defeat or decisively push back the Parthians and bring a measure of
stability to the fragmented power structure of the eastern borders.
For this task, a friendly and subservient Egypt would be an enormous asset. He had therefore sent Q. Dellius, one of his high-ranking
friends, on a special mission to summon Cleopatra to Tarsus. She
was to give an explanation of why she herself had made a contribution to the war effort of the Republicans. The queen, wishing to
preserve her status, demurred: let Antony come to her. But Dellius
had his orders. It was essential, as a first step to manoeuvre her into
submission, that she come to Antony. Bowing to *force majeure*, she
came—but as a woman, and a woman who had already conquered
Caesar. Plutarch's description has been immortalized by Shakespeare:

> The barge she sat in, like a burnish'd throne,
> Burnt on the water: the poop was beaten gold;
> Purple the sails, and so perfumed that
> The winds were love-sick with them; the oars were silver,
> Which to the tune of flutes kept stroke, and made
> The water which they beat to follow faster,
> As amorous of their strokes. For her own person,
> It beggar'd all description: she did lie
> In her pavilion, cloth of gold, of tissue,
> O'er-picturing that Venus where we see
> The fancy out-work nature; on each side her
> Stood pretty dimpled boys, like smiling Cupids,
> With divers colour'd fans, whose wind did seem
> To glow the delicate cheeks which they did cool,
> And what they undid did.

The spectacular stage-management succeeded brilliantly. Cleopatra
knew her Antony from the years between 46 and 44, when she had
been installed by Caesar in a villa on the Janiculum in Rome. They
had first met when she was fifteen, at the time of her father's
restoration by Antony. Now she was twenty-nine, at the height of
her intellectual powers, her charm not yet diminished by the signs
of advancing age. She was not beautiful in a conventional way, in any
case, and fascinated men not by her looks, but by her voice and talk
and manner. Her coins perhaps do her less than justice, lacking any
hint of the vivacity, intensity and variety of expression that the
living woman possessed. According to the romantic Plutarch, the
crowd streamed away from Antony to the river bank until he was left

alone upon his official seat in the town square. She had out-trumped him; and when she refused his invitation to dine and he accepted her counter-invitation, she could be sure that she had saved much of the independence of her kingdom. There was no disgrace for a woman who had been Caesar's mistress in offering herself to a man who was Caesar's successor. In the eyes of her subjects, the goddess-queen could fittingly unite with the conquering Dionysus.

As for Antony, his capitulation is unlikely to have been the effect of blind love. He had very good reasons for favouring Cleopatra. For one thing, Herod and Cleopatra were natural enemies, and Herod was the one prince of whose loyalty Antony could be quite sure; he must prevent them falling out by binding each personally to himself. For another, the influential Graeco-Egyptian nobility of Ptolemaic Egypt were hostile to Rome and supported Cleopatra's younger sister Arsinoe; in fact, they had put Arsinoe on the throne shortly before the battle of Pharsalus. Because Cleopatra lacked this backing at home she needed Roman support and would be more likely to do the bidding of Rome. It was politic, therefore, and easy to dismiss the charges against her; they had been simply a pretext for summoning her. Antony went further. He gave orders that Arsinoe, who had fled as a suppliant to the temple of Artemis at Ephesus, should be assassinated. Thus of the five children of Ptolemy XI only Cleopatra survived: she had seen her father murder her elder sister; her elder brother and consort Ptolemy XII had died in the war against Caesar after Pharsalus; she herself had poisoned her younger brother Ptolemy XIII, with whom Caesar had made her share the throne; and now by her request her younger sister died. There was nothing sentimental about Cleopatra. Her aims achieved, the encounter was over. She invited Antony to spend the winter with her in Alexandria, and departed home.

He occupied the rest of the summer in expelling from Syria many petty rulers established by the Parthians in the past few years. Support of the Parthians, or of Cassius, was sufficient reason for him to levy fines on many of the cities. These were in keeping with the scale of his exactions in Asia; they were so severe that Aradus in Phoenicia revolted, and the Palmyrenes uprooted themselves from their desert oasis and took refuge with the Parthians, on whose trade they depended for their living. But he made no large-scale reorganization of client-kingdoms as Pompey had done twenty years before. There was little point in attempting to build up a secure system of reliable alliances until the Parthian question had been settled. He therefore confirmed on their thrones the two major princes of the area, Ptolemaeus of Chalcis and Iamblichus of Emesa. In Judaea, he appointed the brothers Phasael and Herod to be tetrarchs under the aged Hyrcanus, in spite of the protests of Jewish delegations at Antioch and again at Tyre. He also restored to the Jews some territory which Cassius had taken from them. Then leaving Syria and the Parthian border to the care of the trusty Decidius Saxa, he journeyed at the onset of winter to Alexandria.

He entered Egypt without legions, as a private citizen, the guest of an independent queen. In later years, tales proliferated about his winter with Cleopatra. Plutarch's grandfather knew a doctor who had been a medical student in Alexandria at the time and spun suitably tall stories about the extravagance of the royal manner of living. Cleopatra exerted all her cunning and charm to keep Antony amused, night and day. She drank, diced, hunted, and made love with him. When he went fishing, she arranged that at least he caught a salted herring. When he dressed as a common servant, to be free to explore the multifarious character of the great city, she came with him, so it was said, in the garb of a serving-maid.

There is a core of truth in all this. Antony liked a practical joke. He was not a man who set great store on a dignified public image. His respect for Caesar was sincere and unwavering, and Caesar had been a man who saw through pretentious language and pompous behaviour. Antony had spent a lot of his life with soldiers, in camp, in real wars—not the sort of fortnight's exercise against hill brigands for which men like Cicero were apt to claim a triumph. In such surroundings a man counted for what he was, not for what he pretended to be, and by this test Antony had shown himself the finest soldier of the day. He was perfectly sure of himself, able to indulge his streak of boyish humour and his undeniable appetite for wine and women without a moment of hesitation. He undoubtedly enjoyed Cleopatra; his frank and open character allowed him to accept the affair for what it was, an agreeable diversion mounted for political ends. But whether he was in love with Cleopatra is quite another matter. If he was, he allowed his emotions to influence no other part of his life. But for Octavian, and the wealth of her kingdom, Cleopatra would be no more famous than Glaphyra.

Cleopatra herself appears in the simplified and romantic accounts of the ancient authors as the *femme fatale*, the siren who lured Antony on and made him careless of all great matters of state. She wanted to have at her feet the master of the Roman east, to be the consort of the man who ruled more territories than any Hellenistic monarch since Alexander himself. If this was her aim, she was not successful. Antony departed in the early spring of 40, without a backward glance at the woman who was by then carrying his twins. Cleopatra's real aims were more limited and more tangible: to preserve, and if possible extend, the kingdom of the Ptolemies which she had struggled so long and so ruthlessly to gain. She was not an Egyptian at all, but of the almost pure Macedonian blood that the Ptolemies had preserved. The only royal house into which the Ptolemies married was that established in Syria by Seleucus, who was, like Ptolemy, one of Alexander's Macedonian generals. In the Seleucid house there was Bactrian and Persian blood, whence the oriental cast to Cleopatra's looks. But since her great-great-grandfather's union with the Seleucid Cleopatra I, the Ptolemies had conformed to the ancient custom of this unique country, which expected brother-sister marriages of its quasi-divine rulers. The pride and fire of Cleopatra were her inheritance from the fierce homeland of her race; her cunning and charm, the result of the intrigue and luxury of the Alexandrian court; and her intelligence and ambition, the product of generations of inbreeding. Now her qualities had brought her to the throne. Not a single brother or sister was left to threaten her title. She cared for Egypt and its people; alone of its Macedonian rulers, she spoke to her subjects in their own tongue. It was to win back her kingdom that she had become Caesar's mistress, smuggled into the palace in a roll of carpet when she and her brother-husband were at war. Certainly she had come to Rome and borne Caesar's child. But whatever dreams she may have had about becoming Caesar's consort and mistress of the world were rudely put to flight by his assassination. Antony was no Caesar, that she knew; and where Caesar had failed, would Antony succeed? This time, she would remain in Egypt, certain of her throne and certain that Antony would guard her interests. She had played her cards well. Her kingdom was, for the present, safe from Roman proconsuls, Roman armies, and Roman tax-collectors.

What jerked Antony away from the delights of Alexandria was serious news from Syria. In the summer of 42 Cassius had sent Quintus Labienus (son of the man who had deserted Caesar at the start of the civil war) to seek help from the Parthian king Orodes. The king would not give him an answer, and Labienus remained at his court. When the tidings of Philippi and the crumbling of all Republican resistance in the east reached the winter capital Phraaspa,

Labienus decided to make a fresh career for himself in the service of the enemies of Rome. He won the trust of the old king, and in the winter of 41–40 he and the king's son Pacorus led a two-pronged attack on Roman territory.

Pacorus swung south after they had crossed the Euphrates, while Labienus drove straight on westwards into southern Asia Minor. Antony's failure to take a firm grip on all this area, in conjunction with the ill-feeling aroused by his massive exactions of taxes, meant that there was now no will to resist among the population. Nor was there much spirit in the vastly outnumbered legionaries, some of whom had served no less than four masters in five years—Caesar, Caecilius Bassus, Cassius, and now Antony. Some detachments joined Labienus of their own free will; these were troops of Brutus and Cassius who had known Labienus personally and even now preferred to serve the renegade Republican, however strange his company, than the conquering Caesarian. The others, under Saxa, were easily defeated, and Saxa himself pursued and put to death. Labienus thus made himself master of all the southern part of Asia Minor. He even went so far as to issue coins on the Roman standard, bearing his portrait and the shameful legend IMPERATOR OF THE PARTHIANS. Pacorus was equally successful. In Syria, only Tyre held out for Antony, and in Judaea Hyrcanus was captured and deposed. The faithful Herod fled to the remote and rocky fortress of Masada, where he left his womenfolk in safety, and journeyed on to the strange city of Petra deep in the desert to seek aid from the Arabian king Malchus.

Gravely perturbed by this invasion, Antony reached Tyre in February. He set out for Asia to gather forces for a counter-attack, but after touching at Rhodes heard the shattering news of Perusia. He knew, of course, that his brother and Octavian were quarrelling. A deputation of veterans had been all winter in Alexandria, waiting in vain for Antony to give some clear indication of his views and to resolve the trouble. But the close of the navigating season had interrupted all communication, and he did not know enough about the dispute to commit himself on one side or the other. Now he learnt that his brother, claiming to act in his name, had been defeated and pardoned, and his generals had not stayed to try the issue.

The east would have to wait. Antony had to reassert his position in the only place where it could be undermined. He had no choice but to make for Italy with all speed. At Athens he met his mother Julia and Sextus's father-in-law L. Scribonius Libo, sent with an offer of friendship and alliance against Octavian. Also there were Fulvia and Plancus. It must have been an interesting meeting, but history is silent about it. Antony, unsure of the facts and unwilling to precipitate a breach with his colleague, made a diplomatic answer to Sextus: he was grateful to him for sending his mother, and if there should be war with Octavian he would ally himself with Sextus; but if Octavian should convince him of his good faith, he would attempt to reconcile Sextus with Octavian. He then set out for Italy. At Sicyon, near Corinth, Fulvia fell ill, but he could not wait for her, and travelled on with Plancus and a fleet of 200 ships. His men were few, but he knew that Pollio and Ventidius had legions loyal to him in Italy. Pollio had also informed him that he had won Ahenobarbus to their side. The two fleets, Antony's and Ahenobarbus's, met in the Adriatic. It was a tense moment. Plancus, judging others by his own standards, attempted to dissuade Antony from going ahead with a mere five ships to meet the united and threatening fleet of the last of the Republicans. Antony replied that he would rather die by a breach of faith than save himself by cowardice, and rowed on. The flagships came together, the Caesarian triumvir and the condemned and proscribed Republican greeted each other, and Ahenobarbus's men saluted Antony as general. United, the two fleets proceeded to Ahenobarbus's base at Paloeis and then to Brundisium, probably about the middle of July.

The inhabitants of Brundisium had seen and suffered from Ahenobarbus's fleet too often to mistake it. They hastily barred the port and prepared to defend the town, assisted by Octavian's garrison. Antony, seeing at last with his own eyes the plain actions of an enemy, hesitated no longer. He cut off the town by building a wall across its isthmus, encircled the harbour with a line of towers, and seized the near-by town of Sipontum. He also sent messages to Sextus to move against Italy with his fleet. This Sextus did, descending upon the towns of the Gulf of Tarentum, and his admiral, the Greek Menodorus, seized Sardinia and its two legions.

Octavian sent Agrippa south urgently with instructions to re-enlist the colonized veterans, while he himself proceeded with an army to Brundisium. The veterans were ready enough to fight against Sextus, but as soon as word got round that the enemy was Antony, they turned back. On the road they met Octavian, who persuaded the men from his own colonies to follow him by appealing to their loyalty, respect, and gratitude to him. Such was the bond between commander and old soldiers that they were ashamed to refuse, but they determined to do all they could to prevent Octavian and Antony going to war. It was not eighteen months since the two men had fought side by side at Philippi to avenge the death of Caesar, and in Antony's army there were many of their comrades.

At Brundisium, Octavian could do nothing against Antony, in spite of having superior numbers. He was without his general Agrippa, and Antony was easily able to defend himself on the isthmus without relaxing the assault upon the town. Antony sent for his legions from Macedonia, and meanwhile resorted to the stratagem of sending ship-loads of civilians out to sea by night who returned next day and disembarked in full legionary panoply in the sight of the enemy. Agrippa captured Sipontum, Antony by a lightning stroke a full regiment and a half of Octavian's cavalry. But neither commander was well placed. Octavian could hardly be sure of the loyalty of his men if it came to an all-out war. He controlled more than forty legions; but if Antonian units were excluded, the number shrank alarmingly. No less than eleven had come to him in the last couple of months, the entire garrison of Gaul and Spain delivered over by young Fufius Calenus. His father, an experienced general, a staunch Antonian, and the proconsul of Gaul, had died suddenly, and when Octavian seized the troops and the provinces, the son was too terrified to resist. There were many men, too, who had fought for Lucius, and, as they thought, Mark Antony in the war of Perusia, and many more who had served under Antony at some time in their career.

Antony, for his part, was unlikely to make much progress—at any rate so long as his opponents kept their heads and the loyalty of a substantial number of their men. He knew from the bitter experiences of the autumn of 44 how much the name of Caesar was worth to Octavian. If there was an auction for the services of the soldiers, it would end in a stalemate. Neither of them could credibly promise rewards greater than those they were having the utmost difficulty in providing at the moment. Defeat was unlikely, since he and Sextus controlled the sea and he could easily retreat. On the other hand, even if he captured Brundisium he would be little better off. An invasion of Italy would be profitless unless he could muster the forces necessary to destroy Octavian and at the same time count on the support of the country as a whole. There were altogether too many imponderables in the situation for him to feel at all confident.

Thus when Antony's praetorian cohorts, men whose reliability was beyond question, made moves to approach Octavian's soldiers and enquire of their old comrades why they had come to fight the man to whom they all owed their lives at Philippi, he did nothing to stop them. Such fraternization had done him good before, at Fréjus. So it turned out this time. After mutual recriminations of bad faith and impious alliances, it came out that Octavian's men were unwilling to start a fresh bout of civil war and wanted to bring about an agreement between the triumvirs. Negotiations were then opened on a higher level, through Cocceius Nerva, a friend of both men who had been sent to Antony in Phoenicia the previous summer and was still with him. By pretending to each that his sympathies were with the other, he was able to find out exactly what the grievances on each side were. It had become known that Fulvia had died in Sicyon, and Nerva was artfully able to throw the blame for the Perusine war on her and convince Octavian that she had fallen sick because of Antony's anger with her and wasted away because he would not see her even when she was ill. Not that Nerva neglected strategic arguments: if the triumvirs failed to agree, the fleets of Sextus and Ahenobarbus had the coasts of Italy at their mercy. The persuasion of Nerva and the sentiments of the veterans were decisive. More formal negotiations followed, with Maecenas representing Octavian, and Pollio Antony. The veterans let it be known that they had no interest in the various accusations, only in the restoration of peace. The triumvirs were reconciled, proclaiming amnesty for the past and friendship for the future. The only casualty of importance was Salvidienus. It was discovered that Octavian's best marshal, a man who had stood with him since the early days, had been in treasonable communication with Antony. He proposed to desert, bringing with him the armies and the provinces of Spain and Gaul. The agreement undid him. Had there been a war, his treachery must have proved decisive. His reward would have been a place beside Pollio, Plancus, Ventidius, and Ahenobarbus, in a party that united the survivors of the murderous quarrels of the last four years. As it was, Antony revealed his overtures, perhaps as a pledge of good faith, and Salvidienus, who was consul-designate, was brought before the senate and condemned by that body, to which he did not even belong. The moral of the tale was clear to the imperial historian Velleius: '. . . though of the most obscure origins, he thought it too little to have won the highest honours and to have done what only Pompey and Caesar [Octavian] had done before him, namely, attained the consulship without being a senator—or rather, he would have done this, if he had not climbed so high that he looked down upon Caesar and the state.'

MARCUS AGRIPPA

Relief sculpture of a Roman warship, with fighting-tower and legionaries. The crocodile was a symbol of Egypt and this ship may therefore be one of Antony's from some otherwise unknown monument depicting the battle of Actium. *Photo: Mansell Collection*

The renewed alliance was cemented, once again, by a marriage-tie.
Octavian, who had long dithered over a marriage to replace that
repudiated when he sent Clodia back to Fulvia, had hastily allied
himself with the relations of Sextus in the aftermath of Perusia. He
took as wife Scribonia, sister of Sextus's father-in-law Scribonius
Libo, a woman many years older than himself who had already had
two consular husbands. Where Antony had observed the strictest
propriety in answering Sextus's offer of help against Octavian,
Octavian was ready to play a political trump card in order to win a
proscribed and exiled enemy of long standing to his side. The
difference was typical of the attitudes of the two men, the one
reluctant to pick a quarrel, the other making sure it would turn out
in his favour. Octavian himself, then, was not available for the marriage stakes, but his sister Octavia had recently and opportunely been left a widow by the death of her husband, the consular
C. Marcellus. What more suitable wife could there be for Antony,
similarly bereaved? The match was duly made, and Virgil's celebrated fourth Eclogue was written in a spirit of profound thankful-
ness for the restoration of peace on earth again. The offspring of
such a union of the great ones was surely destined to be no ordinary
mortal. The hopes and aspirations of this Messianic poem reflect the
war-weariness and sense of guilt for the apparently unending
slaughter of citizen by citizen that oppressed sensitive Romans:

> The final age has come of Cumae's Sibyl's song;
> The great procession of the passing centuries
> Now starts afresh, now virgin Justice comes again,
> And Saturn's ancient sway returns, and from the vault
> Of heaven above a new-born child comes down to earth.
> Lucina, pure goddess, bless the birth of this boy
> And the end of the men of Iron; now comes the race of Gold
> In all the world; Apollo, your own Apollo, is king.
> You shall be consul, Pollio, when this glorious age
> Begins in splendour, and the great cycle of the months
> Starts soon to turn; under your leadership the earth
> Will shake off the shadow of our crimes and lose its fear.
> The boy will mingle with the gods and the great heroes who
> Consort with them, and they shall see him rule the world,
> The son of those whose deeds have granted peace on earth.

The promised son turned out to be a girl, the elder Antonia, born the
next year. Pollio held his consulship for the remaining months of 40,

departing from Italy before the end of the year to undertake a campaign against a local tribe, the Parthini, on the borders of his province of Macedonia. The rising poet Virgil passed from his patronage to that of Maecenas, leaving this poem to puzzle the commentators of antiquity and convince the Middle Ages that Virgil was a Christian before his time.

The new partition of the Roman world between the triumvirs confirmed the *de facto* situation. Octavian was to control the western provinces, with Illyricum, Antony the eastern and Macedonia. To Lepidus was granted Africa; Octavian had sent him there after Perusia to take a firm grip of the province, disputed by Caesarian, Republican, and Antonian governors since 44. The war against Sextus, unless some agreement were reached with him, fell to Octavian, while Antony was to undertake the long-deferred project of punishing the Parthians for the defeat they had inflicted on Crassus in 53—not to speak of their present and far more serious invasion of Syria and Cilicia. Italy, as the homeland, remained in theory common ground. But since it was plain that Octavian would in practice be its master, it was formally agreed that Antony had the right of recruiting as many soldiers there as Octavian. Once again, as with the agreements of Philippi, Antony had no means of enforcing these arrangements if Octavian decided to ignore them.

It was desirable, in the interests of new-found harmony, that the Antonian generals who had threatened Octavian in the Perusine war should go elsewhere. The most embarrassing of Antony's allies, Ahenobarbus, had been sent away to govern Bithynia as soon as the negotiations had started. Though he had not in fact been an accomplice in the murder of Caesar, in will and spirit he was one of the Liberators; and in his determination to fight on, he outdid them all. Antony prevailed upon Octavian to join him in pardoning Ahenobarbus. Pollio, promised the consulship, had been instrumental in bringing about the agreement. Respected for his independence, his honesty, and perhaps his literary tastes, Pollio was not obnoxious to Octavian. Even so, he did not linger. Plancus was sent to govern Asia, where his lack of courage would not seriously impair the support he could organize for the fourth of the Antonians, Ventidius. Ventidius was the true professional among them, and was fittingly entrusted with the task of driving the Parthians out of Roman territory. The elimination of those who had opposed Octavian in 41 was completed when Antony put Manius to death, allegedly for inciting Fulvia to act against his interests. Fulvia's death had indeed been convenient for Octavian. If she had been with Antony at Brundisium things might have turned out far otherwise. Her ambition, her shrewdness, and her political experience might have saved her husband from too great a trust in his young, good-looking, and devious colleague.

Antony married Octavia in Rome, after the conclusion of the treaty in October, and they stayed there through the winter. Antony's promise to Sextus, that he would try and reconcile him with Octavian, came to nothing. After Sextus's admiral Menodorus had captured Sardinia, Octavian's lieutenant there, another Greek freedman named Helenus, repossessed the island by a sudden attack. Menodorus drove him out again, and this so incensed Octavian that he would not hear of coming to terms with Sextus. Negotiations were perhaps already in progress, in which case Octavian's anger may be explained as provoked by a breach of faith. He had nothing to gain by repulsing Sextus, as the events of the winter made clear. Menodorus and his fellow-admiral Menecrates harried the coasts of Italy, raided Etruria, and gravely interfered with the supplies of corn to the city of Rome. Antony's fleet had dispersed with his commanders to the provinces of the east, and the triumvirs could do little. Popular indignation mounted against them. There were riots in the city. Octavian was stoned at a public meeting, and Antony, more popular because of his known willingness to make a treaty with Sextus, was able to save his colleague only by calling in a strong force of soldiers. His personal authority was no use. The discontent was aggravated by special taxes, for the triumvirs urgently needed money to prepare war against Sextus. A tax was placed on slaves, equal to half the amount exacted by the same means before Philippi, and another on legacies, which demonstrated the eternal unpopularity of death duties. The people tore down the edict and complained bitterly about being stripped of their private property to enable the triumvirs to prosecute their personal feuds and add to their own power.

The complaints were fully justified. The policies, if any, of the protagonists were no different. At any rate there had been an underlying conflict of principle between the two sides that fought at Philippi, however much it was obscured by the personal nature of Roman politics. Philippi was a conflict between men who wished to preserve the old order of the state and the traditional privileges and influence of a metropolitan oligarchy and men who were prepared to accept the consequences of the social revolution that had slowly overtaken Italy in the previous hundred years. But Sextus, the one party to the present troubles who could lay any claim to be representing the old Republic, had long since lost any right to that claim. In spite of all the Republicans who had joined him after the proscriptions and after Philippi, his only concern was for personal power. He had already murdered Bithynicus, with whom he had nominally shared the governorship of Sicily in the first months of his occupation. Murcus, who took his fleet to join Sextus after Philippi, met a like fate through the jealousy of the Greek admirals. Sextus had been as willing as Octavian to contract a marriage alliance through Scribonia. Both had thereby abandoned the pretence that they were fighting for a cause. As for Antony, he was the most honest, and the most respected, of the three of them; but even in his case the matters of dispute that had nearly led to war with Octavian were concerned with his own power and position. The one real cause that touched the welfare of any large section of the population had been that for which his wife and brother had gone to war the year before, but it was a cause that he could not possibly take up. It was the support of the army and of the colonized veterans which had carried him to joint leadership of the Caesarian party and victory at Philippi. He was as committed as Octavian to satisfying the demands of the soldiery. If he had given Lucius's war his open approval, and annihilated Octavian and his supporters, he would have found himself, in the end, repeating those very acts which had led Lucius to take up arms.

For once, the people of Rome exerted a will of their own and refused to be the chopping-block of the ambitious and power-hungry. The popular unrest and the bankruptcy of the treasury forced the triumvirs to negotiate. Even Sextus was not immune from public opinion in Rome. His mother Mucia still lived there, and there were hostile demonstrations outside her house. At the instigation of Antony, the obvious go-between Scribonius Libo came on an exploratory mission. When the people heard that he was on his way and that his ship had dropped anchor at the island of Ischia, there were more demonstrations in Rome, urging Octavian to grant Libo a safe-conduct and hold talks with him. The upshot was that the three principals agreed to a conference, to be held at one of the seaside places on the Bay of Naples. Antony and Octavian travelled down to Baiae, and preparations for the meeting were put in hand.

From one of the luxurious villas of this select resort, with the famous oracle of the Cumaean Sibyl at their backs, the triumvirs could look out across the bay of Puteoli to Naples and the splendid cone of Vesuvius. On the left, the cliffs of Pausilypon—'Sans-Souci' —the houses less thickly clustered then than now; on the right, the mountains of the Sorrento peninsula stretching out towards Capri. No wonder Octavian and his family later chose this spot for the imperial seaside palace. But for the present, the sublime view had an unusual foreground—a cluster of boats and barges engaged in driving piles for two platforms set in the sea. Sextus would not trust himself to the land, nor Antony and Octavian to the sea. Hence the compromise, comic if it had not been so important. Antony and Octavian were to occupy one platform, Sextus the other, and the two platforms were close enough together to spare the participants the discomfort of having to decide the fate of the Mediterranean world at the tops of their voices.

Sextus did not miss the opportunity to impress his enemies, arriving towards evening in his magnificent flagship, a 'six',* accompanied by a large number of his best ships. He sailed insolently into the bay of Puteoli before anchoring in the harbour of Ischia. In the morning he and Libo occupied the seaward of the two platforms, the triumvirs the landward. But the elaborate preparations were in vain. Sextus had come believing he would be admitted to the triumvirate in place of Lepidus, while the most that Antony and Octavian had thought of conceding was his return from exile. Deadlock occurred, and they separated. Negotiations continued through friends, since it was plainly in the interest of both parties that they come to some sort of settlement. The greatest stumbling-block was the terms to be offered to those who had been proscribed and had fled to Sextus. Sextus claimed full restitution of their property, in addition to repatriation and recovery of full citizen rights. This placed the triumvirs in an uncomfortable position. To pardon the proscribed cost nothing; but their property had been sold at auction and would have to be bought back, and money was what the triumvirs did not possess. The most they felt able to concede to the proscribed was the restoration of one quarter of their property. Sextus held out for more, but the proscripts themselves accepted these terms. Sextus was not a leader who induced confidence, especially

* The number given to an ancient ship indicates the number of men employed on each vertical group of oars. The number of banks of oars never exceeded three (this is disputed). A 'six' would have either two banks of oars with each oar worked by three men, or three banks with two men to an oar—or, conceivably, one bank with six men to each oar.

after the murder of his most eminent recruit, Murcus; nor was Libo anxious to waste the possible benefits of his recent marriage connection with Octavian.

Sextus himself was furious at what he regarded as a betrayal. The proscribed were at once the most respectable and the most committed of his followers. They had no one else to whom they could turn, and the very fact of their proscription meant that they were men of some prominence, either by wealth or by political opinions. In addition to the proscripts, there were also a considerable number of refugees, leading men who had feared that they might be proscribed but in the event were not. Here the triumvirs were on less financially embarrassing ground, for those who had appropriated the property of such men had acted illegally; since they had paid nothing to the state for their acquisitions, they could without ado be dispossessed. It was easy for Antony and Octavian to offer full restitution (except for movables), and Sextus must have expected to lose this part of his support under any sort of an agreement. But for the proscripts to settle for a paltry quarter undermined his own status and negotiating position.

Angry he might be, but there was nothing he could do. If he broke off discussions, those of his followers—and they must have constituted a considerable proportion of his citizen following—who were covered by the triumvirs' offer would abandon him at once. They were with him from necessity, not from conviction, and they wanted most of all to return to Italy, to their families, friends, and property. The core of Sextus's support lay with the Spaniards who had fought for him in 45 and 44 and accompanied him to settle in Sicily in 43, and with a few of his father's freedmen and followers who had survived the battle of Munda and had seen no place for themselves in Caesar's Rome. Impeccable Republican though Sextus was by birth and record—always excepting his strange failure ever to co-operate with others who proclaimed the same cause—he lacked credibility as a representative of the republic. To a Roman, the republic was as much a matter of great names as of political theory, more so perhaps. Names were what Sextus lacked to back him, names with the ring of famous deeds and long prominence in the service of the state about them: Domitius Ahenobarbus, Valerius Messalla, Licinius Crassus, Cornelius Lentulus. But those who currently bore these names were all elsewhere, with Antony or with the new Caesar. For a very good reason: power and influence were their objectives, and they judged that Sextus had neither.

What Sextus did have was undisputed mastery of Italian waters, and it was thanks to this that in the end he wrung very favourable terms from the triumvirs. The three men met again, this time on the mole of Puteoli. It was agreed that peace and free commerce would be restored. Sextus was to remove the garrisons which he had placed —such was his strength—at various points on the Italian coast. In exchange, he was to have the governorship of Sicily, Sardinia, Corsica, and the Peloponnese, so long as Antony and Octavian held similar authority elsewhere. His status was to be made nominally equal to that of the other two, in that he was created a member of the ancient and respected college of Augurs, and was permitted to hold the consulship—but in absence, through any friend he might select. Octavian was evidently willing to concede the title to his enemy, but baulked at letting him occupy the office in person at Rome. The example of Lucius Antonius was too recent and too painful. As for Sextus's veterans, they were to be treated in the same way, upon discharge, as those of Octavian and Antony, and any slaves who had served with him were to become free men, thus escaping the severe punishments to which runaway slaves were liable. Finally, the agreement named the consuls for the next four years. The last pair, for 35, were to be Antony and Octavian, and it was expected that constitutional government would then be restored.

The concordat was sealed by the betrothal of Sextus's infant daughter to the three-year-old nephew of Octavian, and celebrated by a series of banquets. Antony and Octavian entertained Sextus in a marquee on the mole, but the guard-ships that had been stationed around it during the negotiations were still present. When it was his turn, Sextus moored his six alongside the mole and the masters of the world dined on shipboard, each with a dagger concealed about him. Menodorus, it was said, meditated treachery, reluctant to throw away such a chance; but Sextus would have none of it and his flagship remained safely beside the mole. It is a nice story. In fact Sextus must have realized, and the others must have known he realized, that to murder or imprison them would only bring odium upon himself. In their places would spring up other leaders, crying for vengeance. He had been too long an exile, and patronage was not his to give. As for any Republican pretensions he might have, they were a flimsy façade. He had barely known the republic. He had been only twenty-five when Caesar crossed the Rubicon, much too young to have taken any part in political life. His true aspirations, which matched those of Octavian, were revealed by the name he used. His legitimate republican style was Sextus Pompeius Magnus Pius, but he turned the soubriquet he inherited from his father into a first name of unique splendour, and became Magnus Pompeius Pius. Alone of the war-lords who met at Puteoli, Antony knew and understood what had passed away with the formation of the triumvirate; and alone of them he did not look forward to monarchical rule.

Chapter X

THE ALLIANCE STRAINED

THERE WAS general rejoicing at the news that agreement had been reached. It was more than five years ago that Caesar had died, and ever since then there had been civil war or threat of civil war. The Roman people were profoundly and deeply thankful for their deliverance from perpetual emergency, requisitions, disturbance of agriculture, and famine. Sextus returned to Sicily, Antony and Octavian to Rome. Their popularity restored and Italy at last free from troubles, the triumvirs could turn their attention to external matters. Agrippa had been busy in Gaul since the end of the previous year quelling some disturbances. Octavian departed to join him. He must have looked forward to the prospect of a victory over men who were not his fellow-countrymen.

Antony had more serious matters to see to in the east. Ventidius, a deputy even more efficient than the admirable Agrippa, had been extraordinarily successful in pushing back the Parthians. It was not for nothing that Ventidius had served with Caesar. But there were associated political problems. Antony had to face a task that demanded his presence in the eastern Mediterranean and could not be hurried. This was nothing less than the consolidation of the line of client-kingdoms which served as a buffer between the provinces that Rome administered directly and the unruly hinterlands of Arabia, Mesopotamia, and Armenia. During the years of civil war, princes great and small had grown careless of Rome's interests, intent only upon their own. Antony had to re-establish Roman authority and pick men to rule these small but important kingdoms who would be both loyal to Rome and acceptable to their subjects. It was a matter of some delicacy, and much diplomacy, calling for acute judgment of character. Herod was the only monarch appointed by Antony as early as 39; but Herod had special claims, as has been seen. He had found his way from Petra to Rome, and there at the end of 40 the senate had conferred upon him the throne of Judaea, in spite of the fact that he had not asked for it. He knew that Rome preferred to avoid dynastic troubles by choosing members of the existing royal house, and sought the throne only for his future brother-in-law, the grandson of old Hyrcanus. But everything was in his favour. Octavian supported him, for he had given aid to Julius Caesar; he was personally friendly with Antony; and two eminent Antonians, M. Valerius Messalla Corvinus and L. Sempronius Atratinus, neither of whom cared greatly for Cleopatra, thought him a more reliable bastion of Roman influence than the Queen of Egypt and spoke up in his support.

Not that Herod was able to take possession of his kingdom straight away. Antigonus, whom the Parthians had put upon the throne, allegedly for a bribe of a thousand talents and five hundred women, was a nephew of Hyrcanus and enjoyed considerable support among the Jews. Jerusalem was a difficult place to take, and Roman support, at any rate in the shape of legions, was weak until 37. Antony may perhaps have been unwilling to act decisively against a legitimate member of the royal house until the outsider Herod had at least gained a semblance of respectability by marrying into it. This he did with his long-delayed wedding to Miriam, granddaughter of Hyrcanus and niece of Antigonus, in Samaria in the winter of 38–37. The next year Roman help was forthcoming on a proper scale and C. Sosius, proconsul of Syria, took Jerusalem and established Herod on the throne.

Antony could excuse his failure to give Herod substantial support earlier. The chief preoccupation of his commanders was with the Parthians. Ventidius defeated Labienus at the Taurus range, won possession of Cilicia, and forced the pass through the Amanus mountains that divided Cilicia from Syria; Labienus himself fled in disguise but was later captured in Cyprus. Ventidius then marched south into Judaea but made no attempt to aid Herod's followers. For the moment it was enough if his presence squeezed money out of Antigonus and demonstrated the power of Rome. He left his lieutenant Poppaedius Silo to keep an eye on affairs, and turned north again for a reckoning with the Parthians. At the start of 38 he tricked Pacorus into crossing the Euphrates at a point that suited the Romans, and at Gindarus lured him into an over-confident uphill attack on his position. Pacorus was killed and his forces routed. The death of Pacorus was decisive, for it was to his moderation and personal popularity that the Parthians owed their support among the princelings and peoples of the Syrian region. Ventidius sent his head around through the various cities, and Syria became Roman once again.

It only remained to deal with Antiochus, King of Commagene, which lay on the borders of Syria between the Taurus mountains and the upper Euphrates. The survivors of the Parthian army had fled to Antiochus, but that was a minor matter. Commagene was important for its control of the Euphrates crossing, and for its mounted archers which any Roman expedition against Parthia would do well to number in its ranks if it wished to avoid the fate of Crassus and his army at Carrhae. Further, Antiochus's daughter was married to the Parthian king Orodes. Ventidius therefore marched against the capital, Samosata, and laid siege to it. Antiochus, in true Oriental style, offered Ventidius a thousand talents to go away. Ventidius was willing to negotiate, but the business was too important to settle on his own authority. He ceased siege-operations, thereby incurring suspicion of bribery, and waited for Antony to arrive in person. Antony was determined to dethrone Antiochus, whom he judged unreliable, and replace him with one Alexander. He sent Ventidius back to Rome to celebrate a well-deserved triumph—the first ever recorded against the Parthians—and pressed on with the siege. But two events caused him to change his mind. First Herod arrived in Samosata with an urgent request for Roman legions to capture Jerusalem. Not only his own reputation, but that of Rome was at stake. Second, old king Orodes, broken by the death of his favourite son Pacorus, abdicated in favour of another of his thirty sons, Phraates (IV). Intrigue, suspicion, and mass murder followed in the royal house, and among the victims were Antiochus's grandchildren, potential rivals of Phraates for the Parthian succession. Thus the bond between Antiochus and Parthia was dissolved, and Roman troops were needed elsewhere. Antony compromised, confirmed Antiochus on his throne, and allowed him to kill his rival Alexander.

This excursion to the banks of the Euphrates was the only occasion between the autumn of 39 and the spring of 37 that the affairs of the east took Antony away from Athens, and Octavia. He spent the two winters blamelessly and soberly, enjoying the company of his beautiful bride. Although she was already the mother of three children by her first husband, she was still in her middle twenties. She gave him two more children, both girls, and seems to have been genuinely fond of the man whom high politics had brought to her. He put her portrait with his on the coins issued in these years from the mints of Asia Minor and Greece. She thus became, in the eyes of the east, the bride of the new Dionysus. The ivy-wreath and berries

of the god appear around Antony's portrait, confirming the acclamation first given to him at Ephesus in 41 and repeated by the
Athenians in 39. Octavia herself may even have played the part of the
goddess of Athens, Athena Polias, in a representation of a sacred
union of Athena and Dionysus enacted at Athens in the winter of
39–38. Certainly the Athenians honoured Antony and Octavia with
the title of 'Beneficent Gods', and to the Hellenistic world there was
nothing extravagant about the idea—even if it did cost the city a
thousand talents to dower its goddess.

While his legates or governors—the constitutional niceties of the
distinction between a commander responsible only to his superior
and one responsible to the senate are ignored under the triumvirs—
undertook specific tasks and set their provinces in order, Antony kept
an overall watch on the whole area from Greece round to Egypt, and
waited for the moment to undertake the long-deferred expedition
into Parthian territory. To drive back the Parthians, as Ventidius
had done, was not enough. Roman pride demanded that the legionary eagles lost at Carrhae should be recovered and the Parthian
punished in his homeland. To do this, Antony needed a stable
frontier supported by loyal client-kings, money to finance what was
likely to be a long and costly campaign, and enough legions to leave
an adequate guard in the three provinces of Asia, Bithynia, and
Syria. But he could not wait indefinitely. To be away from Rome for
too long was to endanger his own position—granted the premise that
Octavian was as much his rival as his colleague. Twenty years in age,
the sieges of Mutina and Brundisium, and the revolutionary activities
of Octavian in 44 stood between them—hardly guarantees of the
trust necessary to make their division of the empire work.

The pact of Puteoli was highly satisfactory to Antony. By neutra-
lizing Sextus, it denied to Octavian the chance of a victory that
might bring him great popularity in Rome and Italy. To Octavian
and his chief generals, Agrippa and the noble Domitius Calvinus, fell
the task of dealing with irruptions of barbaric tribes into partially
pacified Gaul and with descents of wild mountaineers into the
settled and Romanized areas of Spain. No great glory was to be had
there, nothing comparable with Antony's ultimate hope of a
Parthian triumph. Sextus would also be a convenient watch-dog and
counterpoise to Octavian during Antony's inevitably long absences
in the east. Conversely, the pact was unsatisfactory to Octavian, even
if he chose to forget the fact that the new entrant to the triumviral
club was the son of his 'father's' great opponent. In reality, the

agreement was built on sand, since Sextus had lost the respectable part of his following under the amnesty and received no position except that of consul-designate, while Octavian had plainly been Antony's unwilling partner in the negotiations and would take the first propitious moment to restart the struggle. His excuse was to hand, for those of Caesar's murderers who were with Sextus were to remain unmolested; how long could Caesar's son allow this to endure? Most ominous of all, there was no way in which Antony and the Libonian republicans, who were the true beneficiaries of the pact, could enforce a peace if Octavian and Sextus fell out.

We only have Octavian's version of what happened. Predictably, this throws the blame for the breach of treaty upon Sextus, with an irrelevant story of some dispute over the arrears of taxes of the Peloponnese. Hence mutual recriminations, and preparations for war. This may be true. The real reason for the outbreak of war was mutual distrust and Octavian's impatience of any rival, let alone one of Sextus's stamp. A signal of what was to come was the divorce of Scribonia late in 39. But if a *casus belli* has to be found, the treachery of Menodorus will serve. Prompted by a private agent of Octavian who voyaged to Sardinia ostensibly to buy corn, Menodorus indicated that he was willing to hand over the island along with Corsica, three legions, and a large number of auxiliary troops. Octavian sent an urgent message to Antony in Athens, asking him to meet him at Brundisium on a particular day. He wanted Antony's approval to lend some respectability to this treaty-breaking. Meanwhile he set in train preparations for war, bringing ships from the fleet base at Ravenna, summoning an army from Gaul, and concentrating equipment and supplies at the ports of Brundisium and Puteoli.

Antony came as arranged, but found no one. He did not approve of the war, and he was not a man who cynically broke faith when it suited him. But Octavian's war preparations were evident. Antony, realizing there was no way of stopping his colleague if he were determined on war, angry at journeying from Athens for a broken appointment, and anxious to join Ventidius in Syria, did not wait. He wrote to Octavian not to violate the treaty, which left Octavian perfectly free to justify a war by alleging Sextus's violation of it, and threatened to treat Menodorus as his own runaway slave. Octavian of course ignored Antony's wishes. He knew that the only thing Antony could do to stop him was to join Sextus against him, and that was clearly out of the question.

Octavian moved with speed. He accepted Menodorus's desertion and put him and the squadron that he brought with him under his admiral Calvisius Sabinus; not for Octavian the elevation of Greek freedmen above Roman nobles, however good their seamanship. Still uneasy about public opinion in Rome, which was firmly against this gratuitous war, he spread his own version of Sextus's misdeeds among his soldiers. He alleged piracy, and said that Antony had refused to surrender the Peloponnese to Sextus because he was aware of his intended perfidy. He then travelled south to Tarentum to take command of the force that had by now been assembled there, and left Calvisius and Menodorus in charge of the main fleet. This was to sail south from its present station on the coast of Etruria—for Sextus's naval strength had made even the Bay of Naples unsafe.

Disaster followed. First Menecrates, in command of the major part of Sextus's fleet, fell upon Calvisius and the traitor Menodorus in the Bay of Cumae and won a clear-cut victory—this in spite of Calvisius's attempt to turn the engagement into a land battle by beaching his ships. However, Menecrates himself, badly wounded, chose death by jumping overboard when his ship was captured by Menodorus. His lieutenant Demochares, another Greek freedman, was so demoralized by this that he failed to press home his advantage and sailed for Sicily immediately. At least, that is Appian's story. It is more likely that Sextus had given orders for the fleet to return, in order to beat off the expected crossing by Octavian's land forces. These had by now arrived in Rhegium, accompanied by a large fleet. Sextus lay opposite, at Messana (modern Messina), with a mere forty ships. Octavian's advisers urged him to seize the moment and attack, but he preferred to wait for Calvisius. He did not yet know that Calvisius had been defeated and was making his way cautiously south, hopping from bay to bay with his reduced fleet.

Then Demochares and his ships arrived to join Sextus, and with them came the news of Calvisius's defeat. Octavian at once set out to meet Calvisius. Sextus let him go, then as he was rounding Cape Scyllaeum fell upon his rear. Octavian, knowing his fleet was no match for Sextus's in open water, resorted to the same tactics as Calvisius at Cumae, and with equally unfortunate results. The shore was rocky, and he could not actually beach his ships, so that when they were driven back or dashed against each other they were holed and began to fill. Octavian himself took to the land, while his admiral Cornificius, abandoning what was evidently a senseless tactic, moved out to the attack. This sally met with some success. Then the Pompeians caught sight of the ships of Calvisius and Menodorus coming in from the open sea. Unwilling to risk an encounter with fresh forces as dusk was falling, they stood off and made for harbour at Messana.

Octavian, not knowing that Calvisius had arrived, spent a depressing and uncomfortable night on the mountainside above the strait, in company with those of his men who had imitated his example and swum ashore. The morning brought the good news about Calvisius, but gloomily confirmed the extent of the previous day's defeat. The sea was littered with sails, rudders, and tackle, and the surviving three-quarters of the fleet had suffered considerable damage. While Octavian was engaged in hasty repairs, protected by a screen of Calvisius's squadron, a southerly gale of extraordinary ferocity suddenly came up. Sextus's ships were safe in harbour the other side of the strait. No doubt his admirals could read the signs. On Octavian's side, only Menodorus was experienced and seamanlike enough to know what to do. Long familiar with these tricky waters, he judged, correctly, that the gale would increase in violence. He took his ships out into deeper water where the seas were less short and steep, and rode at anchor. Even so, his crews had to row into the wind to prevent the anchors dragging. The carnage was terrible among the rest of Octavian's fleet, thrown by the breaking surf against the rocks of a lee shore. The ships that managed to avoid destruction in this way were caught in the vicious rip of the strait's current, shaken up, and dashed against each other. The wind tore away the commands of the officers unheard, and numbed thought and action. With the onset of night it freshened still more. It was the worst gale within the living memory of the inhabitants of those parts. As the dawn came up, it died, leaving only the swell to pound the wreckage of Octavian's fleet against the inhospitable shore.

Octavian had lost more than half his fleet. He hurried away to Vibo and northwards even before day broke. He was afraid that Sextus would seize this opportunity and invade the mainland. He had little confidence in his support for this personal vendetta against Sextus. The letters he wrote to his friends and military commanders urged them to take precautions against the possibility of a coup to depose him. He had strained the charisma of Caesar's name to the limit. But he was lucky. Sextus, once again, thought it enough to defend himself. As for opposition in Rome, it was a case of once bitten, twice shy. No Antonian was ready to be a second Lucius, especially as Antony was on the banks of the Euphrates and even less accessible than he had been at the time of Perusia. The man who had been prepared to stand by his colleague against his wife and brother was hardly likely to abandon him for Sextus.

Nevertheless, Octavian was still in severe difficulties. The people of Italy were no more enthusiastic about the war than they had ever been. There was a chronic shortage of money, exacerbated by the refusal of the Romans to pay the special taxes imposed after the treaty of Brundisium. What was left of his fleet was of little use. He needed to build up his naval arm again from scratch, unless he could get help from elsewhere. In this crisis his political cunning never left him. As Appian says, 'He was always very good at seeing what was to his advantage.' He decided to swallow his pride and approach Antony for assistance. Antony had made it quite plain from the beginning what he felt about the war, and recriminatory letters had passed. Relations between them were very strained.

To heal the breach and once again mollify Antony, Octavian sent the ever-diplomatic Maecenas, cultured, urbane, and wealthy; Maecenas, sprung from an ancient Etruscan family that claimed royal blood, disdained the senatorial toga, the paraphernalia of military command, and the ladder of public office. He preferred to serve Octavian in less obtrusive and more subtle ways, as befitted a man with a taste for the scurrilous, the unusual, and the luxurious. He took ship for Athens, leaving Octavian pondering upon desperate plans to attempt a landing of Sicily from slow and cumbrous merchant ships. It was not necessary. Maecenas, perhaps aided by Octavia, persuaded Antony to forget his differences with Octavian and come across to Tarentum in the spring with a fleet of 300 ships. At the same time Octavian heard that Agrippa had won a notable success in Gaul, which did something to restore the public esteem of his régime. Agrippa declined the imperatorial salutation, and later refused to celebrate the triumph that he was offered by Octavian. The coins which he struck in Gaul bear witness to this concern for his leader's credit. For the first time Octavian is described as IMPERATOR CAESAR instead of CAESAR IMPERATOR—a small change, but a momentous one. The statement of fact, the mention of the accolade, has become a kind of permanent attribute. It is, implicitly, a claim to be *the* Imperator. This innovation in title is reinforced, also for the first time on the coinage, by the words SON OF THE DIVINE JULIUS. Caesar had been a god since 42, but Octavian and his friends had found no need to stress the fact. That they did so now reflects the effectiveness of Sextus's manipulation of his own names and the credibility, after the battle and the storm, of his claim to be the son of Neptune. Sextus went so far as to don a dark blue cloak and offer sacrifice to his newly adopted father: horses and, some said, men as well.

It was uncomfortably apparent that Octavian's military abilities deserted him when Agrippa was elsewhere. Salvidienus executed, Calvisius discredited, Domitius Calvinus experienced but unsuccessful, Octavian was forced to recall Agrippa, who had proceeded to start operations against some German tribes on the east bank of the Rhine. Agrippa had to rest content with the fame of being the first Roman commander after Caesar to cross the great river. Back in Rome, he declined his triumph, assumed the consulship for 37, and set about preparing a fleet to defeat Sextus. Stern, efficient, and self-effacing, Agrippa preferred the reality of power to its outward trappings. His origins are so obscure that nothing is recorded of them, and he did his best to suppress even his family name Vipsanius and become simply M. Agrippa, like any aristocrat.* This foible apart, he had nothing in common with the republican nobility. Much more than his leader, he symbolized the revolutionary aspect of the Caesarian party—non-Roman, non-aristocratic, and military. After the death of his peer Salvidienus, he stood without dispute second to Octavian; he deserved perhaps to be first, but he knew that could never be, and remained content that his friend's success should be no less his own.

Meanwhile Antony, in fulfilment of his promise to Maecenas, collected a fleet of 300 ships and sailed to Tarentum in the spring. Once again Octavian failed to keep the rendezvous. Agrippa's preparations were going so well that Octavian, it seems, decided he had no need of Antony's ships. His own reverses and the superior military reputation of Antony made it a matter of more than pride to do without his colleague's support. A victory won jointly could hardly do anything but confirm Antony's primacy in the public eye. On the other hand, if he could keep the credit to himself, there were opportunities to pose as the tireless and undaunted defender of the people of Italy from the ravages of the pirate Sextus and his crew of slaves and adventurers. Agrippa's energy, the lack of any serious opposition in Rome, and the consistent failure of Sextus to follow up his successes made the situation in early 37 look much better than it had appeared in the autumn of the previous year. Thus Octavian's snub to Antony is perfectly intelligible—remembering always his early avowal that he would rest content with nothing less than the honours Caesar had won.

* See Appendix.

Why Antony promised to come, and why he stayed after the snub, seems at first sight more puzzling. The war was an unpopular one. Octavian had elected to start it without Antony's approval in breach of an agreement to which Antony had been a party. Why not let Octavian wallow in the pit he had dug for himself? This was an attractive line of thought. Octavian had made trouble for most of his political career, and it would be a nice change to see him hoist with his own petard. But the conflict must sooner or later reach a decision. Though Sextus might be content with the status quo, Octavian never would. It was impossible to imagine that Sextus could ever supplant Octavian. His following was not of that kind, and the decent and substantial Roman citizens who had lent him a certain respectability as a political leader at the pact of Puteoli had largely returned to Rome—if they had not, like Tiberius Nero, openly embraced the cause of his enemy. Simply to consider the possibility of supporting Sextus was to dismiss it. In the long run Octavian must win. The only question Antony had to decide was how he himself could derive most profit from the situation. Plainly, a victory of the allied forces of the two triumvirs (discounting, as always, Lepidus) was the most desirable thing, and he judged that this was as good a chance as was likely to occur. Besides, there was the much-deferred Parthian expedition which he longed to be able to undertake without having always to look over his shoulder at the west.

As to why he stayed, complaining about the expense of maintaining his fleet as it lay idle in the harbour of Tarentum, and making no secret of his annoyance with Octavian, there was a simple explanation. The exigencies of the civil wars had led commanders who were short of legions to disregard the normal qualification of citizen birth for legionary service. The civil wars were over now, apart from the tiresome business of Sextus, and Antony wished to return to the regular practice of raising in Italy the fresh legions he wanted for the Parthian expedition. This had been the agreement of Brundisium, that he was to have equal access with Octavian to the manpower of the homeland. Certainly, there were a number of Roman citizens in the east, and colonies founded by Caesar, by Brutus and Cassius, and by himself. But the colonists were soldiers who had served their time, whose children were still infants, and the others were men of substance and station in their own cities who could hardly be conscripted into the armies of Rome. Antony wanted an Italian army. The best way of getting it was to be on the spot.

There was an additional point: since the beginning of 42, when he had left Brundisium en route for the campaign of Philippi, Antony had spent little more than a year in Italy—from the late summer of 40 to the autumn of 39. Inevitably, he was beginning to lose touch with the political life of the capital—not the turbulent politics of the dying republic, but the shifting attitudes of the senatorial and moneyed classes to their rulers. Monarchical though his position and Octavian's might be in constitutional terms, in practice they owed their eminence to their qualities as party leaders. Lepidus's virtual annihilation as a political force was a clear enough demonstration of the proposition; without friends or influence, he was little better than the proconsul of Africa. What Antony had to guard against was the unobtrusive undermining of his support in the capital. The free working of the constitution suspended or made mock of, the plebs indifferent or hostile, and the soldiery temporarily satisfied, the struggle for personal supremacy now moved back on to its old battlefield, the upper strata of Roman society.

Even before the end of 39 Octavian was extending the basis of his party. As soon, probably, as Antony left Rome for Athens, he started to court the 'respectable' republicans who had returned from their exile in Sicily. These would more naturally have gravitated towards Antony, indeed many of them were refugees from the war of Perusia. But Octavian desperately needed men of this class to give his following some solidity and something of the aristocratic republican flavour which Antony's possessed. His popularity among the people had sunk dangerously low. The heights that he had reached required more sophisticated support. This he found with a marriage that lasted to his dying day, unpropitious though its beginnings were. He divorced the tedious Scribonia—though she had presented him with the only child he ever had—and took in her place Livia Drusilla, six months pregnant by her existing husband Ti. Claudius Nero. Nero obligingly divorced his young wife—she was not yet twenty—and took the part of her father at the wedding on January 17, 38 B.C. This was indeed a match with the old aristocracy. Livia's father had been one of those who preferred suicide to surrender after Philippi. Though bearing the name of Livius Drusus, he had in fact been born into the still more splendid family of the Claudii and adopted in infancy. Livia's two sons, Tiberius the future emperor, and his brother Drusus, were thus of Claudian blood on both sides. It can hardly be an accident that in this same year 38 the names of an Appius Claudius Pulcher and a Marcius Philippus (son of Octavian's stepfather) appear in the consular records. The aristocracy, or some of its members, judged that the young adventurer had come to stay. By 37 the adhesion of Libo, Nero, the young and brilliant Valerius Messalla Corvinus, and others of their class, was starting to give a veneer of senatorial respectability to the revolutionary military party so well characterized by its leaders: Octavian, Salvidienus, Agrippa, Maecenas. The resources of triumviral patronage were considerable; high offices and high priesthoods, still the targets of noble ambition, lay in Octavian's gift.

So Antony stayed, and through the mediation of his wife eventually prevailed upon Octavian to meet him. Although the latter was ready to make a healthy show of independence, he could not at this stage afford a rupture with Antony. That might come, but he was not yet strong enough. The war with Sextus had alienated the sympathies of the people. They insisted on electing to an aedileship one Marcus Eppius who had saved his aged father during the proscriptions; when he refused the office because of its heavy financial obligations, private citizens contributed to enable him to give the customary games and meet his other expenses. There were also in circulation some couplets about a scandalous banquet at which the guests impersonated the twelve gods, Octavian taking the part of Apollo. Suetonius, who tells the story, goes on: 'The scandal created by the dinner was increased by the acute shortage of food and money at the time. Next day there were shouts "the gods have eaten all the corn", and "Caesar may be Apollo, but he's Apollo the Crucifier"—under which name the god was worshipped in one of the districts of Rome.' Octavian's well-known weakness for dicing was lampooned too:

> 'He's lost his fleet, and lost the battle, twice;
> Some day he'll win; why else keep throwing dice?'

The terms agreed on were that Antony gave his approval to the war against Sextus, who was stripped of his promised consulship and the augurate conferred on him at Puteoli. Antony would also lend Octavian two squadrons (120 ships) in exchange for which he would receive 20,000 legionaries (four or five legions). With these extra ships, plus the survivors from the debacle of the previous year, Octavian might well have been able to invade Sicily straight away. Partly because he did not wish to share the command with Antony, partly because Agrippa's preparations for an entirely different sort of campaign were in mid-course, he deferred operations against Sextus until the following year. He was certain that Antony's preoccupation with the Parthian expedition would take him east before the onset of winter. As it was, Antony had lost a year by Octavian's appeal for help, and could not possibly think of collecting together and leading an army on the long march into Parthia before 36. Not for him a short sail across the Tyrrhenian Sea to engage the enemy, but a slow and arduous circuit around the headwaters of the Euphrates. Octavian lost nothing at all by postponing his offensive.

The final matter of agreement was the renewal of the triumvirate, which was now prolonged retrospectively from the start of 37 for another five years. The original five-year term had expired some months before, probably on December 31. It was a sign of the despotic nature of the triumvirs' power that they had not bothered to give their continued exercise of authority any legal justification. There is apparent here an air of hand-to-mouth improvisation that had in fact characterized the triumvirate all along. Antony and Octavian had taken sweeping powers to enable them to fulfil a common but limited aim, the punishment of Caesar's assassins. After Philippi the situation had dictated their next aims, the settlement of the veterans and the wars against the Parthians and against Sextus. So long as the wars dragged on, there was some kind of reason for keeping their special powers; and it was no doubt in virtue of some general recognition of this fact that they had not in fact laid these powers down at the start of the year. But the time was drawing near when both wars would be over. What was to happen then? Would both men be willing to lay down the supreme power to which they had become accustomed? Antony perhaps; but hardly Octavian—twenty-six was too young to retire in glory and let others aspire to guide the destinies of the state. And if Octavian was unwilling, was it likely that Antony would step down in favour of this man who had rebelled against him, sought alliance with him, and quarrelled with him, not once but twice? Could they divide the Roman world between them? But Rome itself, the heart of the empire and the seat of power, was indivisible.

There is no sign in any of the arrangements of the triumvirs that such questions were ever answered, if indeed they were asked. Politics, the art of the possible, do not encourage the long view, the grand design. If this is true of the present age, armed with sophisticated statistical techniques and committed to ideas of social improvement which would have been utterly foreign to the ancient world, how much truer was it of Rome, where great individual achievement remained the prime and almost the only aim of those who entered public life. The *ad hoc* nature of the triumvirate and the failure of the partners to agree on long-term aims or permanent areas of responsibility arose from the very nature of Roman politics, concerned as they traditionally were with specific problems and personal prestige. Thus the question of what was to happen in 32 was left quite open. In theory, the Republic would be restored and the consuls once again become the chief officers of the state. Two of Antony's most notable partisans, C. Sosius, at present governor of Syria, and Ahenobarbus, in Bithynia, were designated to the office for that year, and for 31 the two principals themselves. Beyond that, no man could see.

Such was the compact of Tarentum, reached in the summer of 37. Antony left the 120 ships, and also his wife, pregnant with the younger Antonia. The version of Dio has it that he made a dramatic gesture of repudiation by sending Octavia back from Corcyra (Corfu), an unlikely tale but suitably dramatic in the light of later developments. Antony was bound for Syria and the army that his lieutenants were collecting there for the great Parthian expedition. It was no place for a pregnant wife, who had six children to care for: her own by Antony and Marcellus, and Antony's by Fulvia. She remained loyal to Antony until he divorced her in 32, and it is quite likely that she hoped to be able to guard her husband's interests in Rome while he was necessarily incommunicado (or virtually so) in the marches of the east.

Chapter XI

THE STRUGGLE FOR MILITARY GLORY

WHILE THE negotiations of Tarentum dragged on, Agrippa put in hand an enormous project designed to bring about the ultimate defeat of Sextus. Octavian's forces suffered from three disadvantages: the ships were no better than those of Sextus's; they were not so well handled; and there was no secure and protected harbour on the west coast of Italy. With characteristic energy and efficiency, Agrippa set himself to remedy each of these deficiencies. He began to build a completely new and improved fleet. History does not record whether he consciously drew his lesson from an earlier episode of Roman warfare in these very waters, but he adopted the same solution as his predecessors at the time of the first great war against Carthage, then the leading naval power of the western Mediterranean. If he could not defeat Sextus's sea-captains by skill and seamanship, he would crush them by sheer fighting-power. So he built big ships, heavy and difficult to sink, and capable of carrying more than the usual number of marines. His tactics would be to grapple and lay alongside, thus turning the fight into an infantry battle on floating platforms. And to ensure that his dreadnoughts would be properly handled, he put in motion a thorough training programme for his crews. 20,000 slaves were given their freedom, at the price of manning the oars of the new fleet. After weeks on the practice benches, they were taken to sea in all weathers to give them a taste of the real thing.

Agrippa's most spectacular achievement was the construction of a strongly-defended and completely enclosed deep-water fleet base at Puteoli. He opened the crater-lake of Avernus to the sea by a canal through to the intermediate shallow lagoon of Lake Lucrinus, which was in turn connected to the sea by two openings in the dyke that carried the coast road. Lake Avernus then served as the fitting-out basin, where the hulls built at various places along the coast were brought for decking, equipment, and provisioning. In itself, it was safe enough from sudden descents by Sextus's squadrons. But to reach it from the north, it was necessary to round Cape Misenum. This meant passing through the channel between the mainland and the islands of Ischia and Nisida, both held by the Pompeians. To obviate the danger to the thousands of tons of stores and materials which the new fleet, its crews, and its workmen required, Agrippa brought back into use the ancient port of Cumae on the north side of the isthmus of Misenum and drove two tunnels of a total length of a mile under the volcanic hills to provide a level and protected route through to Avernus. These imposing engineering works can still be seen, silent witness to the menace posed by Sextus and his over-whelming superiority at sea. Agrippa even took precautions against a possible siege by constructing galleries in the rock to form vast cisterns capable of holding hundreds of thousands of gallons of fresh water.

Testimony of a different kind to Sextus's strength was given by Menodorus. Some time in the course of 37 he changed sides again, taking a handful of ships with him, and was restored to his position of admiral under Sextus. His grievance is said to have been that Octavian had not given him rank equal to that of Calvisius. This, surely, was a pretext. Perhaps the sailor in him was revolted by Agrippa's huge fighting engines, and convinced they could not possibly succeed. The test was soon to come. On July 1, 36, after a solemn sacrifice on the shore and the equivalent of a blessing of the fleet by the priests, the great armament set out from the bay of Baiae.

Agrippa's fleet was only part of the forces arrayed against Sextus. Octavian and his advisers had planned a three-pronged strategy. Lepidus was bringing twelve half-strength legions and a fleet from Africa, while from Tarentum one of the rising lights of Octavian's party, the Lucanian Statilius Taurus, who had been consul in 37, sailed with the two squadrons that Antony had left behind. Legions under Valerius Messalla were stationed south of Vibo, ready to cross if necessary. For his part, Sextus left a force in the west of the island at Lilybaeum to oppose Lepidus. He himself watched the north and east coasts, and especially the Lipari Islands, which could be a valuable base for Octavian's fleet. Once again the weather took a hand though not so decisively as before. On July 3 a southerly gale blew up. Lepidus lost a number of transports, swamped or capsized, but managed to land and begin operations around Lilybaeum against Sextus's commander Plinius; Taurus was able to get back to Tarentum; but Octavian suffered severely. His rearguard under

Appius Claudius Pulcher was caught rounding the promontory of Minerva and partly wrecked or stranded. The main fleet he got safely into the bay of Elea with the loss of only one great ship. Unfortunately for him, the wind veered to the south-west and the sheltered bay became a trap. The disaster of the Messina straits was repeated, though on a smaller scale: thirty-two ships of the line and a greater number of light Liburnian galleys were destroyed, and many of the rest suffered extensive damage.

It would take a month to put the fleet to rights. Octavian thought at first of deferring the whole campaign until the next year, as it was already well on in the sailing season. But that would mean another winter of unpopularity at Rome, and give Antony the chance to anticipate him with a great victory—all that was known about Antony was that he had at last set off through Armenia. There was also the risk that Sextus might find a way of destroying the great fleet. The news that Lepidus had landed may have been decisive. Lepidus, by next spring, was very likely to have either been defeated or won possession of the island unaided. Neither result would reflect any great credit on Octavian.

He therefore decided to make every effort to finish the war straight away. He sent Maecenas back to Rome to quell the undercurrent of support for Sextus that was running amongst those who had not forgotten Pompey the Great. If the real son of Pompey, who had died fighting for the Republic, were to score another success over the adopted son of Caesar, who had proclaimed the Republic to be a sham, there could be trouble. The crews of the wrecked ships were despatched to Tarentum to man some hulls for which Taurus had no oarsmen, and Octavian himself reviewed the Tarentine fleet and the legions at Vibo. Meanwhile Sextus took no action, preferring to wait for his opponents' clumsy ships to venture into open water and lay themselves open to attack by his faster, more manoeuvrable, and more experienced fleet. What he might have accomplished was shown by Menodorus. Sent by Sextus to reconnoitre the enemy's intentions after the gale, he rowed 150 sea miles in three days and fell without warning on Octavian's guard-ships, capturing them and seizing, burning, or sinking the grain transports whose movements they were protecting. If his other admirals had shown like enterprise, Sextus might have been able to hold Octavian at bay for much longer. As it was, they had neither the brilliance nor the fickleness of Menodorus. It turned out that Menodorus was plotting a fresh desertion and had carried out his exploit in order to enhance his somewhat tarnished reputation. Octavian accepted his desertion, but was careful not to give him any position of command.

At last Octavian was ready, and this time the weather relented. The forces of Taurus and Messalla were concentrated on the mainland opposite the bay of Tauromenium (modern Taormina) in preparation for a crossing. Sextus at Messana guarded the straits, while he stationed a smaller squadron on the north coast under Demochares. Agrippa, in command of Octavian's main fleet, seized the Lipari Islands (thus offsetting a reverse sustained by Lepidus, who lost four legions in an unexpected attack as they were coming from Africa to reinforce him) and moved to engage the main bulk of the Pompeian fleet which came to meet him off Mylae near the northeast corner of the island. His heavier ships proved their worth. Their extra weight crushed the lighter Pompeian vessels, and their extra height was of decisive advantage when it came to grappling and fighting at close quarters. Sextus watched the encounter from a mountain, and when he had lost thirty of the hundred and fifty-five ships he had engaged, he gave the signal to withdraw into shoal water where Agrippa's deeper-drafted fleet could not follow. When Agrippa drew off, because his men were tired and he was mistrustful of the weather, Sextus sailed immediately back to the straits. He knew that Octavian, who was directing operations from that quarter, would try to cross in his absence. So it proved. Octavian had ferried half his forces across and was fortifying his camp south of Tauromenium when Sextus's fleet appeared unexpectedly to seaward, cutting him off from Messalla and the rest of his army. Octavian's alarm was increased when he saw cavalry and infantry on the landward side, and the cavalry mounted an attack on his camp. Fortunately for him, Sextus's commanders, unaware of the panic in his camp and wary of the approaching dusk, did not press home their sally. A naval engagement the next day ended with a decisive victory for the Pompeians, whose superior seamanship was able to prove itself in this encounter with the ships of conventional size and weight that Antony had left.

Octavian himself spent the greater part of the night in a small boat, uncertain whether to take refuge with Messalla on the mainland, or go back to Cornificius whom he had left in charge of the camp on the Sicilian side. Caution prevailed. He reached Messalla's camp despondent and exhausted, but soon pulled himself together, issued fresh orders to his commanders, and again sent Maecenas back to Rome to keep order. Finding events critical in the capital, Maecenas had to take action against some agitators. Time, evidently, was running out for Octavian, and defeat or delay could be fatal now. But once again, Agrippa brought salvation. He had seized the port of Tyndaris, west of Mylae on the north coast, and through it was able to land the combined forces of his and Octavian's commands, a total of twenty-one legions with their associated horse and auxiliaries. Cornificius was rescued in the nick of time as he and his men were about to perish from thirst among the lava flows from Etna. Lepidus effected a junction with Octavian and camped near Messana. The forces of the two triumvirs and Agrippa now ringed Sextus, who had withdrawn from Mylae and been reinforced by the troops which had previously been opposing Lepidus in the west of the island.

Cut off from adequate supplies, Sextus decided to risk everything on a great sea battle. Both sides had 300 ships—or so Appian says: in fact Sextus probably had considerably fewer—equipped with fighting-towers fore and aft and every sort of missile. Agrippa devised a special sort of grappling-iron for the occasion. Nicknamed the 'snatcher', it consisted of an iron claw on the end of an iron-shod eight-foot pole which was fired by a catapult at the enemy vessels. The rope attached to it was then winched in, while the length of the pole and its iron covering prevented the crew of the grappled ship from cutting either rope or pole. Agrippa had learnt at Mylae how essential it was for his ships to come to grips with the enemy and not let them use their superior skill and manoeuvrability.

On September 3, off Naulochus, a little east of Mylae, the final engagement of the campaign was fought. The accounts of it given by Dio and Appian are tinged with reminiscences of the famous description by Thucydides of the critical naval battle that took place in the great harbour of Syracuse under the eyes of the watching armies. At any rate for Sextus's men, the battle of Naulochus was no less important. All that could be seen from the land was a long line of ships locked together, distinguishable only by the colours of their towers. Even Agrippa, as admiral, had no very clear idea of the progress of the fight more than a few ships' distance from him. Sextus's men fought desperately. Many of them were runaway slaves and deserters and could expect impalement or crucifixion if they were captured. But the 'snatcher' did its work well and the Pompeian ships could not break free from Agrippa's heavyweights. Superior manpower and superior strength told in the end. Agrippa lost only three ships sunk to the Pompeians' twenty-eight. The remainder of Sextus's fleet attempted flight, but were all captured or run aground except for seventeen which managed to round the promontory and reach the harbour of Messana. There Sextus met them, having abandoned his army as soon as the outcome of the battle was beyond doubt, and with his daughter set out at once for the eastern Mediterranean to throw himself on Antony's mercy. He knew what he could expect from Octavian.

The portion of Sextus's army that was at Naulochus surrendered at once to Octavian. The others, in Messana, were briefly besieged by Agrippa and Lepidus, then surrendered to the latter, who would not wait for Octavian to come from Naulochus before accepting the surrender. Lepidus's taste of success went to his head. He allowed Sextus's legions to unite with his own army, and attempted to buy their loyalty by letting them join his men in plundering the town. He now had twenty-two legions, more than either side had had at Philippi (their quality was another matter), enough, he thought, to vindicate the ancient glory of the Aemilii and take revenge for his years of exclusion from power.

He tried to make himself master of Sicily, seizing the passes and giving orders to the garrisons not to admit Octavian. But the troops would have none of it. They had not brought one civil war to an end simply to start another, and Octavian had little difficulty in winning them over. When he realized the futility of his short-lived bid for power, Lepidus threw himself on Octavian's mercy. Stripped of his triumviral authority, but still permitted to retain the chief pontificate he had so dubiously acquired, Lepidus returned to Italy to live another twenty-four years in comfortable but inglorious retirement at the quiet resort of Circeii.

Thus Octavian had disembarrassed himself simultaneously of an enemy and of a titular rival. There could now be no possible doubt who was the master of Italy and the west. With the ending of the harassment of the coasts of Italy and the resumption of normal grain shipments to Rome, Octavian could expect the ordinary people to be solidly grateful to him. All danger of a coup in Rome was gone, although there were disturbances and dissension in Campania and Etruria. But almost at once the revolutionary leader found himself faced with the same problem that had very nearly brought his career to an end in 41. As after Philippi, he found himself with an enormous army on his hands. There were no outstanding military tasks ahead —at most, employment for a dozen legions in Gaul and Spain and around the foothills of the Alps, and for a few more on garrison duty in Africa. Yet the combined armies of Sextus, Lepidus and himself totalled forty-five legions, together with 25,000 cavalry and 40,000 light-armed troops. These auxiliary forces were not citizens, and did not constitute a problem. They could be dismissed to their native regions without ado. But the probable number of legionaries now under his command, allowing for the weakness of Lepidus's legions and the scratch nature of Sextus's, was not less than 120,000. Octavian was faced, therefore, by a major task of resettlement. Some tens of thousands of veterans expected the customary, and promised, rewards of success in civil war, land and money—neither of them provided by the defeat of Sextus.

He attempted to stave off trouble by an appearance of generosity. He paid the soldiers a small part of their reward and promised to give them the rest later; he covered up his failure to provide more substantial and tangible benefits by making a lavish distribution of crowns and other honours and by pardoning the Pompeian leaders. The manoeuvre did not work. Led by his own troops, who expected the most favourable treatment, the army revolted, demanding discharge and the same rewards as had been paid to the veterans of Philippi. It was quite impossible, financially or politically, to grant them this. There was not the slightest excuse to expropriate Italian land, and no money to buy it. As for imposing extra taxes, that would be a strange way of celebrating the victory over the pirate Sextus. Nor need any help be expected from Antony, who had had quite enough trouble after Philippi trying to wring money out of the eastern provinces—and that was when those regions could with superficial justice be accused of having given their support to Brutus and Cassius, and when Antony was well-disposed towards him.

Octavian was in an extraordinarily awkward position; but he managed to extricate himself by a mixture of demagogic skill and strong-arm tactics. He made fresh promises of payment—which he extended to Antony's troops too 'when they should return'—and tried to browbeat the mutineers by reminding them of their military oath and the sanctions of military discipline. When this threatening attitude failed to have any effect, and they hurled in his teeth the promises he had made to them, he broke the core of the opposition by suddenly agreeing to discharge his own veterans of Mutina, and any others who had served ten years. These numbered 20,000 in all. He shipped them out of the island straight away, and split them further by giving an assurance to the Mutina veterans only that he would nevertheless honour his previous promises to them. The remainder were left to fend for themselves. They were not numerous enough to cause trouble if the rest of the army could be placated, and each man still hoped that he might in the end be included among 'the worthiest' whom Octavian had astutely promised to treat in the same way as the veterans of Mutina. The main trouble-makers thus disposed of, Octavian praised the loyalty of the remainder and gave them a substantial bounty—which he exacted forthwith from the unfortunate Sicilians. The soldiers who had been serving with Sextus were somewhat half-hearted in supporting the mutiny, since they feared that the generous terms on which they had surrendered might not be ratified. Octavian also suppressed one Ofellius, a centurion who had described the extra honours and privileges that Octavian had been distributing as 'children's playthings', and had been applauded for demanding land and money. At least, it was inferred that Octavian suppressed him. He was not seen again, and no one cared to step into his shoes.

The danger thus quelled, the problem remained: too many soldiers, too little for them to do, too few resources to reward them as they hoped and expected. Temporary or partial solutions were found: a few of the veterans were settled in Provence; some on what public land could still be found, and around Capua and Rhegium; and a campaign to occupy, and perhaps reward, the remainder was planned for the following year—against the tribes of Illyria at the head of the Adriatic gulf. In other respects, it was an autumn of triumph. Agrippa, chief architect of victory, was granted a unique honour, a golden crown adorned with the rams of ships. Octavian himself approached divinity more nearly than before: his statue appeared in the temples of the loyal towns of Italy. In Rome, he paid due honour to the gods by consecrating to Apollo the site he had selected for his own house, while to himself honours more in keeping with the dignity of ancient precedent were voted: a column, adorned like Agrippa's crown, supporting a golden statue and bearing an inscription commemorating the re-establishment of peace on land and sea; annual sacrifices to mark the day of his victory; an ovation; and for himself the personal and semi-sacred inviolability of a tribune of the people—this last a foretaste of his eventual solution of the problem of how to hold autocratic power beneath republican forms. At the same time, he proclaimed his readiness to lay down his triumviral power and restore the ancestral constitution as soon as Antony had returned from Parthia and agreed to do likewise.

As for Octavian's chief supporters, men who emerge from his shadow for a moment to reveal themselves, in the Roman fashion, as commanders of fleets and armies in the Sicilian campaign, they were repaid in appropriate manner. The college of fifteen augurs was already full; no matter, Messalla was created a supernumerary member. Cornificius, who had advertised his regard for the memory of Caesar by prosecuting the absent Brutus in 43, became consul in 35. Statilius Taurus, perhaps already one of the inner circle, succeeded to Lepidus's triumviral portion, governing first Sicily and then Africa. Q. Laronius, like Taurus a man from the south, but otherwise without record, reached the consulship in 33. C. Carrinas survived from the days of the dictator and had already been dubiously honoured by holding the first triumviral consulate. Such names, new to the annals of Roman history, marked the final stage of the long struggle of the people of Italy to wrest the control of the government from the ancient oligarchy of Rome and Latium—though it was to be another hundred years before the grandson of a veteran of Pharsalus from the Sabine country became emperor. Alongside the new men, the old aristocracy appear, tenacious of influence and lending respectability to revolution. Apart from Messalla and Appius Claudius Pulcher, there was Paullus Aemilius Lepidus, son of the man who had been proscribed by his triumviral brother; Paullus reached the consulship in 34, sufficient proof of his value to Octavian.

But of all this Antony, for the moment, knew nothing. The eighteen months that followed his departure from Brundisium in the summer or early autumn of 37 appear in retrospect to have been decisive. What his thoughts were as he watched the Italian coastline disappear from sight, we can never know. But it is a fair guess that he was disillusioned with his young associate in power. Octavian had manoeuvred him into first consenting to, and then actually supporting, a war of which he had never approved. The legions which Octavian had promised to give him in return were not immediately available; he might have to wait a long time for them. Nor would it be easy to recruit on his own account while Octavian needed men for a war nearer at hand and less uncertain in its outcome. As for Octavia, she was beautiful and fond of him; but she had not yet given him a son, and there is no sign that the much-married Antony found her unusually attractive. On the other hand, to be left behind was the frequent fate of the wives of Roman notables in search of military glory, and there was nothing sinister in the fact that Antony was travelling east without her. As yet, no breach between her husband and her brother could be discerned. Antony had gone out of his way to humour his colleague, and relations appeared to be more amicable than at any time since the autumn of 39.

Antony's first business, when he arrived in Syria, was to summon the Queen of Egypt. Plutarch speaks with the voice of Augustus: 'As he drew near to Syria, there again flared up with fresh force his passion for Cleopatra, a terrible affliction which had been slumbering for a long time and seemed to have been laid to rest and charmed away by better considerations. Finally, like Plato's stubborn and unmanageable beast of the soul, he rebelled against all that was good and might have saved him, and sent Fonteius Capito to bring Cleopatra to Syria.' That was not quite how it seemed at the time. Antony had business to do with one of the wealthiest, most loyal, and most important of Rome's vassal rulers. That this ruler was a woman and had borne children—whom he had never seen—to Antony, was an interesting and mildly scandalous detail, but of no political significance. What mattered at the moment was that Antony needed to be quite sure of Egypt. He was about to place on the thrones of Galatia, Cappadocia, Pontus, and Judaea men whose ability was proven and whose loyalty to Rome was beyond question—but they were men who were not of royal blood, and in two cases not even natives of their new domains. If his judgment either of the men, or of the political situation in these kingdoms, was wrong, he might leave an uncomfortable situation behind him as he advanced into Parthian territory the following summer. The stability of the whole area, the stability he had been patiently working for ever since 39 by military and diplomatic means, could be threatened. By an irritating combination of circumstances, Herod, the king who was personally closest to him, was also the one most likely to meet opposition both internal and external—for Cleopatra was his enemy. She was casting greedy eyes on his kingdom. Yet Antony's governor of Syria, C. Sosius, had just captured Jerusalem for Herod and brought the rival king Antigonus in chains to execution—not the way royalty was normally treated by Roman captors. For Antony, there could be no going back on his policy of supporting Herod. It thus became a matter of great political importance to conciliate Cleopatra.

Questions of state, then, brought Cleopatra to Antioch again. Historians have spoken of a 'marriage' and explained the gifts of territory that Antony now made to her as a 'wedding-present'. It is said that she wished to reconstitute to its full extent the ancient kingdom of the Ptolemies as it had been in its heyday in the third century B.C. That may be so. More to the point is what Antony

Entrance to the Gulf of Ambracia. The circuit of the walls of Nicopolis can be made out south of A, immediately to the west of and almost the same size as the lagoon

- A   Hill of Mikhalitzi, site of Octavian's camp
- B   Promontory of Actium, site of Antony's camp
- C   Conjectural site of Antony's advance camp
- D   Entrance to the Gulf (the forts are to left and right of the letter)
- E   Octavian's anchorage and landing-beach
- F   Antony's fleet's anchorage

View south from Octavian's camp. In the right foreground, ruins of the theatre of Nicopolis; in the distance, Leucas

View south-south-west from the north shore of the entrance to the Gulf of Ambracia: Leucas and (extreme left) the hills of Acarnania. The very low point in front of the latter is part of the promontory of Actium   *Photos: the Author*

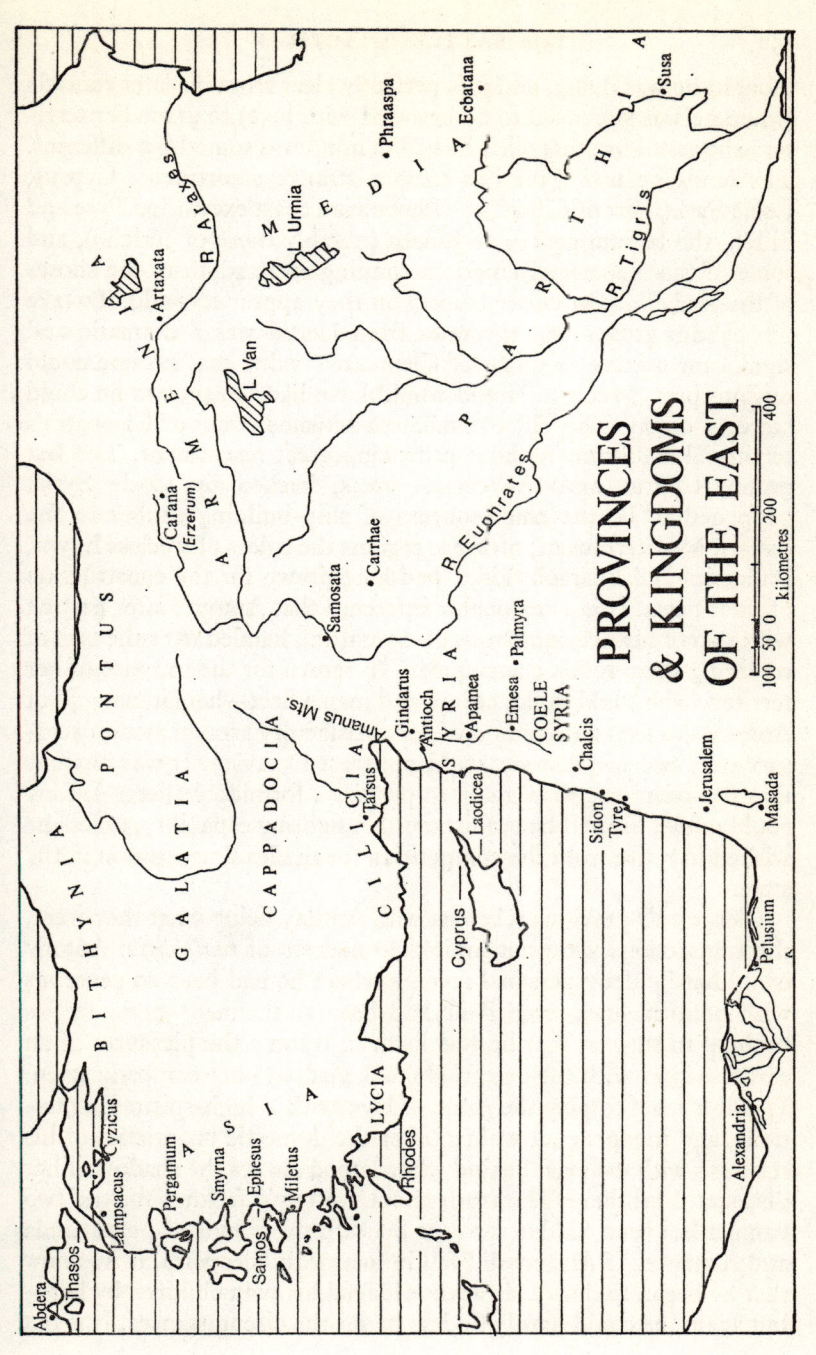

PROVINCES
& KINGDOMS
OF THE EAST

thought he was doing, and it is perfectly clear from his later refusals (when he was supposed to be besotted with love) to grant her territory she asked for, that what he had in mind was something different. The lands he now gave her seem a strange assortment: Cyprus, Coele Syria, part of Cilicia, the Phoenician coast except for Tyre and Sidon, the balsam groves of Judaea (notably those of Jericho), and some of the Nabataean kingdom running away south to the shores of the Red Sea. On closer inspection they appear less odd. To take the balsam groves and revenues from Herod was a dramatic and significant gesture, a token of Cleopatra's value that no one could misinterpret. Much as Herod would have liked to protest he could scarcely do so. The gift of Nabataea satisfied some of Cleopatra's territorial ambitions without provoking great resentment. The last group, Cyprus and the coastal areas, backed by Coele Syria, happened to be the chief sources of ship-building timber in the eastern Mediterranean; on these regions the rulers of treeless Egypt, Ptolemies and Pharaohs alike, had long drawn for the construction of their fleets. It is a reasonable inference that Antony, after parting with two of his five squadrons at Tarentum, handed over the task of replacing them to his client-queen. In return for the increase of her territory, she could build, equip, and man a fleet—hers in name, but Antony's to use: an economical and satisfactory arrangement, necessary only because Antony could not trust Octavian. It was obvious that Octavian was soon going to possess a formidable fleet. Antony could not let himself be outdistanced in fighting capability, unless he wished to retire from the competition for the leading position in the state.

Cleopatra's previous relations with Antony being what they were, the transactions were not limited to matters of *realpolitik*. Antony could hardly deny personal favours where he had been so generous with political ones, even if he had been so inclined—and there is nothing to suggest that he was loath to resume the pleasures of an earlier winter with the queen. He took gladly to her company again. Was it a relief to play the game of love with a high-spirited, ambitious, and independent woman after the domestic proprieties of his relations with Octavia, behind whom stood always the shadow of her distasteful brother? The truth about Antony's feelings for the two women has been hidden for ever beneath the clouds of propaganda and romance. If Antony did fall in love with Cleopatra, it was now that he began to do so. He acknowledged his twin children by her—but again, he could hardly do less under the circumstances. It is not becoming for a queen to have fatherless children. The boy was christened Alexander Helios ('Sun'), his sister Cleopatra Selene ('Moon'). Since there had not been an Alexander in the royal house of the Ptolemies for two hundred years, the imperial implications of the great name were patent. The boy's other name 'Sun' carried associations that were more spiritual and more cosmic. Many men, both in east and west, believed that a Golden Age was soon to come. This Golden Age was firmly associated with the rule of the sun, and the sun in its turn with the idea of all-seeing, all-pervading, and all-quickening justice which Hellenistic god-monarchs claimed to dispense. In Egypt, the name was specially appropriate, for the goddess Isis, according to an inscription in her shrine at Sais, had given birth to the Sun; and Cleopatra took seriously her role as Isis upon earth. For the little girl to be called 'Moon' was less striking, since she had predecessors of the same title. It may be nothing more than a coincidence, in view of this, that the Parthian king against whom Antony was so soon to march, called himself 'brother of the Sun and Moon'; but it was a peculiarly happy one, if Antony intended to place his son upon the Parthian throne.

There was nothing in any of these transactions to cause surprise or resentment in Rome. Octavia knew, when she married Antony in 40, that Cleopatra had given birth to his children. For him to recognize them now was important for them, and for Cleopatra, but not for Octavia. In Roman law Antony could have but one wife, and any union he might contract, even under the forms or customs of a foreign nation, with a woman who was not a Roman citizen remained an illegitimate liaison. Conceivably, Octavia's pride may have been wounded, but she could scarcely complain that Antony was treating her any differently from Fulvia—or even that Antony was failing to follow where Caesar had shown the way. As to the rest of the business, the only reason why the world knows more about the lands Antony gave to Cleopatra than about those he gave at the same time to his three new client-kings—Amyntas of Galatia, Polemo of Pontus, and Archelaus of Cappadocia—is the later course of Octavian's propaganda. It was within Antony's powers, in fact demanded of him if he were to establish a viable system of buffer-states under client-kings, to reallocate principalities and petty kingdoms. It is nonsense to say he 'gave away' Roman territory. The only one of these regions that had ever been directly under Roman control for more than a year or two was the part of Cilicia called Wild—if 'control' is the word. It was a province the Roman government was better off without, being trackless, unexploitable, and apt to shelter pirates.

The winter, then, passed in the diplomatic restructuring of such of the east as was not directly administered by the provincial governors of Bithynia, Asia, and Syria-with-Cilicia, and in preparation for the campaign against Parthia. Antony perhaps missed a chance to recover by negotiation the eagles lost at Carrhae, when a certain Monaeses, a leading member of the Parthian nobility, deserted to him. There was dissension between the Parthian king Phraates and his nobles, which Antony might have exploited for his own ends. As it was, he promised Monaeses the Parthian throne and made a gift of some lands to him and his followers in return for the expectation of their support in the coming invasion; whereupon they made up their differences with Phraates, and Monaeses rode off in the spring to be placed in command of the Parthian forces for a defensive war. Of course, it may all have been a carefully-worked out ruse to discover Antony's plans. If so, it was scarcely necessary. The king of Armenia, Artavasdes, nominal ally of Rome but Parthian by sympathy, culture, and geographical proximity, was a far better source of information. In any case, Antony's general line of attack needed little guessing. Unless he was eager to repeat the disaster of Carrhae, he could not advance across the plains of upper Mesopotamia—at least, not without cavalry in far greater numbers than he possessed to beat off the Parthian mounted archers. The only alternative was to make a circuit through Armenia, past the great inland seas of Lakes Van and Urmia, and strike southward through Media towards Ecbatana and Susa. That this was his intention was made perfectly obvious by the activities of P. Canidius Crassus, his chief general, who was operating with a substantial force against two peoples of the Caucasus in the spring of 36, after spending the winter in Armenia.

Late in the spring or early in the summer Antony left Antioch, having heard not long before that Octavia's expected child had turned out to be another daughter. Cleopatra accompanied him as far as the Euphrates, then returned to Alexandria by way of Jerusalem (doubtless enjoying the negotiations by which she leased to her enemy Herod the balsam gardens which should have been his). Later in the summer, she gave birth to her third child by Antony, a son whom she named Ptolemy Philadelphus after the greatest of his kingly ancestors.

Antony marched on up the Euphrates to meet Canidius at Carana (modern Erzerum) near its source in central Armenia. There he held a review of his army. It numbered 100,000 men. The core consisted of sixteen legions, slightly below their full strength; apart from these 60,000 heavy infantry there were 10,000 Spanish and Celtic cavalry and 30,000 horsemen and light-armed troops of other nationalities, of which the most notable contingent was supplied by the Armenian king himself. 300 wagons carried the siege train, which included a battering-ram eighty feet long, for Antony knew that good timber was impossible to find in the high country of Media and Parthia.

It was already after midsummer when the great army set out from Carana. Men who were wise after the event said that it was too late, that Antony should have wintered in Armenia, that his besotted passion for Cleopatra made him impatient of delay. More plausibly, modern writers have argued that he needed military success to counterbalance Octavian's expected victory over Sextus. But such a victory was scarcely a foregone conclusion, in the light of what had happened in 38, and Octavian had not even begun operations when Antony left Carana. It seems much more likely that Antony intended to capture the Median capital Phraaspa, winter there in security, and use it as a base from which to conduct operations south and east into Parthia in the following campaigning season. Fighting on these bleak uplands in winter was out of the question.

It was when he failed to capture Phraaspa that Antony was in trouble. Though he may be acquitted of any gross error in the timing of his great campaign, he miscalculated how long he would need to get his full army with its enormous siege-train over the long route to Phraaspa. In his anxiety to start the siege, and so be sure of reducing the town before winter set in, he left the siege-train to make its own way with a guard of two legions and some of the auxiliary contingents, and pressed on with the remainder of his forces to Phraaspa. It was a fatal mistake. While he was labouring to build earthworks against the town, the Parthians descended on the inadequately guarded siege-train, annihilated it, and took King Polemo prisoner. Artavasdes, whether he was in collusion with Phraates all the time, or whether he simply judged that Antony's case was hopeless, forthwith abandoned the Roman camp and rode off home with his 6,000 cavalry and 7,000 foot. Antony had thus lost not only a quarter of his total force, but also the indispensable and largely irreplaceable siege engines which he had counted on to obtain him winter quarters.

The one hope lay in a pitched battle. Antony attempted to bring one on, and for a moment the Romans thought they had won a decisive victory. But the Parthians did not stand and fight like more conventional enemies. A pursuit of many miles yielded the Romans a mere eighty victims and thirty prisoners—and no escape from the perpetual harassing by the horse-archers as they made their despondent way back to camp. Antony had no alternative but to retreat. Supplies were getting short. The equinox was past, and an ominous crispness was in the air. After an attempt to bluff Phraates into returning the captured legionary eagles as the price of his withdrawal, Antony started to lead his army back. He went by a shorter and more mountainous route, under the guidance of a native of the region, and thus escaped offering his men as an easy prey to the mounted archers who hung on his flanks all the time. The one determined engagement his rearguard risked was nearly disastrous. All he could do was march in hollow square, with slingers and javelin-throwers and cavalry on the flanks and rear, and beat off the attacks when they came. The farther the army went from Phraaspa, the less intensely did the enemy harry them—but the worse grew the privations from lack of food, and, on one occasion, water. Roman discipline held firm until the last night march to the river Araxes, which was the boundary between Media and Armenia. Some sudden panic, it may be the rumour that Antony had been killed, or that the Parthians had at last attacked and routed the other part of the army, led to a wild outbreak of looting and murder which did not spare even Antony's own baggage-carriers. Antony contemplated suicide, but the assurances of his guide that the river was just ahead, and the information transmitted to him by the devious Monaeses that he need fear no pursuit beyond the river, encouraged him to carry on.

Monaeses had spoken the truth. The Parthians unstrung their bows and made no attempt to stop the Romans crossing the Araxes. Plutarch says they praised the Romans for their courage. Honours were even: Antony and his generals had driven the Parthians out of Roman territory; now Phraates and Monaeses had driven the Romans out of their territory. The Parthians had learnt enough about Rome to know that her rulers did not accept a great defeat, but had to avenge it. Many years might pass, but in the end the day of reckoning would come. It was prudent, therefore, to let Antony escape without too great a humiliation. And so, after twenty-seven days' march and eighteen engagements, the Roman army set foot on friendly soil. 20,000 infantry and 4,000 cavalry had perished, more than half from disease. With some justification, the troops blamed the defection of Artavasdes for their failure and urged Antony to take vengeance on him immediately. But it was out of the question. Antony needed all

Artavasdes's good-will and co-operation if he was to get his starving, weakened, and demoralized force back to the coastlands. Vengeance could wait. He flattered Artavasdes and obtained provisions and money from him, then sent a message to Cleopatra and hurried on to the Syrian coast to meet her while Canidius, Ahenobarbus, and M. Titius, Plancus's nephew, brought the men along the final stages of their winter march. 8,000 more perished in the snows of Armenia before they reached the haven of winter-quarters in the province of Syria.

So ended the great Parthian expedition. Antony had lost two-fifths of his entire force. But for his own qualities of leadership in adversity, he could have lost many more. As it was, his grip on the eastern borders of the empire was so weakened that he felt it necessary to arrange for Cleopatra and her ships to meet him at an insignificant harbour town, Leuke Come. It was possible that the Parthians might have followed up their advantage by breaking across the Euphrates and be once again sweeping through Syria, with the support of the anti-Roman elements in the province. They did not, and Cleopatra came safely, bringing clothing and a little money for the army.

Antony must also have heard, on the final stages of his journey, of Octavian's success against Sextus. No report survives of how he took the news. But whatever his feelings may have been, there was no longer any reason why the legions promised in 37 and now so badly needed in the east should not be forthcoming. With peace in the west established, a debacle in the east narrowly averted, and rein-forcements to be expected next spring, Antony could look forward with some confidence to re-establishing his military prestige on the eastern borders and then arranging with Octavian what was to be done about their position when the triumvirate formally expired at the end of 33. Shortly afterwards, he received a private letter on this very topic from Octavian. Of its contents we know only that it mentioned the Illyrian expedition which Octavian proposed to under-take next year. Antony replied that he was willing to co-operate in this venture, and, surely asked again for the troops for which he had to wait so long.

Chapter XII

OCTAVIAN'S CHALLENGE

AFTER SEEING his troops into their winter quarters, Antony
went back with Cleopatra to Alexandria, which was to be his
winter retreat for the next three years. He could not admit
publicly in Rome that he had suffered a disaster—especially after his
own marshal Ventidius's triumph barely two years previously. The
truth was of course known to Octavian, but he read out Antony's
despatches glossing over what had really happened. Octavian was
not yet ready to pick a quarrel with his senior partner. Besides, if it
were officially admitted that Roman arms had met with a major
reverse in the east, he would not be able to continue with the policy
he had been quietly pursuing ever since 39, of denying to Antony
effective rights of recruiting in Italy. At the moment it was best to
humour Antony, keep him at a distance, and allow his power and his
prestige in Italy to wane with his growing alienation from his native
land and customs. Once inferior to Antony, Octavian had risen now
to be his equal. Given time, a situation might present itself which he
could turn to advantage and so become the master of the Roman
world—fulfilling his proclaimed ambition of 44, not to rest until he
had attained the status of his adoptive father. Until this situation
arose, it would be wisest to maintain apparent concord and keep the
good-will of the public. And so Rome gave thanks with festival and
sacrifice for Antony's 'successes'.

Meanwhile Antony's loyalty to his irritating, and irritatingly
successful, colleague was put to the test. After the battle of Naulochus
Sextus had fled with a few ships in the direction of Greece, pausing
only at the Lacinian promontory of southern Italy to despoil the
famous temple of Hera of its treasure. He made his way by Corcyra
and Cephallenia to the Aegean island of Lesbos, and here at the
beginning of winter he began to make preparations to seize the
mainland that lay across the strait. He was unmolested since Antony
and his army had not yet returned from Media, and C. Furnius the
governor of Asia had neither troops to speak of nor any idea how

Antony wanted him to receive the refugee. Sextus had hopes of making himself master of all Asia Minor if the rumours were true and Antony had perished in Media. When these hopes were disappointed, and Antony returned to Alexandria, Sextus sent ambassadors to him placing himself at Antony's disposal and assuring him of his loyalty and support. Antony had already given instructions to Titius to draft ships and soldiers from Syria and take the offensive against Sextus if he showed himself hostile; but to treat him with honour if he wished to throw himself on Antony's mercy. Antony therefore replied to the ambassadors that if what they said was true, it was strange that Sextus had not come in person with Titius. The reason very soon became clear: Sextus was also in communication with the kings of Pontus, Armenia, and Parthia, and his embassy to the latter was intercepted by Antony's generals and sent to Alexandria.

Once again, Sextus had shown himself incapable of trusting another man or voluntarily accepting the position of an inferior. He could not bring himself to come as a suppliant to Antony, abdicating the independence that he had preserved for ten years and briefly brought others to recognize at Puteoli. Whatever his claims might once have been to have succeeded his father as champion of the Republic, these had forfeited all plausibility. He had at last become what his enemies had called him long ago: an adventurer and a pirate. He was prepared to find sanctuary and status, like a second Labienus, with the enemies of Rome, if Antony, his one-time sympathizer, refused to grant him what he considered to be his deserts. Antony temporized. His Roman sense of honour made him reluctant to turn on this man. Sextus had so nearly been his ally in an invasion of Italy against Octavian in the year after Perusia; later, Octavian had made war on Sextus against his wishes. Yet he could not receive him as an ally without provoking an open breach with Octavian. He gave no clear answer to Sextus's ambassadors and decided to allow Sextus's actions to speak for him if he would not come himself.

Sextus sealed his own fate, for while the embassy was in Alexandria his warlike preparations roused the suspicions of Furnius. The governor sent for reinforcements from Ahenobarbus, who had just arrived back in Bithynia, and from Amyntas, King of Galatia, and kept a watchful eye on Sextus. The latter, after the failure of a plot to kidnap Ahenobarbus and use him as a hostage in negotiations, resorted to open hostilities. By treachery he seized the city of Lampsacus and by lavish bounties and the magic of the name of Pompey—still potent and unsullied in the east—he recruited a large number of Italian veterans, perhaps once his father's troops, who had been settled there by Julius Caesar. The local inhabitants, too, were not unwilling to support him. They were weary of years of exceptional taxation to finance the armies and the wars of the triumvirate, and saw in him an illusory saviour. But three legions and a couple of hundred cavalry, though they gained him a few successes, were not enough. There arrived first seventy ships, the survivors from those Antony had lent Octavian in 37, then a powerful force from Syria under Titius, who took overall command. Sextus was finally captured as he attempted to fight his way eastward in the direction of Armenia. Amyntas delivered him to Titius, who accepted his legions into Antony's service and put Sextus himself to death at Miletus. Whether he did this on Antony's orders, or on his own initiative, or at the prompting of his uncle Plancus, governor of Syria, is unknown, but it was for ever held against him by the Roman people: M. Titius had been among the proscribed in 43 and had found safety by fleeing to Sextus in Sicily, only becoming an adherent of Antony (doubtless through his uncle's good offices) after the pact of Puteoli, and when, in later years, he put on a show in the theatre of Pompey the Great, the populace rose and drove him with abuse and curses from the building.

Sextus seems to have met his end by midsummer. The news was received with the utmost official enthusiasm in Rome, as might be expected. Privately Octavian was glad that Antony was prepared to honour the implications of the treaty of Tarentum, and publicly the Roman people could scarcely help rejoicing over the final elimination of the man they had been at war with for the past three years. Only the more fiercely independent chose to remember the time, not so long distant, when the triumvir Octavian had been stoned and the statue of Neptune had been wildly applauded at a public procession. And so there were games in the Circus, and Antony was honoured by statues in the forum and also in the Temple of Concord, where, like Octavian, he was permitted to hold banquets with his wife and children.

This last honour was not so trivial as it might seem, nor quite disinterested. It was part of the attempt that Octavian and his sister made in the spring and summer of 35 to prise Antony away from his royal mistress and his near-monarchical position in the eastern half of the empire. At the very moment when it was voted, Octavia was in Athens, unsure whether Antony would leave Cleopatra and return to her. She had come across from Italy in the spring, bringing her husband clothing and supplies for his army, 2,000 picked men, and the seventy ships left from the Sicilian operations. A generous and wifely act, as it was represented in the victor's propaganda; and so it would have been, if Antony had not been owed 20,000 men by his brother-in-law. The ships he scarcely needed, though they were convenient for the operations against Sextus. It was men he was desperate for, after losing a third of the legionaries who had set out for Media and Parthia the year before, 'the finest army' according to Plutarch 'that any commander of that epoch gathered together'. Octavian, then, was holding a pistol at his head. Without men, he was powerless, or would eventually become so. The price he was to pay to get them, and so maintain the army on which his own position ultimately depended, was to abandon Cleopatra.

Such was the plain message of Octavia's mission, and her expectant wait in Athens. There was no mistaking it. Instead of soldiers, Antony was offered his wife. A version of the episode has it that Octavia arranged the whole expedition on her own initiative, begging permission from her brother to take the troops and sail to her husband's support; but it is inconceivable that a politician so astute and so unscrupulous as Octavian would have allowed this to happen if it had not suited him. The implication of the story, in any case, is that Octavian was doing the love-crazed drunkard of later legend a favour by sending him any forces at all. There can be no doubt that Octavian made a deliberate challenge to Antony's freedom of action. Hitherto neither man had made any attempt to interfere in the other's sphere of power. What was it that provoked Octavian to issue the challenge? If it was Antony's relations with Cleopatra, he should have taken offence long before, in the winter of 37–36; but Romans did not go to war over their womenfolk in the manner of Homeric heroes. If it was fear of Cleopatra's ambitions, fear that she and Antony might together be planning to rule the Mediterranean world from Alexandria, it must have been a projection of his own desires; for there was nothing in the behaviour or requests of Antony to suggest such a thing. Antony's preoccupations were those of a Roman of his class, brought up to regard the business of life as the winning of glory for himself and empire for his country by the achievement of great deeds—above all, military deeds. His absorption in the conquest of Media, Parthia, and Armenia was such that he could not find the time to make the slow journey to Rome, where his presence might have done something to counteract the increasing preponderance of his colleague. Octavian cannot really have believed that Antony, whose ancestors included men who had held the highest offices of state, would be induced by an Egyptian queen to lead a Roman army against its own fatherland—in the name of what?

No, what Octavian feared was having to take second place. In pursuit of his own glory and political ambitions he had manoeuvred Antony into unwillingly agreeing to the war against Sextus. The successful conclusion of this war, and Antony's unexpected reverse at the hands of the Parthians and the Armenian winter, had given Octavian, briefly, the advantage in the struggle for prestige to which his whole public career had been devoted. Caesar's heir did not intend to give up that advantage, still less when his rival could claim to be succeeding Caesar in less formal ways by adopting Caesar's mistress and Caesar's plans for spectacular conquest in the east. Ambition, political flair, the eye for a chance, drove Octavian to make this first subtle, but unmistakably hostile, challenge. But more than ambition lay behind it; Octavian also happened to be in possession of a large army, whose quality, though not high at present, could certainly be made so. It was an army which was scarcely needed in the western half of the empire. Employment could perhaps be found for it, fighting against Illyrians, Lusitanians, or the tribes of the high Alpine regions. But armies needed to be paid and fed, and this army needed more: its special rewards for its participation in a civil war. Some of its members had been discharged, some even without their bounty or their land allotments; the major part still remained, unwilling to be fobbed off with settlement outside Italy. Italians they were, and in Italy they wanted to make their homes. The troubles that had led to the war of Perusia, the ugly temper of the troops after the conclusion of the war against Sextus, and the expedients to which he had subsequently had to resort had taught Octavian how difficult it was likely to be to disband his surplus legions. For seven years, from the proscriptions of 43 to the defeat of Sextus in 36, Italy had been in turns taxed, ravaged, and parcelled out to soldiers. The food supply of the capital had been interfered with, its political life—excepting the intrigues of the great—almost entirely suppressed. There was a limit to what Italy would stand. The glorious achievement of ending the Sicilian war might look a little shabby if it were followed by wholesale requisitions and widespread distress among peasantry and landed gentry whose property would be expropriated to make way for the soldiers of the victorious party leader.

Octavian appears, then, as the victim of his own success. He had emerged from comparative obscurity because he was the leader of an unambiguously military revolutionary movement. In part he generated this movement, in part it was the necessary result of a historical development whose origins lay a century and more in the past. But the military revolutionary had reached the point where he had to satisfy his followers. He could do this either at the expense of Italy, or by turning eastward to his colleague's domain. No third course was possible. There were no profitable wars to be fought against outside nations at his end of the Mediterranean, nothing that would bring in the sort of sum he needed to buy land and pay the inflated bounties that had been promised to the veterans of the civil wars. Only the east held promise of that, with the treasure of the Ptolemies—the last unplundered royal storehouse of the successors of Alexander—and the distant mirage of the gold of Media and Parthia. The logical solution to the problem was easy: since he had too many men and Antony too few, all he needed to do was to transfer to Antony the legions not required for the defence of the west. This would bring nearer the long-desired victory over Parthia and relieve him of the odious necessity of creating more veteran colonies in long-suffering Italy. But the whole history of his relations with Antony made the logical solution unthinkable, demanding as it did a mutual trust and respect that had never existed between the two men. To surrender voluntarily to the only man whose status could possibly rival his own in the army through which he had risen to power—this was an impossible notion.

There was nothing to be done with the tiger except ride it. But being Octavian, he rode it very cautiously and with great skill. The first move was to use it as a bargaining counter, to make it clear to Antony, through Octavia, that there was a price upon it. The fact that he owed Antony troops was irrelevant. The situation enabled him to put pressure on Antony and try to force him to abandon Cleopatra and his independence; and if he were successful in this, he could pose as Antony's mentor, as the true Roman who had saved Antony from himself. At the same time, it was necessary to put his army to use. This he had already foreseen, and while Octavia waited in Athens to see if Antony would leave Cleopatra, a major expedition started to move against the tribes of Illyria, in what is now central Jugoslavia. It was a brilliant move. The campaign had some military justification, in that the north-eastern borders of Cisalpine Gaul, beyond the Veneto, had certainly suffered from marauders and needed stabilizing. But Octavian proceeded on a far more generous scale than was strictly necessary, and by so doing he was enabled to give the somewhat motley collection of levies he possessed after the Sicilian war some badly needed discipline and battle-toughening. This conveniently removed the troops from Italy, laid the burden of feeding and accommodating them elsewhere, and provided him with an excuse for not sending them to Antony. The Illyrian campaigns have been well described as large-scale manoeuvres held on enemy territory; and they also served all the requirements of traditional patriotism, which saw troublesome tribesmen as fit victims of Roman armies, and natural providers of honour and glory for the upper class commanders of those armies. There was solid political capital to be won from successful operations against (at last) a palpably foreign foe, whether or not concord with Antony were preserved. Significantly, Octavian ignored Antony's offer of help. Such co-operation did not suit his ideas.

Meanwhile, Antony was struggling with an appallingly hard decision. Should he give in to the blackmail of the young Caesar, or vindicate his pride and his freedom of action by staying with Cleopatra? Octavia refused to obey his first instructions, that she should go back to Italy since he was preparing for a campaign against Armenia in which she could have no part. She sent to him again. The Armenian project was a transparent excuse, since the operations against Sextus were already eating into valuable campaigning time. Octavia knew it would scarcely be possible to mount an expedition of the sort required by Artavasdes's treachery before next spring. Whether by her own wish, or on her brother's instructions, she did not intend to play any longer the game of pretending that she had not been deserted. But Antony refused to change his mind, and ordered Octavia back to Italy. 'It was brutal; a man between two women is likely to be brutal.' Plutarch has a typically romantic and colourful account of how Cleopatra simulated a nervous collapse in order to convince Antony of her love and keep him for herself.

But in truth the women were little more than ciphers when it came to the point of decision. Antony was not infatuated with love for Cleopatra. Later in this same year he refused to yield to her the kingdom of her enemy Herod when she asked for it. He seems to have been perfectly capable of keeping his political and emotional lives separate. The decision to resist Octavian was political, as a Roman understood politics. Octavian had broken faith, and Octavian was menacing his personal prestige; Julius Caesar had crossed the

Rubicon for less. Antony contented himself with sending back Octavia, and her brother will have understood perfectly what that signified. It was not an aggressive act, simply a declaration of independence whose nature could only be interpreted in the light of subsequent actions. Antony's conduct in 35 and 34 shows in fact that he decided to leave Octavian alone in the west and establish his own sphere of influence in the other half of the empire. There was no necessary incompatibility between the roles of Roman overlord and Hellenistic monarch, indeed the combination was to a large extent what was expected of conquering generals in the east. 160 years previously, the Roman commander T. Quinctius Flamininus, after delivering Greece from the dominion of the kings of Macedon, had permitted himself the royal honour of being portrayed upon the coinage of the liberated states. That was in a more modest epoch, yet no one had accused him of overweening ambition or disloyalty to Rome. And in Antony's own case, the role he had assumed of the New Dionysus was not even matter for controversy—how could it be when Julius Caesar received posthumous divinity in his own person, and Sextus claimed to be the son of Neptune? The Romans in the east, generals, administrators, traders, and colonized veterans, knew that this was all play-acting for the benefit of the locals. So long as Antony remained a Roman in his dealings with them and did not betray the dignity and the traditions of Rome, it did not matter very much how he chose to conduct himself towards the native inhabitants or their rulers.

No startling outburst followed Antony's rejection of Octavia. The two principals continued to devote themselves to the matters which already occupied them. In Antony's case, this was Armenia, but the episode of Sextus—although it seems to have been over by mid-summer—prevented him from indulging in anything more than diplomatic activity while he prepared a full-scale expedition for next year. The three impromptu legions that Sextus had raised were a welcome addition to his depleted forces, and he recruited further in order to restore the fourteen legions that had escaped from Media to something like their full strength. This has been described as 'arming' and interpreted as preparation for a civil war he already envisaged; but to distinguish between arming for a civil war and arming for a legitimate and necessary punitive expedition is a difficult exercise.

Octavian certainly took little notice of it. He judged, correctly, that Antony would not move against him unless gravely provoked. Time was on Octavian's side. The longer Antony was cut off from recruiting in Italy, the weaker, or the less Italian, grew the armies of the east. If Antony wished to play the Hellenistic monarch, let him command a Hellenistic army composed not of Roman citizens but of Egyptians, Galatians, Syrians, and Greeks. And the longer Antony remained away from Rome, and the more oriental his forces became, the weaker grew his support among the colonized veterans and the municipalities of Italy, and among the people and senators of the capital. Rome was still the centre of political power; it was to be a hundred years before the secret was revealed that an emperor could be made elsewhere, and three hundred and fifty before Constantine could move the capital. Octavian ruled Rome, dispensed patronage, and courted Antony's supporters. Given time enough, the Antonian party might simply melt away.

Octavian gave every encouragement to this desirable process. The theme of his propaganda was the restoration of the Republic and the re-establishment of peace and its attendant prosperity. He made a great show of legal rectitude in refusing to strip the disgraced Lepidus of the title of Pontifex Maximus, in spite of the fact that it was his 'father' Caesar who had been Lepidus's predecessor in the office; he burned the literature of the civil wars, invective and apologia alike; and, says Appian, 'he entrusted to the annual magistrates much of the management of the state, in accordance with ancestral custom'. Certain taxes were abolished, and all debts—largely, one suspects, bad ones—which were owed to the state from before the civil war were cancelled. The great bulk of the serving army was removed from Italy, and once again Roman governors were seen using the legions of Spain, of Africa, and of Cisalpine Gaul against the natives of those regions who threatened to disturb the Roman peace. The disruption of the agricultural economy of Italy during the civil wars must have been considerable. It was highly desirable, both economically and socially, to encourage the proper and fruitful use of the land. It can scarcely be an accident that Virgil, the protégé of the cultured and powerful Maecenas, produced in these years his *Georgics*, that great poem, disguised as a practical manual, in praise of Italy and of the traditional life of the peasant-farmer. The *Georgics* transcend their time, but what could have stood in stronger contrast to the oriental extravagances currently being credited to Antony?

Fortunate he who knows the country gods,
Pan and the sister Nymphs and old Sylvanus.

Over him the emblems of office have no power,
Nor the purple of kings, nor civil war that inflames
Brother against suspicious brother, nor yet
The plotting Dacian marching down from the Danube,
Nor the might of Rome and kingdoms doomed to decline;
He sees neither poor to pity, nor rich to envy,
He picks the fruit from the branch, the drops that the land
Bears of itself; he misses the law's duress,
The frenzy of politics, and the struggle for office.

Octavian needed to do more than evoke images sanctified by the tradition of Rome, while he made a show of surrendering some of his autocratic powers. It might be desirable to court the favour of public opinion, but it was unwise to rely on it. With characteristic perception of essentials, he took the opportunity offered by the genuine need to rid the country of brigands and roaming bands of discharged and homeless soldiery, to station permanent detachments of troops all over Italy. The pretext was public security; the purpose, complete military control. If there were any who remarked how unrepublican this was, they felt it prudent to hold their tongues. Possessing the personal sacrosanctity of a tribune of the people, the *éclat* of a divine father, and at least a reasonable claim to the gratitude of the people of Italy for having ended the war with Sextus, Octavian was not easy to cast in the role of tyrant. His position was strong, stronger than it had ever been. The one point on which he may have still been inferior to Antony was on the strength of his support among the traditional governing classes. Of his two chief ministers, Maecenas preferred to remain outside the senate, unencumbered by rank and office, while Agrippa scorned noble connections to marry the daughter of the banker Atticus, Cicero's old friend and confidant but no aspirant to public honours. On the other hand, Antony's following stood for the old republic, embracing now not only men like Ahenobarbus who had fought against him at the time of Philippi, but even the murderers of Caesar, for Cassius of Parma and D. Turullius had joined him after the death of Sextus. But in between these two extremes lay a thousand or more members of the senate, amongst whom even Caesar's once-derided new senators must have appeared pillars of ancient respectability. Mutina, Philippi, Perusia, the proscriptions, and the campaigns in Sicily and the east had wrought havoc among the men who had witnessed the stabbing of Julius Caesar. The triumvirs rewarded their followers by filling the

senate with them. It was a cheap and harmless reward, since the
senate was powerless and the quality of its members a matter of
indifference. Perhaps this was why Maecenas refused to join the
order. But amongst this swollen and heterogeneous band there were
still scions of the ancient nobility and new men of ability and indus-
try, to be attached by favours, marriage, or office to the leader or
to the inner circle of trusted intimates around him. Rome was in
transition from oligarchy to monarchy; and the traditions of an
oligarchical society were far from dead—the respect accorded to
family ties and family tradition, the suspicion of outsiders, the
preponderating influence of a few great houses. Before Octavian
could safely restore, or pretend to restore, the forms of republican
political life, he had to be sure that he had a personal following
distinguished enough to enable him to control the senate. This was
not a matter of numbers, but of the quality and the standing of his
adherents. Already in 38, with his marriage to Livia, he had started
the process of winning the aristocracy. The recorded names of those
who were with him in 31 show that his endeavours in this direction
were successful, though our information is too scanty to do more
than indicate a general trend. It is a legitimate inference that after
Octavia's dismissal he used all his political skill to detach Antony's
leading supporters in Rome from him, without as yet showing open
hostility or impugning Antony's good faith.

In spite of Octavian's efforts, there were many who remained
loyal to Antony. Most prominent among them was the consular
Pollio, who stood above the sham of political life under the triumvirate and preferred to devote himself to literary pursuits. Pollio was
bound by friendship to Antony, and made no secret of his dislike for
Octavian. The hall and libraries that he built and endowed out of
the spoils of his campaign against the Parthini were named not after
himself, as was the fashion for commemorative monuments, but
after a deity not much in evidence at the time: Liberty. Of kindred
temper was the historian C. Sallustius, who sought to illustrate the
reasons for the collapse of the republic in monographs whose
judgments contain pointed reference to the earlier and nastier stages
of Octavian's rise to power. Sallust is not known as a partisan of
Antony, but he wrote the oration which Ventidius delivered upon
the occasion of his Parthian triumph. Sallust died in 35, Ventidius
probably earlier. None the less there must have been many obscurer
senators who, remembering the republic, felt as they did, and saw
perhaps that Antony was closer than Octavian to the values and

virtues that had brought empire and glory to Rome. Antony's principal adherents, however, were in the eastern provinces. Ahenobarbus was governing Bithynia; Titius commanded the forces which operated against Sextus in Asia; Plancus had newly replaced Sosius as governor of Syria; P. Canidius Crassus was to be Antony's chief general in the forthcoming Armenian campaign; Q. Dellius was Antony's personal representative at the intrigue-ridden court of Herod. All these men, save the smooth Dellius, had either held consulships or were to hold them in the coming years. Sosius, despatched homewards to celebrate a triumph, made some amends for the absence of these eminent Antonians, and envoys of the calibre of L. Calpurnius Bibulus, son of a father notorious for his opposition to Caesar, kept Antony in contact of a sort with the political centre.

In retrospect, it is easy to see that Antony ought to have returned to Rome, if only for a few months, sometime between the end of 36 and the autumn of 34. Perhaps he did not appreciate the full danger of leaving Octavian complete freedom of political action in the capital. Perhaps, even now, he underestimated how consuming his rival's ambition was, and how strong his position after the Sicilian and Parthian wars. Perhaps his feelings for Cleopatra made the very idea of resuming conjugal life with Octavia distasteful, even though it need only be for a few months; for he could hardly return to Rome and ignore Octavia, if his intention was to win sympathy and strengthen his position. Undeniably, he was anxious to proceed against the perfidious Armenian king—but the loss of a campaign in 35 made it relatively easy for him to journey back to Italy that autumn if he had so wished. An appearance in Rome might have tipped the scales of the political balance in his favour again. But for whatever reason, he did not go, and Octavian was able to play his game without interference and at his own pace.

Chapter XIII

THE FINAL BREACH

THE YEAR 35 was quiet, diplomatically speaking, after the failure of Octavia's mission. The fuse had been lit, but it burned slowly. In the west, the armies of Octavian in Illyria and of his commanders in other provinces fought with routine success against their opponents. Octavian himself took a prominent part in the fighting, hoping perhaps to obliterate the memory of his singularly inglorious role in the Sicilian wars. In the east, Mede and Parthian had fallen out over the division of the spoils of victory, and the Median king had sent his royal prisoner Polemo of Pontus to Antony with a request for friendship and alliance. Antony, delighted, made terms, which included the promise of Median assistance against Armenia, and restored to Polemo his kingdom augmented (in anticipation) by the territory of Lesser Armenia.

Diplomacy being evidently more potent than armies in shifting the loyalties of oriental potentates, in the winter Antony sent the versatile Dellius on yet another mission of the highest importance, to try to bring Artavasdes to his senses. A trip to Alexandria, a token gesture of submission, and the promise of some troops for the Roman army would have satisfied Antony and allowed Artavasdes virtual independence. But the king would not comply. (The reason emerged later: Octavian was in correspondence with him—or so it was alleged.) That left Antony no choice. The honour of Rome and the reputation of Antony demanded that the treacherous ally be brought to heel. There were more practical reasons too, as later imperial history was to bear out: in Roman hands, or under a régime friendly to Rome, Armenia was a powerful bastion against the potential menace of Parthia. Armenia lay on the northern flank of the Parthian kingdom and dominated the headwaters of the Tigris and the Euphrates. No Parthian army would dare to cross the middle Euphrates and attack Syria with a hostile Armenia hanging on its right and rear. Armenia, too, was rich; that is to say, her kings had so far kept their treasure out of Roman hands.

The details of Antony's campaign are obscure, but he moved in plenty of time and massive strength, with an army of at least sixteen legions. He captured Artavasdes, but the king's eldest son Artaxes fought on until he was defeated and fled to Parthia. Antony bound Artavasdes in silver chains 'for apparently', says Dio, 'it was shameful for a man who had been king to be bound with iron', and brought him, his wife, his two younger sons, and a vast mass of booty back to Alexandria. The legions he left in Armenia under Canidius Crassus, no doubt intending to press on to Media and Parthia the next year. With Armenia under control, and Media his ally, he should at last be able to turn the tables on the Parthians. But it was not to be.

The immediate reason why his plans were never fulfilled was the ceremony he staged in Alexandria to mark the conquest of Armenia. The surviving accounts, most regrettably, are not detailed enough for us to know whether Antony really intended to hold a Roman triumph in the Egyptian capital, as his detractors alleged. If this is what he did, a patriotic Roman in truth had grounds for complaint. A triumph was a solemn and splendid honour. The senate granted it, and the presiding deity was Jupiter Optimus Maximus, to whose temple on the Capitoline Hill the triumphing general led his procession. It was a ceremony capable of celebration nowhere but in Rome. That Antony, a Roman noble whose grandfather had earned a triumph in an era when the honour was not lightly granted, should think of counterfeiting one in Alexandria seems improbable at the least. All we know is that he sent his royal prisoners and other captives ahead of him into the city 'in a kind of triumphal procession'. He himself followed, driving in a chariot, and presented Artavasdes and his family, and all the other spoils, to Cleopatra. The queen sat surrounded by a vast throng upon a gilded chair placed on a silvered dais, though the effect was somewhat spoilt when the spirited Armenians refused to do obeisance to her or beg her to intercede for them.

Antony then feasted the populace—a practice traditional after a Roman triumph, but hardly confined either to Rome or to that particular occasion—and on one of the following days assembled them in the sports stadium of Alexandria. There he and Cleopatra sat above the crowd on golden thrones placed side by side, Cleopatra wearing the garb of the goddess Isis. A little below them were thrones for Cleopatra's eldest son, Ptolemy Caesar (nicknamed Caesarion), and her three children by Antony. Antony made a speech in which he affirmed that what he was going to do was in honour of the memory of Julius Caesar, who had been the husband of Cleopatra and the father of Caesarion. He then proclaimed Caesarion joint ruler of Egypt with his mother, and declared Cleopatra Queen of Kings and Caesarion King of Kings. He confirmed their sovereignty over Cyprus and over a wide swathe of client-kingdoms by conferring upon them the overlordship of the territories he now proceeded to give the younger children: to Alexander Helios, who wore a Median costume with tiara and upright head-dress, fell Armenia and (hopefully) Media and Parthia; to Cleopatra Selene, Cyrenaica and Libya; and to little Ptolemy Philadelphus, who though barely able to walk wore a Macedonian costume, the Egyptian possessions in Coele Syria and Cilicia, along with a general suzerainty over the dynasts of Asia Minor 'as far as the Hellespont'. The younger boys embraced their parents and received bodyguards, the one of Armenians, the other of Macedonians. In commemoration, coins were struck with the proud legends ARMENIA CONQUERED and CLEOPATRA QUEEN OF KINGS AND OF HER SONS WHO ARE KINGS.

The cold light of reason can see little in all this beyond a splendid show, in the regal Hellenistic manner, and a certain adjustment of client-kingdoms in favour of a house whose loyalty was secure. With one exception: the claim that Caesarion was Julius Caesar's legitimate son. This struck at the whole basis of Octavian's position, whether or not it was meant to be believed only in the east. It gave Antony children who were half-brothers to Caesar's son, and challenged Octavian in the one domain where his claim to be Caesar's heir was better than Antony's. Antony had appropriated Caesar's mistress and Caesar's dreams of Parthian conquest. He could not be allowed to appropriate Caesar's child as well. The official response in Rome to the news of the conquest of Armenia and the 'Donations of Alexandria', as the ceremony has become known, was a glacial silence. The contrast with the honours decreed for the bogus victory over Media and Parthia reported at the end of 36 needs no comment.

Octavian had been waiting his chance to take the initiative against Antony. He was in no hurry, but this was the perfect moment. Two campaigns in Illyria had toughened his army, and indeed given some still mutinous elements in it a taste of traditional Roman discipline. As at Mutina years before, he had had an opportunity of displaying personal courage and leadership at an unpleasant moment during the siege of the town of Metulus; this was important, since he was not physically strong and it would be disastrous if the soldiers thought him a sickly coward with no chance against the rugged Antony, the veteran general, the lieutenant of the great Caesar. In Rome, it was five years since the people had seen Antony, and though the Antonian Sosius had celebrated his triumph for the capture of Jerusalem on September 3, it had fallen between two others celebrated by Octavian's men—those of Statilius Taurus, from Africa, and C. Norbanus Flaccus, from Spain. Competition for public favour had already broken out with the buildings that Taurus and Sosius were starting to construct, Taurus the first permanent amphitheatre in Rome, Sosius the restoration of an ancient Temple of Apollo. This was a traditional activity of men who had triumphed, but Paullus Aemilius Lepidus, suffect consul in this year, went one better by completing the splendid basilica that had been left unfinished in the Forum by his father.

The news of the Donations found Octavian still in Illyria, probably towards the end of November. His presence there so late in the year is explained by a slow-healing knee wound he received at Metulus; he was convalescing before attempting the journey back to Rome. Taurus had arrived from Rome to take over siege operations, which were still going on in spite of the winter, and perhaps Agrippa, who had been deeply involved (as usual) in the campaigning, was still there. If so, Octavian will have had the chance to discuss his strategy with his two leading marshals before he returned to Rome just in time to enter on his second consulship. On January 1, 33 he held the customary debate in the senate 'on the state of the republic' and took the opportunity to attack Antony publicly for the first time. He criticized what Antony had done in the east, resigned his consulship on the same day—exactly as Antony had done when he had become consul in absence the year before—and hurried back to Dalmatia to be present in person at the hasty but decent winding-up of this no longer important campaign.

Octavian may have communicated his complaints officially to Antony, or he may simply have left it to Antony's friends in Rome to inform him of this dramatic turn of events. The news reached Antony fairly soon and he replied from Alexandria both privately and officially. A fragment of the private letter is quoted by Suetonius: 'Why this change of tune? Because I've been in bed with the queen? Have I made her my wife? Do you think it's a new affair? Didn't I start it nine years ago? Is Livia the only woman you sleep with? I congratulate you, if when you read this letter you haven't had sexual relations with Tertulla or Terentilla* or Rufilla or Salvia Titisenia,

* Perhaps Maecenas's wife Terentia. The others are unknown.

or the lot of them. Does it really matter, where or with whom you copulate?'

One ground of Octavian's attack, then, was Antony's relationship with Cleopatra; to which one may add another, Antony's fraudulent recognition of a fatherless bastard as the son of the Divine Julius. Finally, there were remarks about his autocratic management of Egypt and other territories without proper authority from the Roman people—tendentious and specious, but convenient to the purpose. Antony's counter-accusations, as presented in his official communication, were no less damaging. First, Octavian had given Antony no share of Sicily after he had captured the island from Sextus; second, he had kept some of Antony's ships which had been lent him for the campaign; third, he had without consultation deposed their colleague Lepidus and appropriated his legions, revenues, and territories; and finally, he had distributed the available land in Italy in such a way as to leave the far inferior portion for Antony's veterans. Antony therefore requested a half share in all Octavian's acquisitions of troops and territory, and a similar proportion of the recruits he had raised in Italy, according to the terms of the treaty of Tarentum; as for Caesarion, Caesar himself had admitted paternity.

After sending off his letters, Antony left Alexandria to rejoin his army in Armenia. He had business with the king of Media which he could not postpone. Otherwise he would scarcely have left the Mediterranean seaboard at the very moment when Octavian was turning on him. The indications are that he had planned to invade Parthia in conjunction with the Mede, but decided that the political and military threat from the rear was sufficiently serious to make any thought of such an invasion out of the question. Nevertheless, he could not afford to throw away Rome's advantage and embitter an ally who could prove of the greatest usefulness if the present troubles came to a satisfactory conclusion. The least he could do was to explain to Artavasdes (the Median king had the same name as the Armenian) in person why he could not, for the moment, proceed with their plans. And so he led his army as far as the Araxes—perhaps hoping that the contretemps with Octavian might yet resolve itself—and cemented the alliance by betrothing Alexander Helios to Iotape, Artavasdes's little daughter, and receiving a contingent of Median troops for his army. Artavasdes also restored to him the legionary standards he had captured when he had cut Antony's siege-train to pieces on the way to Phraaspa.

At this point Octavian's reply reached Antony, dashing his hopes.

Its tone was that of a declaration of war, brusquely rebutting Antony's complaints: Lepidus had been justly deposed, because he had been abusing his power; Antony could have a half share of Octavian's territorial acquisitions when he gave Octavian a half share of Armenia; and Antony's soldiers had no claim on Italy, since they had added Media and Parthia to the empire of Rome 'by their noble efforts under their commander'. To reply was futile. Antony at once ordered Canidius to take sixteen legions and march down to the coast. He himself went back to collect Cleopatra and such ships, provisions, and men as she could supply, and then set up his head-quarters at Ephesus where Canidius had been instructed to meet him.

For his part, Octavian had not been wasting the year. The initiative lay with him as the aggressor, and once he had decided at the end of 34 to break Antony's power he knew that he must without fail win public opinion in Italy over to his side. No less than three of the provincial governors of the west celebrated triumphs in 33; such was the eagerness of Octavian to impress that the populace were treated to two triumphs from the same province, Spain, inside five weeks. And to show that the Antonian Sosius had no monopoly of religious piety, two of these men set about the restoration of other dilapidated temples: those of Diana on the Aventine Hill, and of Hercules of the Muses near the Circus Flaminius in the Campus Martius. But all these triumphs lay under the shadow of Octavian's own victories in Illyria and Dalmatia. He had attained the speedy and successful end to his campaigns in these regions that he had counted on when he decided to provoke the breach with Antony. The besieged town of Setovia (Sinj) had at last given in, and the Dalmatians had surrendered 700 hostages. Worth much more in terms of prestige, however, was their surrender of the legionary standards which Caesar's general Gabinius had lost in these parts in the winter of 48–47. In spite of his 'victory' over Parthia, Antony was strangely unable to produce the standards of Crassus. Octavian pressed the point home by modestly postponing his own triumph—no doubt because the preparations, and expense, necessary to ensure a truly Caesarian scale would have been a foolish waste of resources at the present moment—but nevertheless completely reconstructing the portico built by the great Metellus in the middle of the previous century. He added a library to the two temples it enclosed, renamed it the Porticus Octaviae in honour of his sister, and placed the recaptured standards in it. This portico lay alongside the much-frequented recreational area of the

Circus Flaminius, so that it and its contents were a constant reminder to the people of Octavian's public munificence and military good fortune—the latter a quality insistently claimed by all the great leaders of the revolutionary age, from Sulla onwards.

But even Octavian's own building was merely the icing on the cake. His concern for the welfare and convenience of the people of Rome was expressed in a mammoth and entirely beneficial public relations exercise carried through under the supervision of the formidable and faithful Agrippa. Agrippa assumed the office of aedile for the year 33, an office which though it ranked next in seniority below the praetorship had remained unfilled for some years. The holder was responsible for the provision of certain public games and entertainments, as well as seeing to such mundane tasks as the draining and cleaning of the streets. The people of Rome had come to expect lavish and expensive shows as the price of their votes, and the political careerists of the Late Republic had felt that money spent during a year as aedile was money well spent. The triumvirate, by removing the people from the political process, had also removed any inducement to stand for such an expensive and inglorious magistracy. What Agrippa did during his celebrated year as aedile—celebrated not least because it was unheard of for a consular to assume the office—is a commentary on the neglect that the public works of the city had suffered over the previous few years. His main task was to refurbish and supplement the water supply of the capital. He not only repaired the two oldest aqueducts, both more than 200 years old by now, but overhauled and extended the distribution system of the great Aqua Marcia (whose arches can still be seen striding over the Campagna south of Rome) and constructed an entirely new aqueduct. Predictably, this was named the Aqua Julia after the party leader. Not the least of Agrippa's qualities was his lifelong ability to efface himself. Within the city he constructed 700 cisterns, 500 fountains, and 300 distribution chambers, to which no less than 300 statues and 400 marble columns added the necessary touch of civic elegance. He inspected, cleaned, and repaired the entire main drainage system of Rome, even going so far as to voyage up the Great Sewer in a rowing-boat. Bathing establishments to the number of 170 were opened free to the public; these were anything but a luxury in a city consisting largely of blocks of flats entirely lacking running water and sanitation except at ground level. Fifty-nine days of shows and games, with barbers supplied free on festivals, put the concern of the régime for the common man beyond all doubt. The whole amazing programme is a foretaste of the Empire, the bread and circuses with which the monarchs of Rome anaesthetized the once unruly population. Maecenas, too, made his own characteristic contribution by laying out and opening to the public, either in this or the previous year, the spacious and beautiful gardens on the Esquiline that bore his name.

At the same time Octavian and his supporters had set to work to paint a picture of Antony such that no self-respecting Roman could doubt for a moment the justice of a war against him. Public meetings were frequent in the first days of the year, after Octavian himself had departed for Dalmatia. At these Antony was vigorously attacked, doubtless in much stronger terms than the studied reasonableness with which Octavian will have addressed the senate. Thus Octavian, returning to Rome three or four months later, could appear to be moving reluctantly but in clear accord with the wishes of the sovereign people when he started to take active measures against Antony.

The general line of the propaganda attack is all too familiar. It has coloured almost every subsequent account of this final stage of the birth-pangs of the Roman Empire. Another civil war was unthinkable, almost obscene—so much so, in fact, that at least one ancient historian refused to treat it as one, even 150 years after the event: Appian's account of the Civil Wars breaks off with the death of Sextus. Antony, then, could not be the enemy. This was to be no repetition of the personal struggle for power which Caesar, with perfect frankness, had admitted the war between himself and Pompey to be. The villain must be Cleopatra, the evil and subtle Egyptian charmer who had corrupted the noble Antony and laid such a spell of blind passion upon him that he was incapable of remaining loyal to the interest, traditions, and moral standards of Rome. The charmer must also be dangerous, actively dangerous— otherwise there was no need to do more than lament the disintegration of a once great soldier. So Cleopatra is invested with dreams of empire surpassing the wildest flights of a Hellenistic monarch's fancy. It is not enough for her to desire the ancient dominions of the Ptolemaic house, she must cast covetous eyes at Italy, and plan to dine with her Roman lover and her attendant eunuchs on the Capitol of Rome. Behind her are more shadowy foes waiting to join the crusade of the East against the West—the hosts of Armenia, Media, Parthia, and Ethiopia. Ever since Rome's first intervention in the affairs of the eastern Mediterranean the best part of 200 years before, there had lurked in Roman minds a suspicion, ill defined and sinister but never wholly verified, that somewhere in the kingdoms of the east there was a power to match their own. There were prophecies and oracles which gave expression to these fears, like the one which said that the Parthians would never be conquered except by a king. It was not difficult for the enemies of Antony to play on this vague uneasiness, the more so as the last fifty years had given the provinces of the east good cause to hate the rule of Rome. There was more than a touch of plausibility in the vision of Cleopatra as the avenger of the outrages perpetrated by the greedy, unfeeling, builders of empire.

There survives in fact a remarkable prophecy of an unknown Greek, written in this time before Actium, which gives the other side of the picture. It is unique in that it transcends the common motif of revenge and retribution; it promises to the humbled bully, in the end, his share of the blessings and lyrical peace of the world beyond the rainbow that is the prophet's vision:

Vast is the wealth of the tribute that Asia has yielded to Rome—
Three times over shall Rome pay it back, to purge her murderous
    pride;
And for every man from Asia's lands who's served an Italian lord,
Twenty Italians there shall slave, and thousand on thousand be
    damned.
O delicate gilded voluptuous maiden, O Rome of the Latin race,
Drunk with your hundred lovers' embraces, a slave-bride yet
    you'll be,
Your finery gone and your soft hair shorn by a mistress' stern
    command;
And she in whose hands lies justice and doom will hurl you from
    heaven to earth.
But then she will raise you again from earth to the heights of
    heaven above.
And peace all gentle will come upon Asia, and Europe happy will
    be,
And the air shall grant long life and strength, and food and
    nourishment too,
And the birds and the beasts of the earth shall increase and never
    know storm or hail.
O blessed the man and blessed the woman who live to set eyes on
    that time

Like peasants who've not seen a palace before, struck dumb at the
  riches displayed.
For one true order and one true law shall descend from the sphere
  of the stars,
And with them shall come to abide among mortals the thing they
  desire above all:
Concord and harmony, trustful and sane, and brotherly love
  between men.
Far from the world shall poverty flee; constraint and chaos shall go;
And envy and blame, with anger and folly, and murderous
  quarrels and strife,
And theft and destruction, and all sort of evil, shall vanish away
  at that day.

The 'mistress' must be Cleopatra, and the poem, in spite of its rough
style and occasional descents into bathos, gives us a precious idea of
the sort of feelings to which Cleopatra could appeal amongst the
indigenous populations of Asia Minor and Syria. Anti-Roman
sentiment was a real thing. The poem also confirms the spread of
Octavian's propaganda in the east. The image of drunken, lustful
Rome is surely a counterblast to Octavian's distortion of the role of
the New Dionysus assumed by Antony so long ago, but now suddenly
found to be objectionable. Dionysus was the god of ecstatic liberation, and therefore of wine, the chief medium of such liberation.
What easier than to portray Antony as a drunkard, especially as
Cicero had employed the same tactic? The would-be god, lecherous,
full of wine, and enslaved by an unscrupulous and evil queen—this
was the Antony that Italy came to know in 33 and 32. It must have
been hard for the veterans who had served under him at Philippi and
Brundisium to believe it, but perhaps anything could happen to
a man in five or six years in the east.

Antony and his supporters were not silent in his defence. Octavian's past was a good deal murkier than his partisans cared to admit
and afforded plenty of scope for exploitation. Unfortunately for the
entertainment of posterity, only a few scraps of the Antonian propaganda have found their way through the sieve of the official version
of the struggle. One cardinal point of Antony's attack was the
legitimacy of Octavian's claim to be Caesar's heir. He started to call
Octavian the 'Thurian', a name by which he had in fact once been
known, which seems to have referred to a minor success of his
natural father against some brigands in the neighbourhood of Thurii

shortly after his birth. Octavian, disingenuously missing the point, wrote back that he had no idea why this old name should be used as a term of abuse. Antony's recognition of Caesarion provoked Oppius, an intimate of the dictator, into writing a pamphlet to disprove Caesar's paternity. Men do not write pamphlets to rebut insubstantial charges. By the same token, the charge of drunkenness was damaging. Antony felt it necessary to issue a defence, entitled *Antony, on his Sobriety*. From this may come some of his counter-accusations in the same general area of personal morality: if Rome wanted an example of misappropriated divinity, it need look no further than the notorious episode of the Feast of the Twelve Gods. Antony provided a pungent commentary on the participants at this sacrilegious and adulterous occasion, and went on to allege that Octavian's sexual appetites were so voracious that 'his friends used to behave like the slave-dealer Toranius in arranging his amusements for him: they would strip married women and grown girls naked and inspect them as though they were for sale'. Such personal invective had not been heard in politics since the war of Perusia. It was a last breath of the free speech of the old republic.

In the realm of public policy Octavian was less vulnerable—and it was here that the real issue lay. Scandal was diverting, and deflated pompous sanctimony; something more solid was needed to swing the loyalties of soldiers and men of experience and influence. Antony cast aspersions on Octavian's potency as a military leader: in the Sicilian war it was Agrippa who had won the victory while Octavian lay terrified and half-conscious below decks. There was plenty of evidence to bolster Antony's thesis, and Octavian was driven to circulate stories illustrating his superior luck: Antony never beat him at dice, the stars were on his side. In an age when Luck was worshipped as a divinity, this was not such a foolish ploy as it sounds. Antony also alleged that Octavian had broken an engagement to Antony's eldest son and betrothed his only daughter Julia to Cotiso, king of the Getae, a tribe who lived north of the lower Danube. By comparison the Median Artavasdes, to whose daughter Antony had just betrothed his son Alexander, was a paragon of culture. Doubtless the story that the Armenian Artavasdes had been approached by Octavian with a view to a mutual alliance against Antony belongs to this same period. It may even be true.

Such accusations can only be a fraction of those current, once the clash was seen to be imminent and inevitable. But the skirmishing was not confined to propaganda, important though that was. While

the two men had been in harmony, the constitutional machinery of
the state had been of little importance; but now, with the legal period
of their triumviral authority due to expire at the end of the year,
under circumstances which would make renewal most improbable,
senate and consuls assumed a forgotten significance. The consuls for
32, agreed on years before at Tarentum, were to be two partisans of
Antony, namely Sosius and Ahenobarbus, men of substance and
reputation. It is unlikely to be pure coincidence that in 33 there were,
apart from Octavian himself, the unprecedented number of seven
consuls or suffect consuls, of whom the majority were his men and
had connections with the last generation of the free republic.
Consulars with names redolent of the past might once again be
support worth having. War was a last resort, and in any case the
usual manoeuvring to force the other to take the first violent and
unconstitutional step was bound to take place in the senate.

In the event, the manoeuvring was brief. Although Antony had
made no reply to the letter of Octavian that had reached him in
Armenia, he wrote later in the year to Sosius and Ahenobarbus.
This despatch contained a full statement and explanation of his
actions, and asked for them to be ratified immediately. But the
consuls, when they entered office, judged that to read this out would
only lose sympathy for Antony. Antony, it seems, had miscalculated
the temper of senatorial opinion, whether because of his prolonged
absence or because of the effectiveness of his enemy's propaganda.
It is certain that during 33 Octavian had deliberately contradicted the
general lines of Antony's settlement of the east. Antony, so it was
said, was 'giving away' Roman territory and granting Cleopatra the
authority that the senate and people of Rome should hold. This was a
gross slander, since no part of the territories Antony had distributed
with such lavish generosity at the Donations had ever been a worth-
while part of the Roman dominions. His arrangements were no more
unpatriotic than those of Pompey in the 60s—and, like Pompey's,
suffered the fate of being attacked for reasons that had nothing to do
with their intrinsic merits. The case of Bocchus, the client-king of
Mauretania, is instructive: he died in 33, and Octavian, instead of
installing a successor, made this unremunerative tract of ground a
Roman province. This was a shrewd move. To public opinion in
Rome, this was a return to the old days when the republic had
grown great by conquest and annexation. After Actium, Octavian
acknowledged the wisdom of Antony's settlement by confirming on
their thrones the most important of his client-kings. But at the

present time, the merits of his solution were irrelevant. Party politics was all. Antony was the enemy, therefore Antony was wrong. That the annexation of Mauretania was inspired by partisan motives is put beyond all doubt by one fact: eight years later it was given back to another client-king, Juba.

On entering office, Ahenobarbus was for proceeding cautiously. The vicissitudes of his career had taught him to be prudent. January, when he was in charge, passed in sparring between Octavian and the consuls. Octavian urged them to read out Antony's account of the Donations, and when they would not, prevented them reading his despatches about the Armenian king, which would certainly have added to his prestige. With the coming of February, the *fasces*, insignia of executive authority, passed to Sosius. More hot-headed than his colleague, he moved to the attack at once. On February 1 he harangued the senate in praise of Antony, and proposed a motion against Octavian, who had anticipated such a move and absented himself not merely from the senate, but from Rome. In this way he avoided meeting his opponents on their own ground, where his position was weak; for the first time for ten years he did not hold lawful power of command and ranked simply as a consular, even if an unusually prestigious one. His absence had another advantage. It gave him time to observe the reactions of the public as well as the senate, and to ponder what course of action was best. He left it to a loyal tribune, one Nonius Balbus, to interpose his veto and prevent the consul taking a vote on any matter detrimental to him; Antony himself had played exactly the same role at the outbreak of war between Caesar and Pompey.

Thus Sosius's assault came to nothing. There followed exchanges between the two sides, but by mid-February it was clear that reconciliation or compromise was out of the question. Octavian, rather than step down, took the law into his own hands and staged a *coup d'état*. Surrounding himself with a guard of soldiers and friends who carried daggers beneath their togas, he went in to the senate and delivered a lengthy and reasoned statement in his own defence. He ended with accusations against Antony and Sosius. No one dared to reply, whereupon he named a day on which the senate might reconvene to hear the documentary proof of his case. The consuls and between three and four hundred senators, unable to resist and unwilling to acquiesce, left Rome and fled to Antony, Octavian, who was never slow to take a political trick, at once paraded his magnanimity in allowing his enemies to depart unmolested, and encouraged their sympathizers to do likewise. He hoped to clear Italy of Antony's important supporters and leave himself a free hand in the none too easy task that lay ahead, of finding some constitutional justification for leading an army against his erstwhile triumviral colleague and against the consuls of the Roman people.

their subordinates in the libraries. He hoped to relax the load, reserve important operations and leave himself a free hand in the more formal task that lay ahead, planning some combination of legislation for founding an army against his erstwhile surrender colleagues and against the enemies of the Roman people.

Chapter XIV

PREPARATIONS FOR WAR

THE REFUGEES from Italy found Antony and Cleopatra still in their winter-quarters at Ephesus, engaged on the final stages of mustering the army and navy that was shortly to contend for the sovereignty of the civilized world. Canidius Crassus had brought his sixteen legions down the long road from Armenia and across the Anatolian plateau to the coast, leaving the forces of Polemo and the good-will of the Median king to guard the borders of the high country. As the garrisons of Macedonia, Bithynia, and Syria had been reduced to very low levels to bolster the striking force in the east, and Antony could not leave unguarded either his rear or his African flank, the newly arrived consuls raised some four legions in Asia Minor, not hesitating to follow the established practice of the civil wars by granting the Roman citizenship to natives of the region in order to qualify them for service. Thanks to these extra forces Antony was able to take nineteen legions to Greece. The rest of his army was made up of the detachments of the client-kings, now called upon to pay the price of their thrones: Archelaus of Cappadocia, Amyntas of Galatia, Tarcondimotus of the Amanus, Mithridates of Commagene, Deiotarus of Paphlagonia, Rhoemetalces and Sadalas of Thrace, Bocchus of Mauretania (Bogud the Moor, King of Western Mauretania being a refugee from Octavian, was in a different category). There were in addition troops sent by Herod, by Malchus the Nabataean, and even by the Median king. In all, Antony's army numbered 75,000 legionaries, 25,000 non-Roman light-armed infantry, and 12,000 horse; and to convey this huge force he had assembled, by the spring of 32, 500 warships and 300 merchantmen.

Cleopatra, we are told, provided 200 of these ships, as well as 20,000 talents* and supplies for the whole army for the forthcoming campaign. Egyptian rowers also formed a very large part of the fleet's manpower. Without Cleopatra's contribution, Antony's military strength would have been less formidable, but his moral

* A legion cost 40 to 50 talents per annum to maintain.

strength much greater. Here was a fatal weakness—not his love for the queen, but his dependence on her. He had already lost the services of the faithful Herod because Cleopatra would not have him in camp with her and preferred to see him embroiled in a petty war with Malchus over her balsam revenues, from which she hoped both kings would emerge weakened. But it was when the consuls and the Antonian third of the senate arrived that Antony realized how much of a liability his mistress was going to be. Ahenobarbus in particular had never cared for the queen, and he and others of like mind persuaded Antony to order Cleopatra back to Egypt. Antony might order, but she would not go; and there were many like Canidius who thought it unjust that she, whose contribution far exceeded that of any other client-king, and whose temperament and Macedonian blood fitted her to take an active part in the war, should be deprived of the right to be present at it. Antony lost the battle of wills. He must have known how gravely Cleopatra's presence in his camp injured his cause; but if she was determined to stay, there was little he could do unless he were prepared to forswear a substantial part of his resources, above all the immense riches of the Ptolemaic treasury.

The result was a division of his supporters into pro- and anti-Cleopatra factions, or 'Romans' and 'monarchists', the former following Antony because they saw in him a truer representative than Octavian of the old governing class of the republic, the latter because they were committed to him personally and had no objections to his liaison with a queen or to the monarchical nature of his relations with the dynasts and peoples of the east. The tensions thus created in Antony's camp were damaging and deep, leading to ill-will and finally to desertion among his leading officers. The presence of the queen was to Ahenobarbus a contradiction of all that he hoped Antony stood for. It had been said of Ahenobarbus's grandfather that 'it was not remarkable that his name was Brazenbeard (*Ahena barba*) since his countenance was of iron and his heart of lead'. The grandson matched him in proud self-confidence and disdain: he alone refused to salute Cleopatra by her title. Nor was Ahenobarbus convinced of the necessity for war. Antony called a kind of anti-senate (a term perhaps more justly applied to the large rump left behind in Rome) soon after the arrival of the refugees and of the news of Octavian's coup. At this meeting, Dio says, there were many who spoke for peace, Ahenobarbus without doubt amongst them. But Cleopatra knew, and Antony knew, that one certain price of peace was her dismissal and the reinstatement of Octavia. This was unthinkable, now, after all that had happened. Antony was a prisoner of circumstances. He settled for war, but still put off the final step of divorcing Octavia. It was still remotely possible that some solution could be found, if Octavian ceased to be intransigent and provocative. No formal ground for war yet existed.

The underlying tensions in Antony's camp remained then, suppressed as best they might be for the moment. Meanwhile the immense operation of gathering and transporting the army to Greece went forward. Antony has been criticized for not moving to the attack with greater speed and bringing on an engagement before Octavian had had time to gather his forces and rally the loyalties of Italy. It is difficult to see what more he could have done. It was not till the middle of 33, when he was beside the Araxes at the uttermost edge of the Roman world, that he knew the true nature of Octavian's challenge and realized he must be prepared to fight. He immediately gave Canidius orders to take the army down to the sea, but even so the march of something approaching 1,400 miles can scarcely have been accomplished before November at the earliest. It was possible for him to have fought Octavian somewhere in Greece in 32, if Octavian had wished it. What was not possible was to invade Italy in 32, for reasons both political and military. Politically, an invasion would be a dangerous gamble, particularly if it were carried out in association with Cleopatra. It would confirm all Octavian's propaganda, and could easily result in a wholesale swing of public opinion to his enemy's side. Militarily, too, such an invasion would not be easy. There were only two harbours his fleet could use on the south and east coasts, Brundisium and Tarentum. How difficult it might be to take either in face of determined opposition he had learnt at Brundisium eight years before. An invasion was not, therefore, something to be essayed late in the summer, with little time in hand before winter made military operations difficult and communications across the Adriatic hazardous. Even if the political risk were worth taking he still required a full summer campaigning season; and that he could not possibly get before 31. In fact, it was Octavian who dictated the pace of events, and Octavian who gave Antony a year in which to take up his position in Greece—for very good reasons of his own. Octavian needed to let time elapse so that Antony could be seen to be taking up a threatening and warlike posture: otherwise how could he plausibly declare war? This was no holy crusade, as the campaign of Philippi had been, a solemn act of vengeance against impious and faithless murderers. The people of Rome and Italy required some semblance of evidence that the alliance of degenerate triumvir and ambitious queen spelt danger to themselves. By the logic of the situation, Antony could not fail to provide that evidence. Every move he made in self-defence could be interpreted as aggression, and defend himself he must—or submit. One cannot help admiring, wryly, Octavian's nerve and diplomatic skill.

By April, Antony knew there was small chance that Octavian would force the pace and bring on an encounter in Greece or Macedonia that year. For one thing, there had been no declaration of war. Nor can he have been unaware, from information transmitted to him by friends and connections of his followers, that Octavian was making no evident moves to assemble and transport an army across the Adriatic. Strategically, therefore, the initiative lay with Antony. Octavian was inviting him to pick the ground for the decisive struggle; and once again, as in 48 at Pharsalus and in 42 at Philippi, that ground was Greece. Like Pompey and like the Liberators, Antony lay as far forward as he could from his base in the east and waited for his opponent to attack. Greece and the Balkan peninsula formed the natural boundary between the two halves of the Roman world; the town that was agreed to mark the division of the triumvir's domains was Scodra, which lies in modern Albania. By choosing to remain in Greece, Antony not only avoided appearing as the naked and shameless aggressor Octavian made him out to be, but forced his opponent to operate at the end of what past experience had shown to be a vulnerable supply route across the Adriatic.

Geography, political considerations, and strategic analysis might lead Antony to the same broad conclusions as his predecessors. But his detailed appreciation of the problem was different. Where they had taken up, or intended to take up, more northerly positions astride the Via Egnatia that led across the base of the peninsula from Apollonia and Dyrrhachium to Thessalonika, Antony chose to centre his forces in the area of the Corinthian Gulf. One reason for this southward shift of defensive position was his need to guard Egypt and to secure and shorten the supply route from the Nile to Greece. Antony could not let himself be outflanked to the south, whereas neither Pompey nor the Liberators had been concerned to protect any particular point in their rear—the corollary being that, when defeated, they had no refuge. The other reason was that this was to be as much a naval as a military campaign. Both sides possessed large fleets, and both expected to use them. Antony therefore chose a coast with plenty of good anchorages: the Ambracian Gulf itself, the east coast of Leucas, Cephallenia, Zacynthos—to mention only the most obvious. These form an arc from the north round to the west of the entrance to the Corinthian Gulf and offer the opportunity of harrying mercilessly an enemy fleet attempting to support its land forces on the west coast of the mainland. North of Corcyra (itself an excellent harbour) the picture changes. Octavian himself was nearly wrecked on this coast returning to Italy from the east in 29. It is rocky and inhospitable or else shallow and sandy—in both cases equally dangerous—as far north as Scodra. The one harbour which might be suitable for a large fleet, the bay of Valona, is not sheltered from every quarter. Antony's intention to use his naval arm would by itself have kept him south of Corcyra. There was another incidental advantage in lying farther to the south: it lengthened the voyage from Octavian's Italian ports of Brundisium and Tarentum.

But in the spring of 32, the detailed dispositions were a thing of the future. It was the general strategy which was clear, deciding Antony to ferry his army across to southern Greece rather than take Xerxes's route around the head of the Aegean. The operation took place, in all probability, in April and May, and may well have consumed the best part of two months if two convoys were necessary. As Antony had a very large number of cavalry, and one horse (at least according to the German general staff of the nineteenth century) takes up as much room as four men, it seems almost certain that one convoy would not have been enough. The army cannot have been deployed in Greece much, if at all, before the end of May. Antony himself transferred his headquarters first to Samos, in April, and then to Athens in May. On Samos a great festival was held in honour of Dionysus, perhaps in conscious recollection of Alexander the Great who had organized similar gatherings before some of his campaigns. All the dramatic artists—actors, musicians, and singers —'were commanded', says Plutarch, 'to appear at Samos and while practically the whole world about them was lamenting and groaning, this one island was filled for many days with the sound of wind and stringed instruments and the theatres were thronged and choirs competed with each other. Every city sent an ox for sacrifice, and the princes rivalled one another in the splendour of their receptions and presents, so that the word went round, "What sort of victory celebrations will these people stage, if they lavish such festivals on the preparations for war?"' Antony, well pleased with the occasion, commemorated his patronage by settling the artists as a guild at the city of Priene, and sailed on to Athens.

In Athens he succumbed to the pressure that Cleopatra must surely have been putting on him ever since the previous winter to divorce Octavia; at some time in the Macedonian month of Daisios, which corresponds to May/June in the Julian calendar, he formally repudiated his wife. The Athenians had been particularly complimentary to Octavia, and it was in Athens that Antony had spent the greater part of the time which he had actually passed in his wife's company. When official inscriptions commemorating Octavia were still visible, one can understand why Cleopatra, faced with the ghost of her rival, was driven to insist that Antony take the step he had refused to take two or three months previously. It was not enough for Cleopatra to be voted honours that equalled or surpassed those conferred upon Octavia. She needed an emotional victory too, and an end to her ambiguous status.

The results of the divorce were immediate. Two of Antony's most prominent supporters, Plancus and his nephew Titius, took it as a sign that the cause was hopeless and deserted to Octavian. One hesitates to speak of principles in the case of Plancus, a man labelled for all time by Velleius's phrase 'diseased with desertion'; but his political judgment had never been wrong, and in so far as he had a position it must have been one that favoured compromise. For those who could read the signs, his defection was ominous. It was the beginning of a long process of sapping of morale amongst those who had decided to support Antony rather because of their political beliefs than from any personal ties. In the end, even Ahenobarbus, who had no time for Plancus, was to succumb. But Plancus and Titius brought more than moral advantage to the other side. Standing high in Antony's counsels, they had intimate knowledge of his intentions and his affairs, amongst them the matter of his will. They were able to reveal to Octavian that Antony had deposited this in the safe keeping of the Vestal Virgins, the seven taboo-hedged guardians of the sacred flame of the goddess Vesta, lifelong virgins whom it was sacrilege to violate or threaten. There should have been no safer place in Rome for the custody of this sensational document. But Octavian desperately needed political ammunition. Indignant though he had grown at Octavia's divorce and her forcible ejection from her husband's house, there was no concealing the fact that this, like the marriage, was a matter of politics, not a moral outrage. It was not a credible *casus belli*. Italy still remained to be convinced that Antony, with his following of old Caesarians, republicans, and younger nobles, was a threat to the traditional interests and ideals of

the Roman state. Admittedly the divorce did something to confirm
the thesis that Cleopatra was daily gaining a firmer hold over Antony
and bending him to be the tool of her imperial desires. Antony
countered with offers to lay down his triumviral authority if Octavian
would do the same. More honest than his enemy, he continued to
use the title of triumvir; Octavian pretended to observe constitutional legality by not doing so, while he toiled in his self-imposed
capacity of honest private citizen to find a ground for civil war.

The will might perhaps provide that ground. Overriding religious
scruple in the name of public interest, Octavian seized the will from
the Vestals. No eyes saw the text except his own, no audience heard
any save the damning passages he marked to be read out. A shocked
senate learnt that Ptolemy Caesar was indeed the true son of the
dictator, that Antony's children by Cleopatra were to receive great
legacies, and that Antony wished his body, even if he should die in
Rome, to be sent to Cleopatra in Egypt after the funeral procession
through the Roman Forum. Octavian laid great stress on this last
provision. Here at last was displayed that contempt for his birthright
that he had been seeking to fasten on Antony. Here was the proof of
Antony's moral treachery to Rome, the proof of his enslavement by
the snares and potions of the foreign queen. Alexandria, not Rome,
was to be the capital of the world. To proclaim his own devotion to
the traditional primacy of Rome, Octavian embarked on the construction of a mighty mausoleum in the Campus Martius beside the
Tiber. Whether he was to die in the forthcoming struggle, or live to
uphold the interests of Italy, his ashes at any rate would repose upon
ancestral soil. The mausoleum was a statement of confidence in the
people of Italy. Its form, a massive tumulus of earth, supported by
great concentric rings of concrete, may have recalled the splendour
of ancient Etruscan monarchy; but this can scarcely have been
Octavian's intention at this particular moment. More to the point
were the echoes of the world of the Homeric heroes, from one of
whom, the Trojan Aeneas, the Julii claimed their descent.

The divorce of Octavia, the defection of Plancus and Titius, and
the terms of the will—these, taken together, were enough to give
colour and substance to the charge that Antony was a traitor to
Rome. The propaganda battle which had been raging for the past
twelve months and more now reached its zenith. Antony, through
his agents, distributed largesse to the civilian population and to the
soldiers, forcing Octavian to secure the loyalty of the latter with a
donative that he would rather not have paid. To conduct an auction

for the services of the military undermined his attempt to fabricate a just war. He was also short of money. Extra taxes had to be imposed, causing him great unpopularity and giving bite to Antony's allegation that it was Octavian's fault that the Republic had not yet been restored.

Antony's supporters in Rome did their best for him; before Octavian had won over the public, they sent C. Geminius, a senator who might be described as an Antonian neutral, on a special mission to urge Antony to dismiss Cleopatra. From Italy it was easy to see the damage the queen's presence was causing. To convince Antony of it in Athens was another matter, and Geminius had to return without accomplishing anything. Even so, the Antonian cause was far from lost. There were many veterans of Antony's settled in the triumviral colonies in Italy, and many men who had served with Caesar in the days when Antony was one of his senior officers and Octavian an insignificant stripling. There were, too, Antony's clients, both individuals and municipalities, bound to their patron by ties of loyalty and gratitude that were often inherited. Greater clans than the Antonii claimed to be the patrons of whole districts of Italy, but although the Antonii could not match the Domitii or the Pompeii, there is no reason to suppose that Antony's *clientela* was negligible. All the advantages that Sallust ascribed to the republican oligarchy were still available to him: 'long-standing nobility, great deeds of ancestors, resources of connections and relations, many clients'.

What constitutional legality there was, Antony possessed—though it could be claimed that the consuls should not have left Italy without the passing of a technical enabling law, since they were still in office. Octavian needed to find a higher legality, such as had been invoked on his behalf by the misguided Cicero to support his earliest revolutionary activities. With this in mind, he scorned appointment to a dubiously legal suffect consulship in place of one of the refugees. That questionable honour he left to two inconsiderable partisans whose names cast a sunset glow of the republic upon the nascent monarchy: L. Cornelius Cinna and M. Valerius Messalla. His own status needed to be above constitutional quibble. He therefore resorted to a device which had precedents in the last sixty years, though it had never been pressed into service with the scope and thoroughness now displayed. This device was the personal oath of loyalty, a spontaneous expression throughout the length and breadth of Italy of the trust and confidence placed by the nation in him, in his policies, and in his judgment of the true interests of the state.

His own words describing this political master-stroke, written forty-five years later, are: 'The whole of Italy, of its own free will, swore loyalty to me, and asked for me to take charge of the war that I won at Actium. The provinces of the Gauls, the Spains, Africa, Sicily, and Sardinia swore in the same way.'

The spontaneity of the oath is a pious fiction. The people of Italy were weary of civil war and resentful of the fresh taxes imposed upon them to finance this quarrel of their masters. Wealthy freedmen were first of all called upon to show their gratitude to the society which had given them freedom and riches, to the tune of one-eighth of their capital assets. This proving insufficient, income tax at 25 per cent was levied—for one year only—on the entire free population, including the freedmen. Riots, arson, and murder ensued, which were not finally suppressed until the winter. It was only Octavian's military grip on the country, and the reflection on the part of the property-owners that they might end up by losing their all if they did not co-operate, which prevented more serious trouble.

Italy had no interest in the faction fight to dominate the Roman state. Whichever side won, would make little difference. Nor had Italy any real unity, but remained a collection of disparate districts marked off by differences of language, population and culture. 'All Italy' was a geographical term, no more; the units contained within it had each their own ties with Rome, in the shape of communal or individual client-patron relations with one (or more) of the great political families. Hence certain cracks in the façade. We know that Octavian excused the town of Bononia from swearing the oath, because the Antonii had long been its patrons. And Bononia was not an isolated case: after his victory Octavian 'expelled from their homes those communities in Italy which had taken Antony's side, and granted the towns and their lands to his soldiers', as Dio informs us. Evidently the enthusiasm of 'all Italy' for its Caesar left something to be desired.

Of the form of words employed we have some idea from later versions of the imperial oath. The taker bound himself to have the same friends and enemies as Octavian, to fight with body and soul, by land and sea, against anyone who should threaten Octavian, to report treason seen or heard, and to consider himself and his children less dear than the safety of Octavian; and if he should break his oath, then let Jupiter visit him and his children with exile, outlawry, and ruin. No mention here of senate and people of Rome, no word of corporate loyalties or public enemies—and with good reason, for its purpose was to ensure unquestioning obedience to the chosen leader.

As to the way in which it was administered we have no direct evidence. It is a reasonable supposition that it was a part-military, part-diplomatic operation. The diplomacy came first, discreetly suggesting to leading men in communities and districts known to be loyal to Octavian, above all the military colonies, that some kind of demonstration of the depth and sincerity of public support for him would be most opportune. And what better demonstration could there be than an oath? Once a few had led the way, many followed. To hold back, in such a situation, was to be marked out. It cannot have been unduly offensive to swear an oath to one whose statues already reposed beside those of the gods in the temples of Italy, a visible claim to more than mortal status and foresight. If the powers of persuasion of Octavian's adherents did not prove sufficient to win over their tenants, their neighbours, their fellow magistrates, and their town councils, there remained the threat of force from the soldiers.

Of the loyalty of the army, there could be no doubt. Ten years had passed since the soldiers of Antony and Octavian had fought together at Philippi. The subsequent division of forces and the settlement of many of the veterans meant that there was hardly a man left in the armies of the west who had once owed allegiance to Antony or his generals. The serving soldiery of Italy had no doubt where they stood. Their personal advantage was linked with that of their *imperator*, benefactor, and patron. They must have been amongst the first and most enthusiastic to take the oath and provide him with a moral and personal basis for the authority so inexplicably denied him by the workings of the political struggle, but which he manifestly still deserved to possess. The garrisons of soldiers stationed about Italy will not have been tolerant of opposition to their leader.

The people of Rome itself retained a memory of the turbulent freedom of the dying republic until many years after Actium. Their numbers and their traditional role as the ultimate source of constitutional authority encouraged them to an outspoken independence not found amongst their betters. They may not under the triumvirate have realized that their days of influence were over for good. They had not hesitated to condemn the war with Sextus and to show violent disapproval of the master of Italy. But their demonstrations, though annoying, could be ignored, since they lacked a leader. Octavian's power was secure, resting as it did on a loyal army, political patronage, the ramifications of clientship and connection all over Italy, and the rock-like strength of ruthless and devoted friends of the calibre of Marcus Agrippa, Statilius Taurus, Calvisius Sabinus, and Gaius Maecenas. No mere demagogue could challenge him. The people of Rome could no longer make and unmake the careers of the great, and painfully the anachronism by which a city-state controlled an empire was being corrected. Not that the people were to be despised or their grievances thoughtlessly ignored. Once the war with Sextus was over, the burdensome army disbanded or removed from Italy, and the corn supply restored, the popularity of Caesar's heir returned. Agrippa's aedileship showed a concern for the welfare of the people of Rome that made previous patronage of this type look niggardly. Once again, as when he entered upon his inheritance in 44, Octavian could claim the population of the capital as his clients—and this time in his own right.

Finally, there were men of substance and sophistication, neither proletarians to be won with bribes or tendentious half-truths, nor loyal supporters whose fortunes were already closely bound up with those of the party. Numerically, they were a small proportion of the population, but much of the wealth of the country lay in their hands. They were financiers, contractors, shippers, wholesalers, agents, bankers, small manufacturers, speculators, traders. Above all they were landed gentry—or if not gentry, at least landed, for land was the only secure investment in the ancient world. Many of this class will have had a perfectly clear idea of the true nature of the struggle between Octavian and Antony. The traders of Campania in particular had had close connections with the Aegean world for a century and a half. They were familiar with the nature and scope of Hellenistic monarchy. They knew how Romans were expected to behave in the east. Then there were men like Cicero's friend Atticus, respected, influential, wealthy, but admitting exclusive allegiance to no one party. Where did the true interests of this upper and middle class lie? Best of all would be no war; but given that the situation allowed neither peace nor personal neutrality, the answer was clear: with Octavian. His victory would entail no further revolution, merely the consolidation of the status quo. To support him was to swim with the tide, a course politically easy and financially prudent. There was also a practical consideration of foreign policy. Octavian, by annexing Mauretania, had advertised his belief in the republican tradition of imperialistic annexation; this allowed Italian businessmen the protection of direct Roman rule for their activities and opened up the possibilities of new business, like contracts to collect the state taxes. Antony, by creating a hierarchy of autonomous client-kingdoms and keeping the area of Roman rule to a minimum, was implementing a policy much less favourable to Italian trading interests. His one deviation from this policy illustrates the point nicely. He made Armenia a Roman province after conquering it in 34, and in the two years that it remained a province it acquired a substantial immigrant community of Roman citizens. These paid dearly for their commercial enterprise when Artaxes, Artavasdes's eldest son, was restored by Phraates while Antony was occupied with Octavian. Artaxes took his revenge on Rome by massacring them all.

Neutrality was almost impossible. Perhaps only Pollio achieved it, and the words of Velleius are a fitting comment: 'Let me not omit the memorable conduct and memorable saying of Asinius Pollio: for after the peace of Brundisium he stayed in Italy, never set eyes on the queen, and did not associate with the party of Antony after love had demoralized him; but when Octavian asked him to go with him to the war of Actium, he said, "My services to Antony are the greater, his to me the better-known; and so I shall stand aside from your quarrel and be the victor's prize." '

Those communities which were brave enough to stand out for Antony were perhaps more truly 'the victor's prize'. But they were not numerous enough to destroy the fiction of 'all Italy', and towards the end of the year Octavian announced that Antony was not fit to hold the consulate which the two of them were to hold as colleagues in 31. He stripped Antony of his powers, and proceeded to declare war with all ancient and ritual solemnity upon the Queen of Egypt. Neither Antony nor his followers were outlawed: it was foolish to make the path of the deserter too difficult.

Chapter XV

THE CAMPAIGN OF 31

MEANWHILE ANTONY had taken up his position on the west coast of Greece. He made some sort of personal reconnaissance up the coast, a little beyond Corcyra, doubtless to make sure that Octavian had not stolen a march on him. He placed his most northerly detachment at Corcyra (which had been Pompey's southernmost outpost in 49). The bulk of his fleet lay for the winter just inside the promontory of Actium, at the south side of the entrance to the magnificent land-locked waters of the Gulf of Ambracia. A squadron guarded Leucas and the passage inshore of Ithaca and Cephallenia to the mouth of the Corinthian Gulf and Patras, where he established his winter-quarters. We do not hear of them in the patchy accounts of the campaign, but it would be incredible if there were not ships stationed at Zacynthos, of which Sosius, if one may judge from the island's coinage, had established himself as virtual prince. On the south coast of the Peloponnese, there was a garrison at Methone commanded by Bogud the Moor, and another at Taenarum. A detachment of some kind held Crete, and the southern end of the chain was formed by the four legions of Pinarius Scarpus in Cyrenaica. This relatively powerful force included the garrison of Egypt and lay forward ready to meet the possibility of an attack by the North African legions of Octavian under Cornelius Gallus.

Both sides passed the winter in final preparations. The propaganda campaign continued with unabated violence. Antony struck coins at Patras which asserted his claim to the consulship of 31 but also advertised his association with Cleopatra—one side bears in Greek abbreviation his name and title, the other Cleopatra's. He circulated promises to lay down his power within six months of victory, and restore to the senate and people their full authority; while Octavian derided Antony's prose style, seeing in its luxurious decadence an echo of his style of life, and issued a comic-opera challenge to him to withdraw a day's journey on horseback (about fifty miles) from the sea, allow Octavian's army to land, and come to battle in five days—

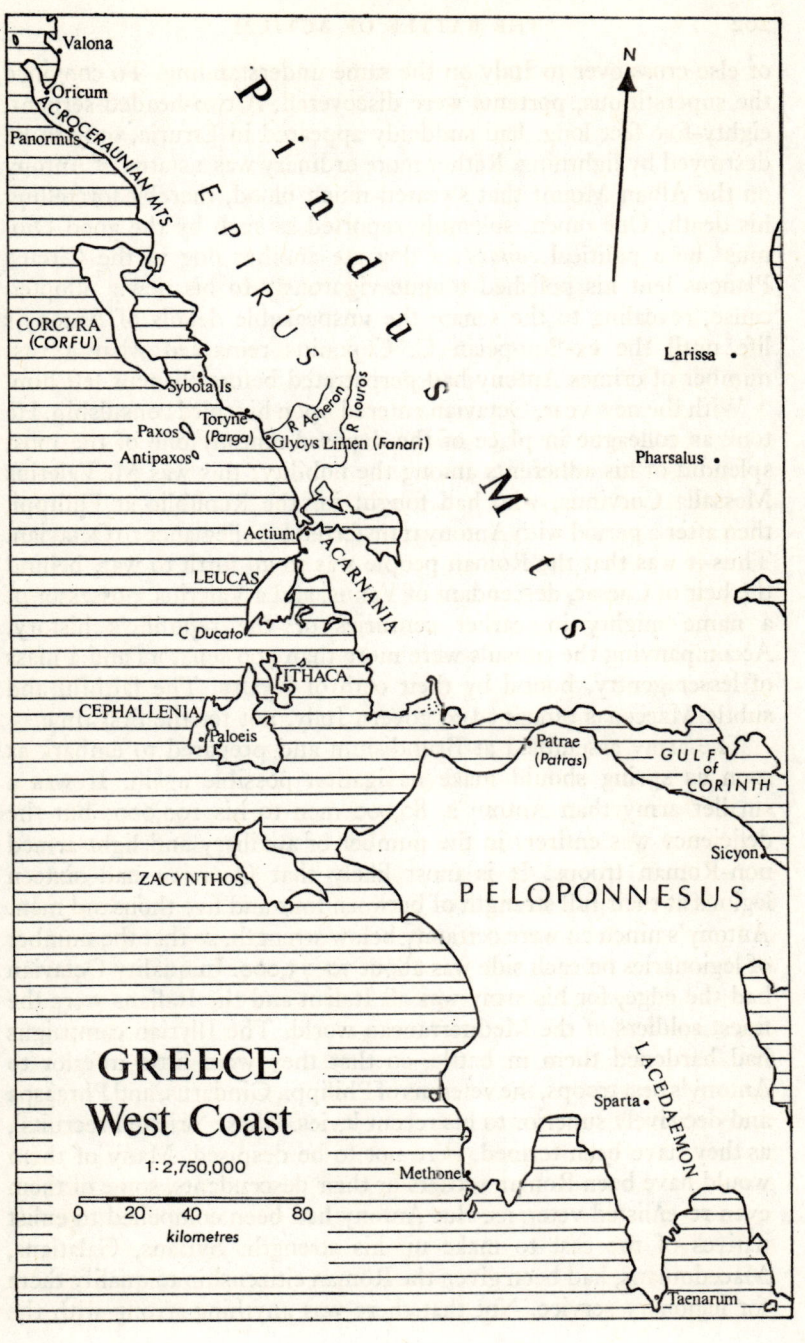

GREECE
West Coast

1:2,750,000

0   20   40   80
kilometres

or else cross over to Italy on the same understanding. To convince the superstitious, portents were discovered. A two-headed serpent, eighty-five feet long, had suddenly appeared in Etruria, only to be destroyed by lightning. Rather more ordinary was a statue of Antony on the Alban Mount that sweated much blood, thereby foretelling his death. One omen, solemnly reported as such by the good Dio, must be a political *canard*: a dog ate another dog in the Circus. Plancus lent his polished tongue vigorously to his newly adopted cause, revealing to the senate the unspeakable details of Antony's life until the ex-Pompeian C. Coponius remarked what a vast number of crimes Antony had perpetrated before Plancus left him.

With the new year, Octavian entered upon his third consulship. He took as colleague in place of the deposed Antony one of the most splendid of his adherents among the nobility; this was M. Valerius Messalla Corvinus, who had fought for the Republic at Philippi, then after a period with Antony transferred his allegiance to Octavian. Thus it was that the Roman people was to go forth to war, behind the heir of Caesar, descendant of Venus, and a Valerius, possessor of a name mighty in earlier centuries of the republic's history. Accompanying the consuls were more than 700 senators and a mass of lesser gentry, bound by their oath of loyalty. The faithful and subtle Maecenas remained to govern Italy, not for the first time.

The army assembled at Brundisium and prepared to embark as soon as spring should make navigation possible again. It was a smaller army than Antony's, 80,000 men to his 100,000; but the deficiency was entirely in the number of auxiliary and light-armed non-Roman troops. It is most likely that Octavian had sixteen legions at their full strength of between four and five thousand men. Antony's nineteen were certainly below strength, so that the number of legionaries on each side was about 70–75,000. In quality Octavian had the edge, for his army was all Italian and the Italians were the finest soldiers of the Mediterranean world. The Illyrian campaigns had hardened them in battle, so that they were little inferior to Antony's best troops, the veterans of Philippi, Gindarus, and Phraaspa and decisively superior to his recent levies. These 'oriental recruits', as they have been termed, were not to be despised. Many of them would have been Roman settlers or their descendants, some of them even re-enlisted veterans. But Antony had been compelled to enlist natives of the east to make up his strength. Syrians, Galatians, Macedonians, had been given the Roman citizenship to qualify them for legionary service. Not that there was anything wrong with the courage or fighting abilities of these peoples, but they did not share the Italians' personal involvement in this struggle to decide who their future master was to be. Nor had they been tested in battle like Octavian's men, since the great mass of them cannot have been recruited until after 35 when Antony realized that he had no longer any hope of recruiting more men from Italy. They numbered perhaps as much as a third of his legionary forces.

In cavalry, too, Octavian took care to match his enemy—almost as if he had prescience of what was to happen. The temptation to try to overwhelm Antony by sheer weight of numbers must have been strong. Octavian had at his disposal at least as many men again, but to supply, manoeuvre, and command such an enormous force might not be easy. There was also the problem of transport, awkward enough in any case: first across the Adriatic, subsequently perhaps in Greek waters. It is tempting to see the confident and experienced hand of the great Agrippa in the decision to take a smaller number of (one infers) choice troops. Agrippa himself assumed command of the fleet; as in the campaigns against Sextus Pompey, the naval arm was the more important. Any victory that Antony might win on land would be indecisive unless his fleet could defeat and destroy his enemy's. Without doing so, he could not cross to Italy, and there still remained Octavian's massive reserves of manpower, both serving legions and veterans, in Italy and the western provinces. Conversely, if Octavian were victorious by land he might still be gravely embarrassed by losing control of the sea—unable to follow up his advantage, his supply lines cut, and Egypt quite out of reach while his enemies prepared for a second round.

Though the details of the campaign that followed are not entirely clear, the broad outline is secure, thanks partly to Plutarch, who has preserved some precious hard facts in his romantic story, but above all to Dio, writing a safe 250 years after the event. Actium has been called 'the birth-legend in the mythology of the principate'. The poets and panegyricists of Octavian-Augustus and his immediate successors were not interested in the military manoeuvring by which the great victory was won. The fact was all that mattered, the moral lesson all that needed to be driven home: Roman virtue, Roman piety, Roman courage, and Roman gods were a match for all the barbarous levies of the east, the threatening posturings of would-be kings, and the bestial deities of Egypt. The truth about Actium was prosaic, a little unspectacular for the weight of enthusiasm it had to bear. Octavian, supreme politician though he was, was required by the tradition of public life at Rome to be also (what he was not) a supreme general. The famous lines of Virgil give us this ideal picture:

> Here, Caesar Augustus leads the Italian race to war,
> With him senate and people, the gods of his hearth and of
>   heaven;
> He stands high up on the poop, his radiant forehead framed
> By a pair of flames and crested above by his father's star.
> Over there can be seen Agrippa, redoubtable, leading his
>   column,
> The gods and the winds behind him; his proud emblem of war
> Gleams on his head—his crown adorned with the rams of ships.
> Facing them, fresh from his conquests over the tribes of the East
> And the shores of Arabia, Antony trusts in barbarian arms,
> In the motley might of the Orient, levies from Egypt and
>   uttermost
> Bactria's lands—and with him (o shame!) his Egyptian wife.

The facts of the matter, as we shall see, are rather different.

Operations in 31 got off to an early start. Barely had the sailing season opened when Agrippa with a strong squadron made a swift and unexpected crossing well south of the usual route and attacked Methone, taking it and killing Bogud. It was a brilliant stroke. Antony, lying as far south as he did, can hardly have expected the first attack to fall upon his southern flank—indeed, one of his objects in taking up the position he did may have been to invite Octavian to make the much shorter crossing to the coast of Epirus north of him, and thus to give his fleet some chance of intercepting the armada. Antony may be criticized for not blockading the coast. But under the conditions of ancient naval warfare such a blockade, off an unfriendly coast, and starting as it would have to in late winter, would have been almost impossible to maintain. The squadron he had stationed at Corcyra was the best he could manage in the way of an advanced guard. Octavian apparently made some move to sail to Corcyra, intending to occupy it and use it as a base for an attack on Antony's main force at Actium, but tried this sortie too early in the year and was driven back by a storm. It was left to Agrippa to dispose of the Corcyraean squadron; he kept a force at Methone to harass Antony's corn-ships as they laboured round the Peloponnese from Taenarum to the shelter of Zacynthos and the

Gulf of Corinth, and sailed north attacking Antony's other outposts and drawing off the ships which should have been guarding Corcyra.

Under cover of this diversion Octavian was able to ferry his whole army across without hindrance from Brundisium to a port under the Acroceraunian mountains, probably Panormus (modern Palermo), less probably Valona. The latter, though a more protected harbour, is a good deal farther north and the essence of Octavian's plan was speed. Once the army was disembarked, he took his 230 warships and descended on Corcyra, only to find the garrison gone. This meant that the easy inshore passage, between the island and the mainland, was his already, and there would be no danger to his flank or rear when his forces arrived at the entrance to the Ambracian Gulf. He sailed on to the little port of Fanari at the mouth of the river Acheron, a place known in antiquity as Glycys Limen (Sweetwater Harbour). There he met his army, which need have taken no more than four days to cover the ninety miles from Panormus. The speed and unexpectedness of these operations caused consternation at Antony's headquarters. The first news to reach Antony was that his enemy held Toryne, a small place on the coast somewhere between the southern end of Corcyra and Fanari. Antony's guardships, patrolling northwards from Actium to Paxos and the strait between Corcyra and the mainland, will have caught their first sight of Octavian's fleet as it came south of the strait and made for Toryne (modern Parga). From there to Patras is 125 miles by sea, a distance that an ancient ship could not have covered in much less than twenty-four hours, even under the most favourable weather conditions. By that time Octavian and his army were at Fanari, the last harbour before the entrance to the Gulf of Ambracia and the planned assault on Antony's fleet.

But Octavian's lightning success was at an end. He cannot really have expected to surprise the enemy fleet so completely as to be able to force the entrance against a merely defensive holding operation. The entrance is less than half a mile wide, and narrowed by shallows immediately to seaward. Antony's men had erected towers on either side, doubtless in the very spots where the Venetian forts stand to this day, and from these they could deliver a murderous hail of catapulted boulders and fireballs. A block-ship or two only needed to be moored in the channel, and the entrance was impregnable. Octavian offered battle out in the open water, but the Antonians were not so foolish as to accept the challenge, and he had to withdraw. Nevertheless, he had trapped the main part of Antony's fleet and the strategic initiative lay in his hands. Antony could choose no other ground for combat without either abandoning his ships or fighting his way out with them, whereas Octavian was reasonably free to withdraw both fleet and army if he wished.

By the time that Antony arrived, two or three days later, in company with Cleopatra and her women and as many troops as he could embark immediately, Octavian had established himself on the hill called Mikhalitzi, some five miles north of the entrance. Rising to a height of 400 feet, this is the southernmost of a low chain of hills running away to the north and dividing the open sea of the bay of Gomaros from the lower course of the River Louros where it debouches into the lagoons and muddy shallows that form the north-western corner of the Ambracian Gulf. It is a commanding viewpoint, in spite of its modest altitude. As one looks south, immediately in front lies the low and slightly undulating neck of the peninsula, about two miles wide, whose most conspicuous present-day feature is the ruins of Nicopolis, the city Octavian founded here to commemorate his victory. There are Byzantine walls, the remains of a great basilica, and nearer at hand a theatre set in the lower slope of the hill and the long overgrown oval of the stadium. Farther away the ground rises a little and almost obscures the pleasant harbour town of Preveza, the latter-day successor to Nicopolis. On the left of the peninsula, a steep hilly arm runs out to divide the Gulf of Preveza from the wide magnificence of the inner, main, Gulf. The narrow entrance which gives access to both, south of Preveza, is hidden, but beyond it can be seen the flat barren promontory of Actium, lying only a few feet above sea-level. Closing the view to the south-west, twenty miles away, broods the massive bulk of Leucas, an island in name alone, for no ship can sail between it and the mainland. Three and a half thousand feet high and falling in sheer cliffs into the sea along its north-western side, it is the most arresting and unmistakable feature of the prospect. Inland from Leucas, behind and to the left of the waste of Actium, are the splendid mountains of Acarnania, dark and shadowed in the mornings but changing to sculpted silver-grey with the westering sun. Farther away and farther to the left, at the head of the Gulf, beyond the miles of calm blue water, lies the great range of the Pindus, the spine of northern Greece, stretching endlessly into the distance to north and south. Even in summer the thunderclouds hang over its peaks. Nearer at hand, directly to the north, is a scatter of lower mountains and behind them the whitish heights of the Suliot country. Finally,

out at sea to the north-west lie the distant shapes of the small
islands of Paxos and Antipaxos; and in clear weather it is just possible
to catch a glimpse of the southernmost headland of Corcyra.

It was an admirable site for Octavian's camp. It could not easily
be encircled to the north, and the relatively level ground of the
peninsula of Nicopolis below could serve as a battlefield—if a battle
were desirable. If it were not, Octavian knew that Antony would
never be so foolish as to attack his camp, uphill. But it had two
disadvantages. One was a shortage of good water on the spot; for

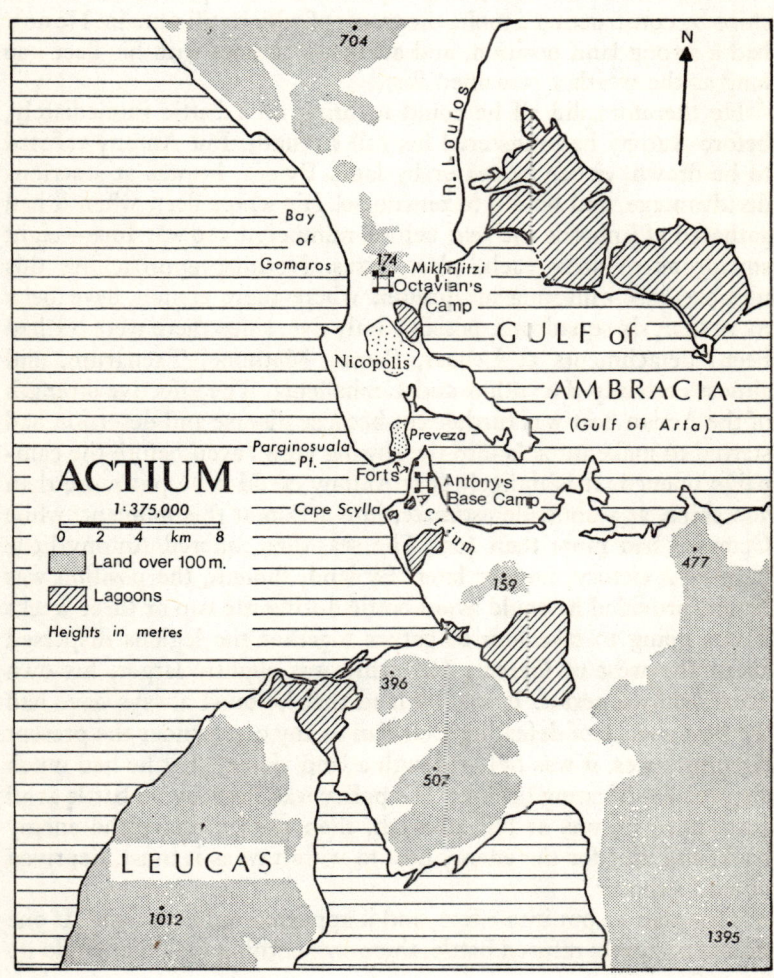

adequate supplies Octavian needed to make use either of the River Louros, or of the two good springs down on the site of Nicopolis. Neither source, however, was far away, and things would have to be going very badly for him before he were deprived of both. More serious was the lack of a good anchorage nearer than Fanari. The bay of Gomaros, though adequate in the fine weather which predominates in summer, was no use in any sort of a westerly storm. Nevertheless, it had to serve as a base for the blockade- and guard-ships and as a supply-point for the army. After fortifying his camp, Octavian built walls down to the beach and improvised some protection for the ships by constructing a mole, the traces of which still remain. He now had a strong land position, and adequate contact with his fleet—so long as the weather remained fine.

He therefore did all he could to bring on a battle immediately, before Antony had mustered his full strength. But Antony refused to be drawn, either by sea or by land. By sea, he was at a serious disadvantage, and bound to remain so. His whole fleet, when it had gathered at Ephesus the year before, numbered 500 warships—eight squadrons of sixty each, plus extras. Nothing approaching this number was wintering at Actium, where there cannot have been more than six squadrons, possibly only five, since there were (or had been) detachments at Leucas, Patras, Methone, Taenarum, and almost certainly Zacynthos and Cephallenia. The effective strength of the Actian fleet was further cut because disease and desertion had started to make inroads into the rowing crews even before the campaign opened. It is unlikely that Antony could have put more than 300 ships, at an outside estimate, into action at this moment, while Octavian had more than 400. The sea, then, offered Antony little hope of a victory, now or later. By land, though, the position was better, provided he could avoid battle during the two or three weeks it was going to take him to gather together the legions dispersed about the west of Greece. His army was slightly larger, his own generalship superior. It was by land that he must always have had the best chance of defeating Octavian in any case; under the present circumstances, it was only through a land victory that he had much chance of extricating his fleet. His policy was clear: avoid battle at all costs until he was at full strength, then engage, drive the enemy back, and wait for the enemy fleet to withdraw as it must, deprived of land support.

This plan he put into effect, and it appeared to be working. If one side persistently refused battle, there was nothing the other could do except resort to subterfuge or siege. Antony lay quietly in camp on the point opposite Preveza and contented himself with skirmishing. His guard-towers on the north shore were sufficiently well fortified to be safe and his fleet lay secure behind the point. For additional protection he joined the beach of this anchorage to the camp itself by long fortification walls like those of Octavian. Some ships lay outside the point, in the roadstead of Preveza, making the entrance quite safe. He had to resign himself to seeing some of his supply-ships captured as they tried to run the blockade, but that was a small price to pay for securing battle on his own terms. Finally, probably about the end of April, his army was complete and he was ready to accept Octavian's challenge. He ferried the men across the narrows, took up a position on the northern peninsula—the slight rise just south of Nicopolis would have been a suitable spot—and offered battle. Octavian refused.

He refused not because he was afraid of the result, but because the situation at sea had changed. While Antony's build-up had been taking place, Agrippa had made a successful attack on the Antonian squadron that held Leucas and guarded the strait between Cape Ducato (the south-western tip of the island) and Ithaca and Cephallenia. This had two results. It gave Agrippa a protected harbour much nearer than Fanari to Actium—for even if the channel cut in previous centuries through the mud-banks of the lagoon dividing Leucas from the mainland had silted up, reopening it was hardly a task to daunt the man who had created Portus Avernus. It also forced any of Antony's supply-ships willing to run the blockade to take the unprotected route seaward of Cephallenia before making their dash for the entrance to the Gulf of Ambracia. Octavian was now established to north and south of Actium, and the risk of losing a large proportion of his ships in a sudden storm had largely disappeared. He could supply his army indefinitely from farther up the coast and from Italy. Antony, on the other hand, in order to rescue a fleet which was a liability until it had been extricated, had been forced to concentrate a powerful army in a physically unhealthy and militarily constricting spot. The longer Octavian could keep him there, the worse his situation was likely to become.

Antony saw this as clearly as Octavian and Agrippa. If Octavian would not accept an invitation to fight, he must be forced to fight. It was impossible to besiege him effectively, since supplies could be landed without hindrance at the temporary port of Gomaros, except in bad weather—and no spell of bad weather would last long enough at that time of year to cause any hardship. All Antony could do was to try to cut Octavian off from his water-supply. This was easily done in the case of the springs at Nicopolis by erecting earth-works and establishing the main part of his army in a regular camp there. It was a healthier site and meant that any attempt to recapture the springs would lead to a full-scale battle. To keep Octavian from the River Louros was another matter. Antony sent a force of cavalry round the head of the Gulf, and for a short time came near to investing his enemy by land; but a sudden and determined charge led by Statilius Taurus and the renegade Titius (now enjoying the consulship that had been the price of his desertion) defeated Antony's cavalry and persuaded Deiotarus Philadelphus, the king of Paphlagonia, to desert him. Octavian also diverted his would-be besiegers by sending off detachments to Macedonia and Eastern Greece, with the double intention of interfering with Antony's land supplies and making him disperse his forces.

Meanwhile Agrippa was winning further successes with his fleet. He followed up the capture of Leucas with an attack on Patras, where Q. Nasidius, who as one of Sextus's admirals had fought against Agrippa and had then transferred his allegiance to Antony, had been left to hold the Corinthian Gulf. Agrippa defeated Nasidius, and took the town. The situation in the Peloponnese looked ominous for Antony, with Methone and Patras in the hands of the enemy and Lacedaemon in revolt. The ruler of Lacedaemon was one Eurycles, the son of a pirate whom Antony had put to death. Not surprisingly, Eurycles declared for Octavian (and when the gamble came off won for himself the Roman citizenship and for the Spartans the honour of presiding at the Actian games that afterwards commemorated Octavian's victory). Later on, though how much later it is impossible to say, Agrippa sailed right up the Gulf and took Corinth itself, though he did not succeed in holding it. These operations of Agrippa, and the forays of the land forces of which no details survive, made Antony's position more and more precarious.

This might not have been so disastrous had morale in his camp been good. But the unresolved conflict between 'Roman-republicans' and 'monarchists' amongst his chief followers poisoned their loyalty and sapped their determination. Ahenobarbus, long an opponent of the queen, finally reached the point where he could bear to stay no longer. Tension between the factions became so great that the 'republicans' offered him the leadership in Antony's place. But he was gravely ill and, faced with an impossibly difficult decision, he embarked in a small boat and was rowed round to Octavian's camp. Antony courteously sent his baggage after him, but Ahenobarbus did not live to repay the kindness. He must have been a victim of the severe disease that ravaged Antony's camp through the long hot months of summer. Malaria and dysentery are the two most likely candidates. The promontory of Actium is infertile, bitter soil, with occasional brackish, stagnant pools. There is no running water, and the sluggish and almost imperceptible tides of the Mediterranean cannot have been able to scour away the refuse of more than 100,000 men—for even if the bulk of Antony's fighting force were encamped on the healthier northern promontory, his rowers who remained with the ships numbered at least 70,000. Even today, a visit to Actium is a depressing experience. The few trees (save for a proud group at the landing stage) are miserable stunted things, the vegetation coarse and tussocky, the lagoon on the seaward side desolate, marsh-fringed, and sinister. Only the distant views redeem it, and distant views are no foundation for the morale or the health of an army. It is scarcely surprising that Antony's army was eroded by disease and desertion, amongst princes, officers, and men alike. Ahenobarbus, though the most eminent, was far from being the only deserter; Rhoemetalces, a king of the Thracians, went over to Octavian; so did M. Junius Silanus, whose tally of desertions over the previous dozen years was impressive, but not unparalleled; and Antony was driven to make an example of two other notables who were about to do likewise—namely Iamblichus, the ruler of Emesa, and Q. Postumius, a Roman senator, both executed.

There had been a shortage of rowers even at the beginning of spring. By midsummer the position was much worse, and Antony was compelled to send forces inland not only to watch and hinder the marauding operations of Octavian's detachments but also to press-gang able-bodied inhabitants for service in the fleet. He was also beginning to feel a shortage of fighting troops, and Dellius and Amyntas were despatched to Macedonia to raise more troops and to try to gain the support of Dicomes, a king of the Getae—no doubt a rival of Octavian's ally Cotiso. It is said that Antony was unsure of the reliability of his subordinates, and that it was for this reason that he set off after them himself. But this episode came not long before the end of the blockade, and a more sensible interpretation is that it was an attempt to draw Octavian away from the hill of Mikhalitzi. Dellius 'true to his own example', as Velleius has it, did indeed desert—but not yet. The diplomat could scent which way the wind was blowing; but if Antony had suspected what was in Dellius's mind, it is barely credible that he entrusted him with an important mission only to shadow him in person. Nor is it likely to be coincidence that Sosius, Antony's senior naval commander, made a determined attempt to break the blockade at the very time that Antony was away. The two things go together, and constitute Antony's first attempt to extricate himself forcibly from the trap that was closing ever more tightly round him as the weeks of inaction, disease, quarrelling, heat, and increasing shortages dragged on. Early in August is the most likely date for it. But Sosius was unlucky. He sailed out of the entrance in a thick mist, fell upon the blockading squadron commanded by L. Tarius Rufus, routed it, and was in hot pursuit when Agrippa came up with the rest of his fleet just in time to turn defeat into victory. A notable casualty on the Antonian side was Tarcondimotus, dynast in the Amanus, a region not noted for its connections with the sea. It looks as though Antony left Sosius with enough fighting men to man the ships, and led the rest off with the intention of meeting Sosius somewhere on the Aegean coast of Greece, whither Agrippa's squadrons had not yet penetrated.

Antony was evidently not prepared to abandon most of his fleet and half his army. When the news reached him that Sosius had failed to break out, he returned to try a different plan. This was the simple tactic of the pitched battle, which neither side had offered since the early days of May. Antony succeeded in bringing on a cavalry engagement, perhaps by the same manoeuvre of trying to cut Octavian off from his water-supply, and certainly with the same result. Earlier it had been Deiotarus, now it was Amyntas who deserted with his 2,000 cavalry. Thus the second attempt to end the blockade had failed.

It was now near the end of August, and Antony's position was becoming desperate. The desertion of Amyntas was a tremendous blow to his morale and his strength alike, and brought jubilation to the other side. Octavian sent a despatch to Maecenas in Italy, and on receipt of the good news Horace penned a poem (the ninth Epode) that eagerly looks forward to broaching the vintage wine when victory is securely won. By itself, Amyntas's desertion would not have been so significant. But Antony was getting very short of provisions too. Plutarch, who was a native of Chaeronea in central Boeotia, says that his great-grandfather used to tell how the citizens of the town were forced to carry wheat down to the Corinthian Gulf at Anticyra, being encouraged in this task by the whip. They had

transported one load in this fashion, when news came that Antony
had been defeated and they were left to enjoy the wheat themselves.
Rowers too were still short. Recruiting had not been able to keep pace
with the depredations of disease and desertion, and starvation was
undermining the strength of those there were. Antony's press-gangs
laid their hands on every able-bodied man, snatching reapers from
the harvest and muleteers from their beasts, and even so he could not
man all his ships.

Antony therefore withdrew his forces from the northern promontory and called a council of war. There were two choices open to him:
he could abandon the fleet and fall back to the eastern side of
Greece, or he could fight his way out by sea with what ships he
could man and hope that the rest of the army might save itself
somehow. Canidius Crassus, the commander of the land forces,
argued for the first course: Antony was not a nautical man; the
victor of Philippi should seek a decisive engagement by land; there
were recruits and allies to hand in Macedonia and Thrace. Cleopatra
was the chief advocate of the second course. The drawbacks of a land
withdrawal were patent: to take a demoralized and weakened army
up through the passes of the Pindus savoured too much of the Athenian
retreat from Syracuse; the fleet would have to be completely
abandoned, since it could not fight without soldiers on board; if the
army did reach Macedonia safely, it would still be cut off from any
hope of an escape to Asia Minor or Egypt by the unchallengeable
naval superiority of the enemy; and Dicomes's willingness to help
was little more than optimistic conjecture. On the other hand, to try
to break the blockade was no more risky than to retreat over the
mountains; and if the attempt succeeded Antony would still be in
possession of a good part of his fleet and, of course, the pick of his
army manning it. The rest of the Actian army might manage to get
away, but if it did not, there were the seven legions of Syria and
Cyrenaica to be added to the four or five that could be embarked on
the fleet. Egypt was easy to defend, a base from which an able and
resolute man might still fight back, and the way to it and to the other
legions lay by sea, not by land.

The case for the sea-fight was unanswerable. It is no paradox that
Antony, the greatest land commander of the day, chose to decide the
struggle by a naval engagement. The logic of the situation forced the
choice upon him. Not that it was his intention to make the battle a
decisive one: outnumbered and undermanned as his fleet was, he
might manage to break through, but he could hardly hope to win a

victory. Plainly, he had to fight to get out, and the more of his
enemy's ships that went to the bottom in the process, the better. But
his primary aim remained to escape with as many ships and men as
possible. After Mutina he had recovered from an equally bad position.
If he could only extricate himself, he was not yet lost. All that
remained was to decide upon his tactics and put them into effect.
Subterfuge was out of the question. Not only were all his troop- and
ship-movements in full view from the northern promontory, but it
was at this late moment that Dellius chose to desert, taking with him
full details of the council of war and exact information of Antony's
strength.

Chapter XVI

THE BATTLE OF ACTIUM

ANTONY FIRST burnt his spare ships. The flames consumed some of the smaller warships and all but a few of the transports. He had not the rowers to man them, and there was no point in making Octavian a present of them. He was left with a fleet of some 230 vessels, which ranged in size, according to Plutarch, from triremes, or threes, up to tens. Florus, who used the lost account of Livy, says that Antony's ships went from sixes up to nines. Perhaps what Livy said was that the majority were of those sizes. A ten was a big vessel—Sextus's flagship had only been a six—and Antony may well not have had more than one or two ships of this rating. Even so, he clearly had the advantage over Octavian in the matter of size; though whether this was because he had deliberately outbuilt him after 36, as Dio says, or because the Hellenistic navies of the eastern Mediterranean had always favoured bigger ships than the west, is impossible to say. But there was no essential difference in kind between the fleets. Octavian had substantially the same fleet as he had used to defeat Sextus. Florus may well be right in saying that it consisted of biremes (twos) up to sixes, but to take this difference in rating figures as indicating a fast mobile fleet ranged against a heavy cumbrous one is wrong. Both sides intended to use the same tactics, the tactics that had proved so successful at Naulochus, of laying alongside and thus turning the ships into platforms from which an infantry battle could be fought. The ships were built accordingly, with massive timbers bound with iron at the waterline to resist the impact of the ram, and capable of supporting towers at stem and stern to give protection and vantage to archers and slingers. Relatively, Octavian's ships may have been the more manoeuvrable, but it was by weight of numbers, not by seamanship, that they would defeat Antony. To Antony's 230, Octavian opposed more than 400.

By August 29 Antony was ready, but four days of storm followed. The wind blew onshore from the west and made it impossible for him to get out of the entrance and round Leucas. Otherwise, he would certainly have taken advantage of the bad weather to run for it in conditions that made interception and fighting extraordinarily difficult. He had done this very thing years before, dodging the Pompeian blockade of the Adriatic in a southerly gale in order to bring badly needed reinforcements to Caesar at Dyrrhachium. There was nothing to be done except wait for the return of the fine weather in which alone ancient naval battles could be fought.

At last, on September 2, the morning came up bright and clear. Antony had four squadrons. One of these was Cleopatra's, which included merchantmen and had the treasure-chest and valuables aboard. Plainly this squadron was not intended to take a serious part in the combat, and though Antony cannot have left it altogether destitute of fighting men, the bulk of the 20,000 legionaries and 2,000 archers that Plutarch tells us he embarked for the battle must have been on the 170 ships of the other three squadrons. Also on board were the sails, a clear sign that Antony intended flight. Sails and their associated tackle were bulky and heavy, and were invariably left ashore before a battle. Antony tried to counteract the depressing effect of taking them by pretending that they were going to be used to pursue the defeated enemy. The senatorial élite of his following—or such of them as were left—came with him on the ships. The rest of the army, reduced by disease and desertion and probably numbering at the most not above 50,000 men, remained in camp under Canidius Crassus. In the event of Antony managing to get away, Canidius's orders were to fall back inland to Macedonia, and so to Asia.

Octavian, well aware (thanks to Dellius) of Antony's intentions, toyed with the idea of letting him sail past and then giving chase. Perhaps he thought that Antony's ships were formidable enough, because of their size and the number of men they could carry, to inflict serious damage on his own smaller ships and still escape afterwards. The action could well develop in constricted water, where his own advantage in numbers and ease of handling might be neutralized. If he let the enemy go, they would inevitably spread out and be open to attack from every side—provided that he could catch them. But it was a big proviso, and the plan carried no guarantee of victory. Octavian allowed himself to be overborne by Agrippa, who pointed out the unnecessary riskiness of such a proceeding and expressed himself in favour of a battle-plan which would block Antony's escape but force him to come out into open water to engage. So he embarked eight legions and five praetorian cohorts (some

40,000 men), and took up his position a mile or so to seaward of the line joining the two outermost points of the entrance, Parginosuala and Scylla. He had on board, then, very nearly double his opponent's number of men; but in keeping with the difference in ship sizes, his average per ship was lower—about 90, compared with Antony's 110–120. In this situation, his tactics must be to lure Antony's fleet out into open water and make it spread out so that two of his sixes could take on each of Antony's bigger ships. His crews, too, had been given constant practice in ship-handling by their blockade duties and by Agrippa's forays southwards. An opportunity to exploit their superior skill was much more likely to arise away from the land.

Antony and his admirals Sosius and Gellius Publicola knew all this as well as their enemies did. So when Antony's fleet had emerged from the entrance to the Gulf, crossed the shallow water of the bar (which cannot have given a ten much to spare under her keel),* and reached the safer depths around the five-fathom line, it halted. Cleopatra's squadron came out last, and stayed at the rear through-out. Antony himself, with Publicola, commanded the right wing, M. Insteius and M. Octavius the centre, and Sosius the left. The names at least suggest the possibility that the biggest ships were concentrated at the two ends of the line, where the senior comman-ders were. If this was so, Antony may have hoped to draw the enemy strength away from the centre, and create a weakness there which would give Cleopatra's squadron a chance to break through and escape. The others might then disengage, if they could. But first, he had to try to bring Octavian to battle. What he wanted was a fight as close inshore as possible, preferably in a position where the enemy could not sail round the ends of his line and so engage him on both sides at once. If he could keep his ships close together the enemy would not have the sea-room to use their superior numerical strength.

A simple calculation can give us a clue to Antony's battle forma-tion at this point. The 170 ships of his three fighting squadrons, if strung out in a line bows-on to the other fleet and stationed as close together as safety and seamanship permitted, would have occupied about two and a half sea miles (assuming an average width of sixty feet per ship over the oars, and thirty feet clear water between). The distance between Parginosuala and Scylla, or rather the outlying rocks of the latter, is about one and a half sea miles. It would be playing

---

* In 1805, there were twelve feet of water on the bar, then undredged (W. M. Leake, *Travels in Northern Greece*, I, p. 180), while N. G. L. Hammond (*Epirus*, p. 42) estimates the sea-level to have risen four to six feet since classical times.

into Octavian's hand to advance much beyond these two points, so conveniently placed to guard his flanks. Antony must therefore have doubled his line and waited. But Agrippa, to whom Octavian had wisely delegated the command, refused to accept the invitation to battle. For a space the two great fleets lay quietly on their oars in the September sunshine, a mile of tranquil sea between them.

The key to what followed is the way the wind behaves at Actium. In fine weather the pattern is consistent enough to be quite predictable—or at least as predictable as a wind ever is. By night a land breeze, which is sometimes quite fresh, blows from the mountains down the Gulf to the sea. The rising sun begins to kill it, by ten o'clock it is faint-hearted, and by eleven non-existent. The sea lies flat, its surface brushed only by little catspaws or furrowed by the wake of a fishing-boat making her way down the dredged channel through the bar. There is half an hour of calm. Then out at sea the almost invisible junction of the hazy pale blues of sea and sky becomes clearer, as though a dark pencil had been drawn along it. The sea breeze is starting to make in as the sun burns up the air inland. A few minutes later, the first stirrings reach the land and begin to rustle the brittle leaves of the gum-trees that somewhat unexpectedly line the beach of Preveza. By noon or shortly after, the breeze is firm in strength and direction, blowing gently but constantly from a little south of west. Over the next couple of hours it increases quite rapidly in strength and hauls round to the north, so that by two or three o'clock there is a brisk sailing breeze (force 3–4) from about west-north-west. In the late afternoon this starts to die with the sinking sun, but its direction remains the same. It is still blowing, gently, at sunset, but an hour later all is calm and the lamps along the quay-side of Preveza are reflected in the glossy black water that waits for the night wind from the Gulf.

The wind is important because it governed Antony's tactics once Agrippa refused to join battle inshore. If the engagement had taken place where Antony wished, it must have been fought to a finish. If Antony had then emerged victorious, he would have been able to make off round Leucas without interference, and the direction of the wind would not have mattered very much. But when Agrippa, as Antony must have anticipated, refused to come inshore, Antony was forced to take the initiative himself and advance into open water. Great generals are realists, and Antony can have had no illusions about his chances of inflicting enough damage on the opposing fleet to make it incapable of pursuit. His only hope was to get into a position where he could use his sails. With these and oars together he could out-distance any pursuer who had to rely on oar-power alone, apart from fast light vessels which could not really expect to stop ships of the line. But he could not use his sails at any time he pleased, even assuming the state of the battle permitted him to disengage and take to flight. The obstacle was Leucas. The great island, stretching its huge mass seaward, stands like a sentinel over the bay of Actium and forces any ship southward-bound from the Gulf of Ambracia to set a course that is almost due south-west.

As is well-known, the square-rigged ship—and all ancient Mediterranean ships of any size were square-rigged—could hardly sail against the wind at all. The best a Roman merchantman could do was slightly less than a right angle (or in nautical language, seven points off the wind, eight points being the right angle); and there is no reason to suppose that Antony's warships, whose sailing abilities were incidental, could do any better. Thus any wind between southeast and north-west made it impossible or very difficult to sail directly from the mouth of the Gulf around Leucas. If the wind is at all south of west, even a modern yacht, which can sail far closer to the wind than any ancient ship, will have very little to spare between herself and the cliffs by the time she reaches Leucas on a straight course from the bar of Preveza. But the farther the wind goes round to the north, the more it blows from astern and the easier it becomes to round the island. Similarly, the farther out to sea a ship starts, the more nearly southerly, and the further off the wind, the course lies. Having spent so many months at Actium, Antony knew exactly what the wind could be expected to do on a normal day of fine weather. Not until early afternoon would it have gone round far enough or be blowing hard enough to be much use to him with his heavy, unweatherly ships. But even with the wind from west-north-west, he would be very lucky to get round Leucas if he started from an inshore position. The course, in such a case, is exactly seven points off the wind, that is, the closest his ships could possibly sail to it; but the closer a ship sails to the wind, the slower she goes, and though Antony's fleet might technically have been able to make Leucas from the bar, its speed at this point of sailing would be very low, probably about two knots; hardly enough to compensate for the extra effort Octavian's oarsmen might produce in their eagerness to catch a fleeing enemy. But for every mile Antony could make to seaward, the angle between the direction of the wind and the western tip of Leucas increased by half a point. Antony therefore wanted to bring on the battle as far out to sea as he could, so as to have the afternoon wind at least slightly behind him when he broke and ran for it. It would also be an advantage if he could make some distance to the north as well.

Antony's tactics now become intelligible. A precious fact preserved by Plutarch is that neither side made any move until noon, when, as he specifically says, a breeze sprang up from the sea. Antony, then, was content to wait an hour or more after it was apparent that Agrippa was not going to allow his ships to come in to the attack. Plutarch has the facts right, but their interpretation wrong, when he says that Antony's men became impatient at the long wait and, feeling confident in their ships, got the left wing to go forward. On the contrary, Antony deliberately waited for the breeze to come in—for there was always the chance that it might not. Nor was there any hurry once it did come, since it was going to be another two or three hours before it swung fully round to the north. The left wing was the first to advance because it lay closest inshore and farthest south, and so had the greatest need to make distance out to seaward. Octavian's right wing, commanded by M. Lurius, backed water so as to bring the Antonians as far out into open water as possible.

From this point on, the ancient writers do not make it at all clear what happened—at least so far as tactics are concerned. Dio has a nonsensical version, whereby it was Octavian who formed his line into a crescent shape and attacked, attempting to outflank Antony and thus provoking him to counter-attack. Dio's narrative continues with picturesque and exciting details of the actual fighting, but of the tactical situation there is no word. Dio, in short, is indulging in the sort of conventional battle-picture that writers of histories were expected to provide. Plutarch, on the other hand, has precise tactical information and little rhetorical flavour. It seems that his account of the battle depends on an eye-witness whose identity is unknown but has been called 'the deserter' since the nature and colouring of the facts Plutarch took from him indicate that he was an anti-Cleopatran follower of Antony who disapproved of the decision to fight at sea and was induced to desert by it.

Plutarch says that, after Antony's left wing had advanced as described, the fleets came to grips with each other. Then Agrippa, who was commanding the left wing so as to be opposite Antony, started to extend his line to the left with the object of outflanking his opponents to the north. Publicola, in tactical command of Antony's right, was obliged to counter this manoeuvre by likewise moving northwards. Outnumbered as the Antonians were, their line had to break, and so the right wing became separated from the centre, which was under attack from L. Arruntius commanding Octavian's centre. In the confusion, with the battle still quite undecided, Cleopatra's squadron hoisted sail and made off through the middle of the combatants. 'The enemy', says Plutarch, 'watched them in amazement as they made use of the breeze to sail away in the direction of the Peloponnese.'

So the great fleet that had come to make war on the barbarian queen gazed open-mouthed as she sailed clean through them? Clearly, something is wrong with Plutarch's account; yet that account—apart from being the only one we have—seems to make sense in its general outlines. Omission, compression, and misunderstanding are to blame. One omission must be the fact of Antony's advance on the right wing, recorded but misrepresented by Dio. Antony had no particular desire to pivot his line on its northern end, and it is a reasonable inference that, although the left wing was the first to advance, the centre and right followed suit. And if Lurius had orders to back water, Arruntius and Agrippa surely must have done the same. The whole purpose of the manoeuvre was to draw Antony's ships well away from the land. In this, both sides were temporarily in agreement; but Antony, once started, had no intention of stopping, and battle was joined as soon as Agrippa ordered his fleet to cease giving way. Agrippa's original position had been a mile from the Antonians. He was probably, then, at least a mile and a half to seaward of the point Parginosuala when he decided to engage. From this position, the course to Leucas bore six and a half points south of west—in other words, flight under sail would become possible for Antony as soon as the wind veered to its full extent.

The fleets came together. The preliminaries were a hail of missiles, incendiary and otherwise, from the catapults, followed by a fusillade from the archers and slingers ensconced in their towers. Then came the moment when the two lines actually met, though the exact manoeuvres employed at this critical stage elude us. There were several ways of disabling an enemy ship: ramming and sinking; grappling and overpowering; sailing close down one side and breaking off the oars; and burning by hurling incendiary missiles. Fire was the most terrible of all offensive weapons, once it got a grip; but it was unreliable and apt to rebound upon the user. It seems to have played little part in this battle. Antony's heavy ships had formidable rams, but were too unwieldy to employ them effectively. His best chance lay in grappling, since the superior seamanship and greater mobility of Octavian's ships gave them the advantage when it came to ramming. Not that Antony had much fear of ramming. The great squared iron-bound timbers with which he had strengthened his ships made them proof against it. The manoeuvre of breaking off the enemy's oars demanded perfect timing and highly skilled crews, who knew exactly when to draw in their own oars. It was a sophisticated gambit more appropriate to the triremes of the fifth century than to the floating fortresses of the first. The celebrated *diekplous* of trireme warfare, which involved sailing through the enemy line and turning back upon it, was evidently not in question. If Antony had been able to sail through, he would have done so, and kept going.

Agrippa's problem was to make sure that the initial impetus of the big Antonian ships was checked without allowing them any chance of a breakthrough. An obvious way of doing this was to double his line, since his superiority in numbers was so great that Antony's fleet, even in single line, could still not outflank him. That he did in fact adopt this formation is indicated by Plutarch, who says that it was only *after* the fleets came to grips that Agrippa tried to work round Antony's right. Publicola, to counter as he did by going to the north, must have had a substantial number of his ships still free to move, not yet locked in battle with their opponents nor seriously damaged. The engagement, then, was still in its early stages when this piece of manoeuvring took place.

From the sequel it appears that Publicola's reaction was a deliberately planned tactic. Whatever Antony's squadron commanders might do, in the end they were bound to be surrounded, outnumbered as they were by more than two to one (Cleopatra's squadron discounted). The only question was whether they let the enemy outflank them, or opened the centre by attempting to stop the inevitable outflanking move. One of Antony's aims, as we have seen, was to make as much westing and northing as he could in the course of the battle. The westing the enemy had obligingly given him by withdrawing; the northing he attempted to gain by advancing his left wing first—and now, by moving to the right when Agrippa started his anticipated outflanking manoeuvre. This meant, quite certainly, that a gap was going to appear in the centre of the line. Antony had reckoned with this. He had put his most powerful ships and his senior admirals at either end of the line, compelling Octavian to do likewise. The commanders of the centre, on either side, were the least experienced in naval warfare—so far as our meagre records enable us to judge. It seems that Antony deliberately intended to play down the centre, open a gap in it, and hope that the battle there would become a tolerably evenly matched mêlée of apparently secondary importance—with plenty of unoccupied water.

Certainly this is what happened. Plutarch does not say whether Publicola prevented his flank being turned. He would have done well to succeed. A quite hypothetical reconstruction, which gains a vestige of support from the way Antony escaped, is that as Agrippa's ships, with the advantage of the wind behind them, gradually worked around to the north, Publicola turned his line more and more from its original north–south alignment towards an east–west one. After this the tactics (if any) of the two sides are unknown. Probably the battle now became the normal series of ship-to-ship engagements, in the manner of the naval battles of the Napoleonic wars. Antony's bigger ships were taken on by two or three of the enemy at once. Grapnels and boarding-bridges came into play, the fighting men struggled to push back their opponents and swarm over their decks, the archers and slingers aloft poured arrows and shot into the sweating, thrusting combatants beneath them, and the rowers below decks waited helplessly at their oars, praying that their ship would not be sunk or burnt. Sea breeze and salt spray were fouled by blood and smoke, the sunny afternoon defiled by shouts and groans and clash of steel on steel. In the centre, which had become disorganized as a result of Publicola's manoeuvre, there developed a fierce and evenly balanced struggle, as Arruntius's ships fell on those of Octavius and Insteius. Antony's fleet was making a good fight of it.

It was at this point, when the battle had been going on for some two hours, that Cleopatra made her celebrated and misinterpreted dash for safety. Treachery, said the official version of these events. What else did one expect of a perfidious sorceress? At the very moment when her misguided lover was giving the last proof of his nobility by fighting for her bold and nefarious designs, she hoisted sail and fled like a coward; Antony himself, faithful to the end, abandoned his fleet and his honour to follow her.

There is a more rational and less discreditable interpretation. Cleopatra's squadron contained merchant ships, lay behind the three fighting squadrons, and made no attempt to intervene. Odd, if it was intended to be a reserve; but quite understandable if the whole purpose of Antony's rightward move was to thin the centre enough to give reasonable hope of success to a determined dash straight through it. To save even sixty ships out of two hundred and thirty was a creditable achievement for a man embayed on a lee shore and vastly outnumbered. But Antony did better, for he seems to have extricated a few of the ships he had with him on the right wing. He was prepared for Cleopatra's sudden, and to the enemy surprising, action. His flagship was too heavily beset to be disengaged, but he was able to transfer to a five and make off after Cleopatra. That he could do this at all suggests that there were some of his ships which were not surrounded by the enemy and lay to southward of them, so that they could break off the engagement, hoist sail, and make towards Leucas without having to force a way through the opposition.

Cleopatra's escape took place between two and three in the afternoon, for by that time the wind had attained its maximum strength and had veered far enough for her to be able to use her sails effectively. Virgil, for what his poetic version is worth, corroborates this. She fled, according to him, 'with the waves and the wind called Iapyx'— that is, the wind that comes from between west-north-west and north-west. After she and Antony had gone, the rest of the fleet fought on for survival. It was not that they did not realize what had happened, nor that they preferred death to dishonour. It was simply that they were not in a position to follow. In particular, the left wing, under Sosius, had always stood much less chance of getting away, and no doubt it was for this reason that Antony himself had taken the right wing. Grappled, disabled, or surrounded, the remainder could not break away to follow their commander. About four o'clock, they started to surrender. They were troubled by the sea kicked up by the breeze, and it seems that a squall caused some damage.

Even by night-fall it was still not altogether clear that the portion of Antony's fleet which remained off Actium was decisively defeated. Octavian himself spent the night at sea in his Liburnian, the light fast vessel that had carried him throughout the battle (for the Sicilian war had taught him a sharp lesson, and he had left the flagship to Agrippa). Not until morning was he sure that victory was his, and only partial victory at that. Antony had slipped away from a nearly hopeless position with his queen, her treasure, and about a third of the ships he had taken into battle. Still encamped on the promontory of Actium was a sizeable army under the experienced and loyal Canidius Crassus. At the time, Actium can hardly have seemed the glorious occasion that it later became. Dio, indeed, does his best to redeem a historically unspectacular battle. His version of the end has it that Octavian, at a loss how to overcome the stubborn resistance of the Antonians, sent ashore for fire and with its aid turned Antony's fleet into a chain of floating pyres. There is not a word of this in Plutarch. Dio's imagination seems to have run riot, seeking a picturesque climax to his rhetorical description, the final touch to make the battle of Actium suitably dire, memorable, and worthy of the beginnings of the Principate.

Meanwhile Antony and Cleopatra made their escape. Although none of the heavy ships from Octavian's fleet could catch them, some Liburnians set off in pursuit and managed to come up with them after Antony had been taken on board Cleopatra's flagship. Antony turned his ships about to face them and scared them all off except for the galley commanded by Eurycles of Sparta, who had his father's death to avenge. Homeric challenge and response ensued, but Eurycles swung away, rammed and captured a second flagship (for one other, presumably that of the centre, had made its escape), and took another ship which was carrying some of the royal impedimenta. This achieved, the Liburnians drew off in the dusk and allowed the Antonian squadron to sail away unmolested to the south. It was a three days' voyage to Taenarum, and during all that time, Plutarch says, Antony stayed in the forepart of the ship in a state of profound dejection and would have nothing to do with Cleopatra. Whether this be true or not, Antony had much to brood upon. He knew his fleet was lost, except for the seventy or eighty ships he had with him. But the land forces might yet manage to escape and unite with the Syrian legions, there were four legions in Cyrenaica, and the coming winter would give him time and opportunity to build a fresh fleet. Egypt was naturally strong, and though his military prestige might have suffered as a result of Actium, his real ability as a general was unimpaired. Whether or not Canidius could lead the rest of the army to safety, Egypt was the only base from which he could hope to fight back against an enemy who now had a decisive superiority in both ships and men.

Nevertheless, Antony waited some days at Taenarum for news and stragglers to arrive. They did, in the shape of heavy transports which had been left behind in the flight or had been in the ports that Antony still held before the battle; some of his friends also managed to make their way to him after the defeat. These brought the news that the fleet was indeed destroyed but that the army seemed to be holding together: an illusory spark of hope, as it turned out. Canidius started his men on the first stages of the withdrawal across to Macedonia, but when Octavian's army came up with them, they halted. Not to fight, however. The soldiers knew their price, and they had an accurate idea of who was going to win in the end. There was no point in blindly following a defeated cause; but equally, no point in casting themselves as suppliants on the mercy of a man whom they well knew would prefer to avoid a battle. Negotiations ensued, which under the circumstances can only be called protracted. Evidently, Antony's army was far from being a spent force. The soldiers bargained for a week. The veteran centurions who spoke for them had seen enough of civil war to know that Octavian would agree to almost any terms to secure their surrender. They held out for equal treatment with the victorious army, and obtained it. On top of this, they made Octavian concede continued existence of six of the legions, instead of dissolving them and inserting the men into his own legions as he did with the rest. The professional officers of a unit such as the famous *V Alaudae*, the 'Larks', had a regimental pride and a regimental tradition that they would not lightly give up. Before the negotiations were concluded, Canidius and his senior commanders, unwilling to follow the example of their men, fled secretly by night. They could not expect Octavian to be generous to them. Plutarch preserves the official version of these transactions, which is a choice specimen of the distortion of the truth systematically practised by Octavian in all that concerned the memory of Antony: 'Antony's soldiers showed such loyalty and bravery that even after his flight was beyond all doubt they held fast for seven days, ignoring Octavian's overtures. But at last, when their commander Canidius had fled by night and abandoned his army, being left destitute of everything and betrayed by their superiors, they went over to the victor.'

Such, then, was the battle of Actium, which became decisive only by the surrender of the army. In military terms, Antony did well to escape from a nearly hopeless position. His fatal weakness was the association with Cleopatra, which rotted the morale of his high-ranking supporters, provoked desertion, and caused a situation where he was forced to abandon the army. The collapse in Greece destroyed his credibility as a leader of a Roman party. The Romans who remained with him were loyal to him for personal reasons, or because they could expect no mercy from Octavian. This Antony seems to have realized. His last act before he left Greece was to send to Corinth those of his friends who wished to follow him no farther. He gave instructions to his agent there, one Theophilus, to hide them safely until they could make their peace with Octavian. He thus discharged, as best he could, the obligations of friendship, and set sail with Cleopatra for Africa.

Chapter XVII

THE END OF THE CIVIL WARS

OCTAVIAN MADE no attempt to strike immediately at Egypt. Not so much because Caesar's heir lacked Caesar's temperament and Caesar's ability to follow up a victory with speed that became proverbial, but because there were more pressing political problems. During the campaign of Actium, young Marcus Lepidus, son of the triumvir and nephew to Brutus, formed a plot to assassinate Octavian on his return to Italy. The plot became known to Maecenas, who allowed Lepidus enough scope to incriminate himself and then put him to death. His wife Servilia (Isauricus's daughter), once betrothed to Octavian, refused to outlive him and swallowed a live coal. Whether inept, or simply unlucky, the conspiracy was a sign that all was not well.

More trouble could be expected when the inevitable demobilization of troops took place. Octavian's experiences after the defeat of Sextus in 36 had taught him a lesson in how to handle a large and potentially mutinous army which considered itself to have at last earned the rewards which had long been dangled before it. As a result of the surrender of the opposing army, he found himself in command of upwards of thirty legions. Of those that had been Antony's, he permitted six to remain in existence. The rest were disbanded and their men inserted into the ranks of his own legions so that there was no longer any formal distinction between his men and Antony's and he could more easily carry out his promise to treat both alike—a promise he had made as long ago as 36, and which he could not go back on now without provoking a serious disturbance. It was important to act quickly, since he still did not possess the resources to satisfy the legitimate demands of all. He reduced his artificially swollen legions by disarming and sending back to Italy all citizen soldiers (that is, he excluded Antony's oriental recruits) who were over a certain age. Once there, they received nothing, but were dispersed in their units, on leave pending formal discharge. There were very soon rumblings of discontent, and he sent back the stern

Agrippa to keep them in order. At the same time he made a conces-
sion to the civilian population by remitting a quarter of the special
tax he had imposed on wealthy freedmen the year before. This went
a little way towards alleviating fears that Italy was destined to
become the prey of the greedy soldiery. From the remainder of the
army, there was no trouble. They had the prospect of rich booty
from the forthcoming campaign against Egypt.

Octavian then proceeded to Athens, where he paraded the correct
philhellenism by being initiated into the Mysteries of Demeter at
Eleusis. From there he went to Samos and established his winter-
quarters on the island. He had time to turn his attention to the client-
kingdoms, and confirmed the soundness of Antony's system by
leaving the heart of it untouched. Amyntas of Galatia, who had
deserted, Polemo of Pontus, who had remained behind, and
Archelaus of Cappadocia, whose eagerness to join the victor may be
surmised, were all confirmed on their thrones. Armenia was irretrievably lost, thanks to the campaign of Actium; Artaxes had resumed
his throne and taken his revenge on Rome by slaughtering all the
Roman citizens who had entered the short-lived province. The minor
princes were deposed and replaced by Octavian's own nominees; and
he distributed rewards, punishments, fines, and occasionally pardon,
to communities and individuals.

He had not been long on Samos when grave news reached him
from Italy. The veterans were mutinous and even Agrippa could not
handle them. Midwinter though it was, Octavian hurried back to
Brundisium, to be met by a carefully organized demonstration in the
best traditions of a modern people's democracy: the whole senate
(except for the tribunes and two praetors who were specially exempted), the vast majority of wealthy non-senators, and many of the
ordinary people, some as official deputations, some as private
individuals, flocked to greet him. So did the veterans, and not so
amicably. Concessions had to be made. Octavian agreed to distribute
land, fully realizing the storm of unpopularity that might break
round him. Since the supply of state-owned land had long ago run
out, and he had not nearly enough money to buy more, the only
solution was to dispossess existing holders. This was the very
action that had led to the war of Perusia. The conspiracy of Lepidus
was a warning that the splendid consensus of all Italy lacked solidity.
The demands of the revolutionary army could yet unseat its leader.
It was the last crisis of the civil wars. Once again, Octavian's extraordinary political skill carried him successfully through. He split the

veterans by distinguishing between those who had been with him 'throughout his campaigns' (in other words since Mutina and Philippi) and those who had joined him later. To the former he gave land and money, to the latter money alone, with the promise of land later. Thus he fully satisfied the hard core of 'his' soldiers, who had known no other commander since the very earliest days and could now be counted upon to support him faithfully once again; and at the same time he kept to a minimum the amount of land he had to find. It sufficed to evict those communities which had taken Antony's side. There was no shortage of land outside Italy: the veterans might not be interested in it, but it served to offer to the dispossessed. If the latter preferred a cash price for their land, they could have it—but at a ruinously low valuation. Many of the evicted chose expatriation, and settled on the Albanian coast or at Philippi. Of protest we hear nothing. It would have been futile.

Octavian spent thirty days at Brundisium, settling this crucial matter. The solution was a stop-gap; he had once again been forced to rely on promises; and the number of soldiers involved was small compared with those he would have to reward after his final victory. That victory would ultimately be his, he can have had little doubt. But almost more important than victory was to lay his hands on the treasure of the Ptolemies, the last great accumulation of wealth left in the Mediterranean world. With its aid, he could escape from the economic strait-jacket that had forced him either to oppress the civilian population or risk alienating his soldiers. At last it would be possible to pay off these useful but embarrassing servants without being called a tyrant, an extortioner, a ravager of his fatherland—and destroying the whole myth on which his successful challenge to Antony had been built.

He returned to Samos, avoiding the dangerous winter voyage around the capes of the Peloponnese by hauling his ships across the Isthmus of Corinth. Once he had missed the chance of following up the victory of Actium with an immediate attack on Egypt, time was on his side. He was in no hurry to move against his enemies. As the months of winter passed, their will to resist could crumble and their remaining Roman supporters desert a hopeless cause. By diplomacy and negotiation, he might yet avert the need for an invasion and the danger of losing the treasure.

In the meantime, things had not been going well for Antony. On leaving the Peloponnese after the flight from Actium, he had separated from Cleopatra and sailed to Cyrenaica to join the four legions of Pinarius Scarpus. But Scarpus had already heard the news of the battle and persuaded his men to declare for Octavian. Antony could do nothing. He made his way to Alexandria, where Cleopatra had put a brave face on her arrival and promptly arrested and executed the most important of the nobility she knew still opposed her. Q. Didius, the governor of Syria, went over to Octavian, and used his legions to prevent the gladiators who had broken out of their barracks at Cyzicus from passing through his province and offering their services to Antony. In this Didius was assisted by Herod, who was not slow to seize a chance of doing a service to the new master of the east. Antony sent Alexas, one of his friends, to try to stop Herod deserting him, but without effect. Herod went to meet Octavian on Rhodes and was gladly accepted as an ally and confirmed on his throne. Octavian had little choice, as Herod had taken the precaution of putting to death old Hyrcanus, his only plausible rival for the kingship.

Antony and Cleopatra wavered between thoughts of flight and resistance. Antony was depressed, inactive, and solitary, brooding like Timon of Athens in his seaside villa and barely roused by the news that gladiators at least were still loyal to him. Minor princes who had once been allies refused their aid, though the Egyptians themselves remained faithful to their queen. Cleopatra had some ships hauled from the Nile over to the Red Sea, so that they could escape to the Arabian Gulf or to India, but her enemy Malchus, king of Nabataea, attacked and burnt them. Spain was suggested as a possible refuge. It had served Sertorius and Sextus Pompey well enough in the past; but Antony lacked the personal ties with the province that those two representatives of a defeated party had enjoyed, and the Queen of Egypt, once again, might prove an incubus. The only practical course was to negotiate, and prepare to fight. They gathered more ships, men, and cavalry. They encouraged the Alexandrians by enrolling Caesarion, who was sixteen or seventeen, and Antony's son Antyllus, who was a couple of years younger, amongst the youths of military age. At the same time an embassy went to Octavian: Cleopatra was willing to resign the throne, if Octavian would agree to place one of her children upon it. Antony is also supposed to have asked for his life and a quiet retirement in Greece; this is barely credible and is probably a story put about to cast a posthumous slur on his manhood. Negotiations continued, with further exchanges of envoys, but they came to nothing and the truth about them is lost for ever in a fog of romance and propaganda.

Hardly before full summer, Octavian moved against Egypt, taking the land route through Syria and Judaea, where he and his entourage were lavishly entertained by a grateful Herod. From the west, Cornelius Gallus advanced through Cyrenaica. He united with the legions of Scarpus, and seized the port of Paraetonium. Antony marched against him with a substantial force and the faint hope that he might manage to win his men over again, for they were his own veterans. His attempts at oratory outside the walls of the town were thwarted by Gallus, who ordered his trumpeters to maintain a steady blare and drown the insidious words. Antony had no better luck with more conventional military manoeuvres and was compelled to withdraw with the loss of a number of ships. Meanwhile Octavian had reached Pelusium, the eastern gateway to Egypt, and taken it from Cleopatra's general Seleucus. Antony hastened back to defend Alexandria. He fell on Octavian's cavalry as, tired from the day's advance, they reached the outskirts of the city, and put them to flight. Once again he tried to subvert the legionaries, by shooting arrows into their camp carrying promises of 6,000 sesterces per head if they would desert. But it was not his ability to pay that they doubted, merely his ability to win.

The decisive engagement took place on August 1, 30 B.C. It was a fiasco, though that did not prevent it later becoming a public holiday 'because' (as the official calendars have it) 'on that day Imperator Caesar freed the state from grimmest peril'. Antony's fleet sailed out to engage the enemy, and at the same time he drew up his infantry and cavalry in battle order on land. The fleet, possibly on Cleopatra's own instructions, much more probably on those of her naval commanders who saw a chance to save their skins and ingratiate themselves with the winning side, raised its oars and surrendered without a fight. The cavalry deserted, the infantry were defeated. Antony, hearing that Cleopatra had killed herself, ordered his servant Eros to kill him too. But Eros turned the blade upon himself and Antony shamed by his example drove his sword into his own stomach.

The wound was not immediately fatal. As Antony lay dying, he was told that Cleopatra was still alive. Anticipating the result of the battle, she had gone to her mausoleum and shut the door, which was designed never to be opened again. In the mausoleum were all the most valuable of her treasures, heaped round with firewood—her last bargaining counter. In spite of the sealed door, it was still possible to enter, for the building was unfinished and a kind of window remained open in the upper part. Antony begged his slaves to carry him to her, and with great effort Cleopatra and her two waiting-women pulled him up by means of ropes. He died in her arms, bloodstained and racked with pain, but not before he had time to ask for a glass of wine and commend Octavian's friend C. Proculeius to her. He bade her not mourn too much for him, for he had achieved great things and met his match only in another Roman. His nobility remained with him to the end, the quality which had undone him; as Appian puts it, 'His thought and spirit were ever direct and lofty and without malice.'

Not long afterwards, Proculeius arrived. Octavian had occupied the city and heard of Cleopatra's flight to the mausoleum and Antony's suicide. He was anxious about the treasure, and wanted to separate Cleopatra from it. It is also alleged that he wished to take Cleopatra alive, but his subsequent behaviour gives the lie to this story. For the moment, though, Cleopatra refused to surrender herself to Proculeius, and he departed, to return with Cornelius Gallus, an envoy sufficiently important to conduct a queen. While Gallus detained Cleopatra in negotiation at the door of the tomb, Proculeius and a freedman put a ladder up to the window, climbed in, and seized the queen and her two women before they could set fire to the treasure.

The treasure safe, Octavian set about encouraging Cleopatra to suicide. She was something of an embarrassment to him. Certainly, he could lead her in triumph through the streets of Rome; but if he afterwards executed her as was the old Roman custom, this would seem an act of barbarous cruelty. Yet what else could he do with her? Exile her to some barren islet, perhaps; but even then he would have to ensure, somehow, that her version of the war of Actium never reached the world. No, she would be safest dead. He allowed her to embalm the body of her lover, then transferred her to the palace. An interview took place, in the course of which she is said (naturally) to have tried to seduce him, an attempt which he (naturally) resisted. Whatever her entreaties were, for her life, her children, even perhaps her death, he refused them and left her with little doubt that she was to be paraded a captive before the Roman mob. Still she did not take her own life, even though he had left her her own attendants. August wore on. Growing impatient, he allowed her to discover that in three days' time he intended to set off through Syria, taking her and the children with him. This convinced her that she could expect no mercy, and she arranged for an asp to be brought in to her, concealed in a basket of figs (or in a water-jar, according to other accounts). She provoked the reptile with a spindle until it sank its fangs into her bared arm, and so she died, deified, as the Egyptians believed, by the bite of the creature that was the minister of the sun-god and had reared its protective head for millennia upon the crown of the monarchs of Egypt. Her two serving-women chose to die with her, and when the guards broke in upon them they found Iras dead at Cleopatra's feet and Charmion still weakly trying to adjust the diadem around her mistress's brow. 'A fine deed, Charmion,' one of them exclaimed. 'Yes, very fine,' she said: 'she was descended from many kings,' and fell dead herself.

Cleopatra was granted her last wish, to be buried beside Antony. Antyllus and Caesarion were both put to death, Antyllus dragged from sanctuary at the shrine that Cleopatra had erected to his father, Caesarion caught as he attempted to flee to the Red Sea. The other children were spared. Too young to understand, they would serve to advertise Octavian's mercy. Cleopatra Selene was betrothed to Juba the Numidian, to whom Octavian later gave the province of Mauretania to be his kingdom. The two boys, Alexander Helios and little Ptolemy Philadelphus, are lost to history, though Alexander walked with his sister in Octavian's triumph. Antony's remaining children, Iullus Antonius and his two daughters by Octavia, had stayed with Octavia ever since their father had departed from Italy in 37 and were absolved from any taint of his guilt. Of Antony's supporters, three at least were killed: the inflexible Canidius Crassus, and the last two surviving assassins of Caesar, D. Turullius and Cassius of Parma. Octavian consented to spare Sosius, who had been found in hiding after Actium, though L. Arruntius had to exert all his old-fashioned gravity and strength of character to persuade him to do so.

The spoil of Alexandria at last released Octavian from bondage to his soldiers. He augmented the treasure of the Ptolemies by fines and confiscations exacted from the wealthy citizens and by the sacred offerings which Cleopatra was alleged to have snatched from the temples. Octavian paid his troops all that he had promised them, and an additional thousand sesterces a head as compensation for not being allowed to pillage the city. In Rome, the joyful news was announced by the consul—none other than Cicero's son, who should have been more than satisfied to proclaim the death of Antony, to whose rancour his father was held to have been sacrificed. Horace produced an ode succinctly embodying the whole Caesarian mythology about Cleopatra, from her insane designs on Rome to her proud death that cheated the conqueror's triumph of a captive queen.

Octavian himself wintered in Asia, putting the finishing touches to his arrangements for the eastern provinces and client-kingdoms. Egypt was too strong and too wealthy to be left to tempt a senatorial governor with delusions of grandeur and power. He appropriated it for himself, and governed it through personal representatives who owed their station and advancement to his favour alone. Cornelius Gallus became the first, soon to pay with his life for a gesture of independence that his master judged out of place. Antony's only two real 'gifts' of Roman territory to the house of Cleopatra, namely Cyprus and Cyrene, became Roman provinces again. To Artavasdes of Media Octavian restored his daughter Iotape; he also granted him Lesser Armenia, thus ensuring that the Median would incur the continued hostility of Artaxes of Armenia, and minimizing the chances of an anti-Roman coalition on the eastern borders of the empire. Artaxes he otherwise ignored, in spite of the massacre of Roman citizens which had taken place in the winter of 31–30, like-wise Phraates of Parthia. He had guarantees for the good behaviour of both—Artaxes's younger brothers, captured in 34 by Antony, and Tiridates, the fugitive pretender to the Parthian throne, whom he allowed to live in Syria. If dynastic insecurity failed to keep the kings in check, then Polemo, Artavasdes, and the legions of Syria could be relied upon to hold the eastern frontier.

At Actium he built on the ancient site a new temple to Apollo, on the low point where Antony's camp had been, and near it set up a novel monument of his victory, a ten-ship trophy. This perhaps consisted of one ship from each of the classes of Antony's fleet, but it was burnt down so soon that not even Strabo, who was collecting geographical material on this coast within a few years of the battle, could describe it. On the northern promontory, where his own tent had stood, he erected a unique dedication: a massive wall built of squared stone and adorned with the rams of captured ships held back the hillside from a terrace in front, where stood an open-air shrine to Apollo. The traveller who climbs the hill of Mikhalitzi can still see the fallen blocks bearing fragments of the inscribed dedication, and the grey limestone wall with its inset row of oddly-shaped apertures, like huge inverted keyholes, where the prows were once fixed. The most grandiose memorial to the victory, however, was the new city of Nicopolis ('Victory-town'). This was an artificial creation, formed by transferring to the excellent site on the level between Mikhalitzi and

Preveza the population of a number of cities in the neighbourhood of the Ambracian Gulf. The forced union was successful—the imperial government could hardly allow it to fail—and Nicopolis prospered well into Byzantine times.

Octavian arrived back in Italy about the middle of 29 B.C., suffering from another of his chronic attacks of ill-health. He spent a little time convalescing in the south before he finally made his triumphant entry to the city of Rome. The entire population, including even his fellow-consul Valerius Messalla Potitus, offered sacrifice for him, though he did not permit to be put into effect a decree of the senate which ordered every inhabitant of the city to go out and meet him. Spontaneous demonstrations were no less impressive, and more desirable. Honours of every sort were showered upon him. On August 13, 14, and 15 he celebrated a splendid triple triumph. First came the deferred Dalmatian triumph, then the Actian, and finally the Alexandrian. The last, as was only fitting, was the most magnificent. It was notable not only for the splendour and quantity of the spoils displayed in the procession, but also for the effigy of the dead Cleopatra lying on her couch with the asp clinging to her arm. Gifts were made to the soldiers, and a hundred denarii each distributed to all adult males. The same sum was later given to boys as well, in the name of Octavian's nephew, and only near male relative, the thirteen-year-old Marcellus. The victor cancelled debts owed to him, and sent back to the municipalities of Italy the money they had contributed for the triumph—money that had in the past been used to provide gold crowns to be carried in the triumphal procession, but had now become tribute in disguise. So much money, in fact, was injected into the economy by the spoil of Egypt that prices at once rose and the standard rate of interest dropped from twelve to four per cent. Octavian was also able to buy up land in order to redeem his long-deferred pledges to his veterans, and in the years following Actium he managed to settle some 50,000–75,000 men without provoking unrest.

Chapter XVIII

AUGUSTUS

THUS OCTAVIAN emerged as sole ruler of the Roman world, in theory the man chosen by the people of Rome and Italy to save them from a foreign queen and their own degenerate general, in fact the leader of a revolutionary party which concealed its true nature behind conventional slogans. The basis of Octavian's power was the army, the pretext for its employment the national danger. Now that the danger had been averted and there were no further foes to conjure with—save the Parthians, a hornet's nest not worth disturbing—some constitutional framework had to be found within which Octavian could continue to exercise the power he had struggled so long to obtain. His temperament and the needs of Rome alike made it unthinkable that he should resign that power. Ambition had not died overnight amongst the upper classes of Rome, and where Sulla, Caesar, and he himself had shown the way, it was certain that another would soon set out to tread the same path. The traditions of Rome, which allowed self-aggrandisement to be an acceptable goal of political action, led inescapably to monarchy. To restore the republic, in the sense that the Liberators intended when they sank their daggers into Caesar, meant entrusting the destinies, not merely of Italy, but of the greater part of the Mediterranean world, to the capricious play of factional politics amongst a few dozen members of the Roman oligarchy. This was undesirable, irresponsible, and in fact impossible. The brief play of republican-style politics between March and September 44 had shown that. The army and the Italians had become a factor in the political life of Rome that proved, to the discomfort of the Roman governing class, that their city was in truth the capital of Italy.

Caesar's solution to the problem had been characteristically direct. The constitution offered, in the dictatorship, an office of absolute power, with certain temporal limitations. He abolished the limitations, and used the office as the vehicle of autocratic rule. A logical procedure, but not subtle enough for a state with a long tradition of political freedom. Octavian had to steer, somehow, between the Charybdis of renewed anarchy and the Scylla of unconcealed despotism. In this, he had one advantage denied to Caesar. Twenty years of civil strife, punctuated by brief intervals of uneasy calm, had left the Romans profoundly war-weary and more convinced of the blessings of peace than of 'freedom'. The same twenty years had carried away a whole generation of politicians, men who understood, even if they did not sympathize with, the motives of Brutus and Cassius. Tacitus, writing of the situation in A.D. 14 when Tiberius succeeded to his stepfather in monarchical fashion, put the celebrated question, 'Who was there left who could have known the Republic?' Even the old men, he says had been born during the civil wars. Already by 29 B.C. this process of the obliteration of the historical memory had begun. For twenty years law and precedent had been ignored and flouted. Any move in the direction of constitutional legality, however specious, would be welcome. Such a move, in any case, became more and more necessary as time went on and all aspects of life returned to normal.

By the end of 28 the immediate tasks of resettlement and reorganization were completed and Octavian felt ready to act. On January 13, 27 B.C., he announced to the senate, which had by now been purged by himself and Agrippa of its vast accretion of unworthy members, that he wished to resign the special powers that he had continued to exercise after the defeat of Antony and to restore the traditional basis of government. In his own words: 'In my sixth and seventh consulships, when I had put an end to the civil wars, having acquired supreme power over the empire by universal consent, I transferred the Republic from my authority to the free disposal of the Senate and People of Rome.'

No doubt the sequel was carefully staged, but we need not for that reason deny all sincerity to the participants. Octavian's speech was greeted with cries of protest and dismay: was the saviour about to abandon his cherished flock? With a show of reluctance, Octavian agreed to retain his consulship, and to take special responsibility for certain provinces, namely Gaul, Spain, and Syria. These happened to contain the overwhelming proportion of the legions retained on permanent service. He was responsible to the senate and people for the administration of these provinces, exactly as any republican proconsul had been. Not so strictly republican was the provision by which he was allowed to appoint deputies with full powers, so that he could stay in Rome, freed from the necessity of exercising his authority in person. None the less, there were precedents for this in the Late Republic, and it was possible to represent the whole arrangement as being essentially a return to republican practices. It would have been tactless to draw attention to the fact that twenty-three out of twenty-six legions were concentrated under the control of one man.

Octavian's special connection with the army was thus given constitutional shape. His parallel claim to be the patron of the Roman people had already been acknowledged, after the capture of Alexandria, when the powers and privileges of a tribune of the people had been conferred upon him. He had possessed the personal inviolability of a tribune since 36. That had been more a mark of esteem for the son of a god than a token of a political relationship. The grant of the other powers symbolized his status as protector and champion of the common people and gave some kind of tangible expression to the bond of clientship which united the people of Rome and their first emperor. One of the most important of the original functions of the tribunes, when that office had been instituted in the founding century of the republic, was to render assistance to the individual and protect him from the arbitrary actions of the upper-class magistrates. This power, though seldom invoked now, remained emotionally potent. That Octavian possessed it, expressed something fundamental about his position. The tribunate also conferred more solid and administratively useful powers, such as the right to propose legislation, but these were largely gratuitous while Octavian continued to be consul.

So Octavian emerged from the 'restoration of the republic' as consul, proconsul, and tribune, though in the case of the two last he had partially or entirely separated the powers of the office from its tenure. Individually, as he himself stated, he held (in theory) no more constitutional power than any of his colleagues. In sum the cumulation was unique and despotic, little veiled by his pretence that he was simply the first citizen, or *princeps*. A final varnish was laid on this mock-republican picture three days later. Octavian required a title, if only to distinguish him from his great-uncle. That title had to be worthy of the second founder of Rome. 'Romulus', which some thought suitable, was embarrassingly monarchical in its associations, but Plancus, as ever, had the right answer. There was a famous line of the early poet Ennius, telling how Romulus, 'By august omen founded the city of Rome' (*Augusto augurio postquam incluta condita Roma est*).

The adjective was propitious and hinted at superhuman greatness, yet embodied nothing that could offend a republican ear. And so the new ruler became Augustus—as did the month which had seen him both enter his first consulship and put an end to the civil wars. The gateposts of his house were decked with laurel, the victor's emblem; above the door was placed a wreath of oak-leaves, the decoration awarded to a soldier who had saved a comrade's life in battle; and in the senate-house a golden shield was set up, whose inscription announced his four prime virtues—courage, mercy, justice, and piety.

The first constitutional settlement, in the event, needed to be modified. We hear all too little of the opposition to the régime—for opposition there certainly was. But it is not in the nature of totalitarian states to publicize disharmony. Only in 23 B.C. do we get any real glimpse of the tensions and personal rivalries that underlay the apparently tranquil surface of the restored Republic: Augustus, gravely ill, his extra-constitutional authority challenged, found it necessary to invent a 'plot' to dispose of the challenger, who was no less a person than his fellow-consul. At the same time Agrippa made it clear that he would not willingly yield second place to Augustus's young nephew Marcellus, who was already being groomed for the succession. The crisis passed. Augustus recovered, Agrippa gained his point, and it was twenty years before another consular needed to be executed—ironically, Antony's younger son Iullus, reared by Octavia and held by the Princeps in equal affection and favour with his own stepchildren.

None the less, it was evident that the system of control devised in 27 had to be improved. One flaw was that Augustus, as consul, had a colleague whose powers, at least in Rome and Italy, were constitutionally equal to his own. Another disadvantage of his permanent occupation of one consulship was that he halved the opportunities for other men to reach it; and even under this new sort of a republic the consulship was still the crown of a political career. For both these reasons, Augustus refused to hold the office any longer, in spite of the violent efforts of the Roman plebs to make him do so. Only in 5 and 2 B.C. did he emerge from 'retirement' to honour his grandsons by becoming their colleague in the chief magistracy of the state. This apparent abdication of formal authority was of no serious constitutional importance. Thanks to the tribunician powers granted him in 30, Augustus already possessed much of the legal competence necessary to enable him to conduct formal matters of state. The parti-

cular powers that he still lacked were voted to him in the course of
the immediately succeeding years. As for the provinces which were
not specifically entrusted to him to administer, but remained in the
charge of senatorial governors, he acquired good warrant to interfere in their affairs. The executive power (*imperium*) which he possessed was enhanced and extended so that he now had legal authority to
override their governors, and this augmented *imperium* (termed
maius, superior) was conferred on him for life.

Thus Augustus in fact tightened his grip on the state; at the same
time he avoided the charge that he was perverting any republican
magistracy by using it to secure his personal supremacy. He had
skilfully built himself a base for his illegally won but now unchallengeable dominance. He had needed to create no new constitutional
powers, but the position he now held was in effect new. It lay outside
the constricted and battle-scarred field on which the savage political
struggles of the Late Republic had been fought. Augustus held no
office. By resigning the consulship, and being compensated later by
the grant of some of its privileges, Augustus completed the process
begun in 36 when he was granted the sacrosanctity of a tribune. He
eventually held all the powers of the major republican offices, freed
of the two checks to which they had been subject: his tenure was not
limited in time, nor did he have an equal colleague endowed with a
veto or other means of constitutional obstruction. His position was
related to and derived from good republican institutions, but placed
him above and outside the framework of the traditional magistracies
—of which Velleius, giving the official view, could say that they had
been 'restored to their ancestral competence'. In keeping with this
necessary pretence, Augustus counted the years of his reign after 23
by the number of years that he had held the tribunician power—the
'label of supremacy' as Tacitus was later to call it. It was wise to
emphasize the link with the Roman people and the defence of their
liberties (though hardly their liberty), and keep discreetly in the
background the true, military basis of the imperial power.

In building an acceptable and secure foundation for his monarchy
Augustus succeeded brilliantly. It was otherwise with the problem
of the succession. The republic recognized no hereditary right to
power. The members of certain great families might have looked
upon the consulship as their birthright, but they had first to prove
themselves and demonstrate to the Roman people that they were
fit to hold the highest magistracy. The consulship, in any case, was
merely the anteroom of power; real power was wielded by the elder

statesmen who had once held that office. Oligarchic politics, in fact, resisted the claim of any one family to monopolize power and invariably produced a counter-grouping capable of shattering such pretensions. Augustus was the first man in the history of Rome not to be thus shattered by a coalition of his enemies (if one excepts Sulla who abdicated voluntarily). His problem now was to ensure that the power he had attained and held could pass smoothly to a successor. If he failed, the Roman world would again know the horrors of civil war.

The difficulty was that, in theory, the problem did not exist. Augustus was simply the Princeps, the first citizen who had by his outstanding services deserved a place of unusual prominence and honour. All around him, honest, loyal, and competent men continued to make the state function as it always had. If Augustus were to die, the only visible gap in the administrative machinery of the state would be among the provincial governorships; and even here the gap would be more technical than real, since Augustus's legates, the deputies he appointed to govern each of his provinces, needed only to have their authority confirmed by the senate. According to the proclaimed ideal of the restored republic, there should be no need for another Princeps. In fact, as everyone knew very well, the restored republic could not do without one. What Augustus had to do was to pick a man capable both of ruling and of being made acceptable to the army and the people as his successor.

His thinking on this point was incurably dynastic. He did once look beyond the members of his immediate family, to Agrippa. But he had very little choice under the circumstances. In the crisis of 23 B.C. the opinion was current that, if Augustus died, Agrippa would not long let young Marcellus enjoy the power the Princeps wished him to inherit. Augustus evidently thought so too. When he recovered, he gave Agrippa an enhanced *imperium* inferior only to his own; this meant that his death would leave Agrippa, in constitutional theory as well as in fact, the most powerful man in the state. As it happened, Marcellus died in the following year, thus saving Augustus some embarrassment. His seventeen-year-old widow, Augustus's only child Julia, was transferred to Agrippa. Son-in-law and heir-presumptive, Agrippa was later granted the tribunician power; he became a deputy Caesar in all but name. Perhaps he scorned adoption, confident in his own qualities and well aware that Augustus owed as much to him as he to Augustus. But after his death in 12 B.C., his successors as imperial heirs, his own eldest son

Gaius and Augustus's stepson Tiberius, were in turn adopted by the Princeps and became the only bearers (apart from the Princeps) of the potent name of Caesar.

It was natural for Augustus to think in this way. He owed his own success to the accident of adoption, and republican politics stressed above all the achievements and reputation of the family to which one belonged. Glory won by an individual increased the prestige of a family, and friends and clients were inherited just like money and estates. Whatever the constitutional façade he might erect, Augustus's power rested on the personal loyalty of the armies bolstered by the support of the people of Rome. These were his clients, on a scale that was undreamt of even at the very end of the Republic, but implicit in the political fabric of the Roman state. The escalating struggle for personal supremacy had merely pushed to an extreme a tendency which had always existed, until in the end one man emerged as the patron *par excellence*. Augustus had inherited this vast *clientela*, in embryonic form, from Julius Caesar; he had nurtured, increased, and transformed it until it was the basis of an unchallengeable power. What he had acquired with a name, he intended to pass on with a name. It is doubtful, in any case, whether he could have done otherwise, for the plebs and the armies shared his preconceptions about the nature and inheritability of political loyalty. Like their ruler, they had been brought up within a framework of social attitudes common to all Italy, and they expected as a matter of course to transfer their allegiance to his heirs and descendants.

Support of this kind was proof against any coup. Augustus's government, like any other, depended on the men who operated it; but none of them could think of challenging the Princeps for first place. Hence Agrippa's lifelong service to a man who was in some ways his inferior. Even from its earliest days, the revolutionary party had possessed but one head. What may have gone on in the inner councils of the party, then and later, is another matter. There may have been men around Augustus who were subtler politicians and wiser strategists than their leader, but if so, the world knew nothing of them. Without him and his Caesarian charisma, their abilities were wasted. This is not to belittle Augustus. He had the supreme genius of knowing how to turn other men to his own purposes. His supporters came from both inside and outside the old senatorial aristocracy, and the composition of his following is a sufficient testimony to his ability to unite old and new. He was able to create a revised form of government whose highest posts were more open to men of talent and whose concern was more for the interests of the governed than had been the case under the republic.

'All Italy' gradually became a reality, and though the Roman state remained in essence an oligarchy, it was an oligarchy more broadly based and less furiously compietitve than before. The highest prizes had been pre-empted. The Princeps monopolized military glory and stood supreme at home. Not the least of Augustus's contributions to the stability of Rome in the next two centuries was to debilitate the ancient tradition whereby military achievement was the high road to success in public life. But his supreme feat was undoubtedly to put real political power beyond reach of competition. In its place, he had to rebuild the idea of a Rome that was worth serving, since it could no longer be dominated. This was in fact the ideal which had sustained the early and middle years of the republic: hence Augustus's programmes of moral and religious reform, which should not be too cynically dismissed as the window-dressing of an astute autocrat; hence the new official art, which emphasizes the power, magnificence, and civilizing qualities of Rome; hence the literature, and in particular the works of Virgil and Livy, which stresses the greatness of Rome and her divine destiny to rule the world. Peace, prosperity, and justice were the noble, if unexciting, objectives of Augustus's mature years. In large measure he achieved them, and for all the unpleasant nature of his rise to power, his rule brought nothing but good to the millions of ordinary citizens of the Roman world. The ancient aristocracy of the city of Rome, their power shattered, passed away—not in Augustus's lifetime, but very shortly afterwards. It might be said that they had extinguished themselves. They paid the price of not adapting their ideals and values to a changing environment. Italy could produce more able and more vigorous men to govern empire.

In what sense, then, was Actium a turning point? It was a turning point in that it brought the completion of a process of historical change whose origins lay at least a hundred years in the past. In these terms, the result of the battle hardly mattered. Its significance was chronological: it marked the beginning of the Roman Empire. If Antony had won, and won not merely the battle but the whole campaign, he would have found himself in much the same position as Octavian after the fall of Alexandria, but with grave disadvantages. The problems that faced Octavian of settling the soldiers and restoring some sort of constitutional government would have been more difficult for Antony, associated as he was with Cleopatra and the east, and lacking the fabulous wealth of a captured treasury. But assuming that he could have overcome these difficulties, it is hard to see how he could have arrived at a permanent solution very different from that of Augustus. Antony might, of course, have abandoned Rome and the west; but the strength of Italy and the history of Rome's relations with the east were such that he can hardly have expected ambitious Romans to acquiesce for long in such an arrangement. If he tried to set himself up as a Hellenistic monarch in Alexandria, he would soon be challenged again. He was well aware that the legions of Rome were the finest fighting force of the Mediterranean world. To try to hold power without them was folly. To see him, then, as standing for a Hellenistic-monarchic principle, and Octavian for its antithesis, is false; it was simply that the west refused and the east demanded the trappings of kingship in its rulers.

The true cause of the civil wars lay in the social and economic troubles of the Italian peninsula. If Antony had failed to satisfy the fundamental needs of the soldiery and of Italy as a whole, sooner or later there would have been fresh unrest and a new revolutionary leader. A real restoration of the republic was impossible, as Antony knew from his own experiences in 44. In so far as he represented any genuine republican elements at Actium, the whole tide of historical development was against him. It was fitting that he lost, and easier for the Roman world that he did so, although he was the more noble and the more open of the two antagonists. The best epitaph of the battle is the family tree of the Julio-Claudian dynasty founded by the victor. In it the blood of Antony, Octavian, and Agrippa is inextricably intertwined.

ROMAN NOMENCLATURE

EVERY ROMAN citizen had a forename (*praenomen*) and family name (*gentilicium* or simply *nomen*). There were a very limited number of forenames and for each there was a recognized abbreviation (see list below). In addition, very many men had a third or distinguishing name (*cognomen*) which had originated as a nickname. This the possessor might have acquired himself or have inherited from previous generations. In some cases this third name was possessed by a group so large that second and even third *cognomina* came into use. Thus the ancient clan of the Cornelii included both Cornelii Scipiones and Cornelii Lentuli, each so numerous that the cognomen no longer served its proper distinguishing function. Thus we find P. Cornelius Scipio Africanus and even P. Cornelius Scipio Nasica Serapio. These second *cognomina* were in fact rarely inherited, except in the case of such famous sub-clans.

In everyday reference, as in Cicero's letters, a man was generally called either by his *nomen* or by his *cognomen*, e.g. Cn. Pompeius Magnus was known as Pompeius, C. Julius Caesar as Caesar. The *praenomen* was used in conjunction with one of these to avoid confusion, e.g. L. Caesar to denote Antony's uncle. Occasionally the *praenomen* was used by itself where the context (or the uniqueness of the *praenomen*) made the reference unambiguous.

The short form of formal reference was by *praenomen* and either *nomen* or *cognomen*, depending on which was generally used for the man in question; the latter combination is practically restricted to the nobility. The full form, never used except in official documents, gave the father's and sometimes the grandfather's *praenomen* before the *cognomen*. Thus Cicero's name in full was M(arcus) Tullius M(arci) f(ilius) M(arci) n(epos) Cicero.

Adoption was common among the Roman aristocracy. In this case the adopted person took the three names of the adopter and added either an adjectival form of his own family name (e.g. C. Julius Caesar

Octavianus) or a *cognomen* belonging to his own family (e.g. Q. Servilius Caepio Brutus, better known under his original name of M. Junius Brutus).

Freedmen acquired citizenship along with their freedom, and thus required names in Roman form. The practice was for a freedman to take the *gentilicium* of his patron (his former owner) and retain his own personal name as a *cognomen*; he might preface these with any *praenomen* he liked, often that of his patron: thus C. Julius Demetrias who was a Greek freedman of Caesar's. The same custom was followed by non-Italians enfranchised for any reason, for example Orientals given the citizenship in order to qualify them for service in the legions (see pp. 107 and 188).

Women were known simply by the feminine form of their family name. Fulvia had no other names. The very late Republic saw the beginning of feminine *cognomina*, e.g. Cassius's wife was Junia Tertia-Octavian's Livia Drusilla, and this practice developed further under the Empire, particularly amongst the womenfolk of the imperial house.

Praenomina (excluding very rare and exotic examples)

A.	Aulus
Appius	(confined to Claudii Pulchri)
* C.	Gaius
* Cn.	Gnaeus
D.	Decimus
L.	Lucius
Mam.	Mamercus (?confined to Aemilii)
M.	Marcus
M'.	Manius
P.	Publius
Paullus	(confined to Aemilii)
Q.	Quintus
Ser.	Servius (virtually confined to Sulpicii)
Sex.	Sextus
Sp.	Spurius
T.	Titus
Ti.	Tiberius

* The old Roman alphabet did not possess a separate letter G and used C to represent both the voiced and the unvoiced sound. Later, when G had been adopted, the old abbreviations were still retained for Gaius and Gnaeus.

SELECT BIBLIOGRAPHY

I. THE SOURCES

Apart from the principal written sources dealing specifically with the period (listed below), there are scattered items of information to be gleaned from the works of a large number of ancient writers. The picture thus built up can be supplemented and corrected by the evidence of contemporary coins and inscriptions. For an introduction to the latter see J. E. Sandys *Latin Epigraphy*, 2nd edn. rev. by S. G. Campbell, Cambridge, 1927 or R. Bloch *L'Epigraphie Latine*, Paris, 1952; for the coin evidence the standard work is E. A. Sydenham *The Roman Republican Coinage*, London, 1952. For a full discussion of the sources see *Cambridge Ancient History*, vol. 10, pp. 866–76. The following brief notes cover the most important of the ancient writers who touch on the events with which this book is concerned.

(a) *Narrative.*

Appian (Appianos, c. A.D. 90–160), an Alexandrian who entered the imperial civil service, wrote in Greek a history of the Civil Wars. The murder of Caesar closes Book II, and Books III–V cover events down to the death of Sextus Pompey in 35. Appian's is the fullest and best of the ancient accounts. His sources remain unidentified, though E. Gabba (*Appiano*, Florence, 1956) has tried to show that he depends very substantially on the lost history of this period written by Asinius Pollio.

Dio (Cassius Dio Cocceianus, c. A.D. 163–230 or later) from Nicaea in Bithynia, senator and twice consul, wrote in Greek a complete history of Rome down to his own times, of which the books relating to this period survive complete (XLIV–LI). He is briefer, less precise, and more rhetorical than Appian. See F. G. Millar *A Study of Cassius Dio*, Oxford, 1964.

Velleius (C. Velleius Paterculus, c. 19 B.C.–after A.D. 31) of

248

Campanian descent, senator and praetor, wrote in Latin a brief sketch of Roman history from the origins to A.D. 30, taking an extreme pro-Augustan viewpoint.

Josephus (T ? Flavius Josephus, 37/8–after A.D. 98), an aristocrat of the Jewish priesthood who was pro-Roman, wrote in Greek on the history of the Jews (*Antiquitates Judaicae*) and on the Jewish War of A.D. 66–70 (*de Bello Judaico*). Valuable for Antony in the east.

[The great history of *Livy* (T. Livius, 59 B.C.–A.D. 17) of Patavium (Padua) survives for this period only in the epitome called the *Periochae* and indirectly in the work of later compilers of brief histories of Rome, such as Florus, Eutropius and Orosius.]

(b) *Biographical.*

Plutarch (Ploutarchos, c. A.D. 46–127), of Chaeronea in Greece, wrote in Greek, as part of his great series of parallel *Lives*, lives of Caesar, Cicero, Brutus, and Antony. These are, historically speaking, unsystematic, and their accuracy is very variable.

Suetonius (C. Suetonius Tranquillus, c. A.D. 69–140), grammarian, and secretary for a short time to the emperor Hadrian, wrote in Latin on the twelve Caesars from Julius to Domitian. These 'lives' are portraits, not biographies in the modern sense, but contain a great deal of information drawn from excellent sources, particularly in the case of Augustus in whom Suetonius seems to have been very interested.

Nicolaus of Damascus (c. 64 B.C.–?c. A.D. 5), court historian to Herod the Great, accompanied him to Rome and met Augustus personally. He wrote in Greek a Life of Augustus, drawing on the Princeps's own memoirs. For text see F. Jacoby *Fragmente der Griechischen Historiker* 90 F130; for text and translation C. M. Hall *Nicolaus of Damascus's Life of Augustus*, Northampton, Mass., 1923.

Augustus himself left a brief list of his achievements which was engraved on two bronze tablets set in front of his mausoleum in Rome. Copies of this inscription were erected elsewhere in the empire, and that from Ancyra in Asia Minor has survived almost complete. It is known either as the *Monumentum Ancyranum* (from the place of its finding) or as the *Res Gestae*. For the Latin text, translation and commentary, see P. A. Brunt and J. M. Moore *Res Gestae Divi Augusti*, London, 1967 (paperback).

(c) *Other.*

Cicero's letters, in particular those to his friend and adviser Atticus, were never intended for publication and are a historical source of the highest value. The fourteen speeches called already in Cicero's lifetime the *Philippics*, delivered between September 44 and April 43, are likewise unique contemporary evidence.

II. MODERN WORKS

The list is divided into two parts, the first containing works relevant to the book as a whole, the second material specifically relating to individual chapters. The chapter bibliographies also contain references for direct quotations in the text. In general, the works here listed are of three kinds: recent books designed for the non-specialist (indicated by an asterisk); fundamental studies; and specialist articles, mostly of recent date, dealing with particular points in the text. For Chapters XV and XVI the list is fuller, but still select; that on Chapter XVIII can only indicate some ways in to a vast subject.

(a) *General*

* BALSDON J. P. V. D. (ed.) *The Romans* (London, 1965)

BROUGHTON T. R. S. *The Magistrates of the Roman Republic*, 2v. (New York, 1951–2)

COOK S. A., ADCOCK F. E., and CHARLESWORTH M. P. (eds.) *Cambridge Ancient History*, vol. X (Cambridge, 1934) (reprinted from chs. I–IV of this is TARN W. W., and CHARLESWORTH M. P., *Octavian, Antony, and Cleopatra* (Cambridge, 1965)

* EARL D. C. *The Moral and Political Tradition of Rome* (London, 1967)

GRANT M. *From Imperium to Auctoritas* (Cambridge, 1946)

HADAS M. *Sextus Pompey* (New York, 1930)

LEVI M. A. *Ottaviano Capoparte*, 2v. (Florence, 1933)

* MCDONALD A. H. *Republican Rome* (London, 1966)

REINHOLD M. *Marcus Agrippa* (Geneva, N.Y., 1933)

SYME R. *The Roman Revolution* (Oxford, 1939)

* VOLKMANN H. *Cleopatra, a Study in Politics and Propaganda* (London, 1958)

The East

BUCHHEIM H. *Die Orientpolitik des Triumvirn M. Antonius* (Heidelberg, 1960)

JONES A. H. M. *The Cities of the Eastern Roman Provinces* (Oxford, 1937)

MAGIE D. *Roman Rule in Asia Minor*, 2v. (Princeton, 1950)

Social and Economic

BRUNT P. A. 'The equites in the late Republic' in *Trade and Politics in the Ancient World* (Second International Congress of Economic History, Aix-en-Provence, 1962) (Paris, 1965)

— 'The Roman mob' *Past and Present*, 1966, 3–27

FRANK T. *An Economic Survey of Ancient Rome, I : Rome and Italy of the Republic* (Baltimore, 1933)

TAYLOR L. R. 'Freedmen and freeborn in Imperial Rome', *AJP*, 1961, 113–32

YAVETZ Z. 'The living conditions of the urban plebs in Republican Rome', *Latomus*, 1958, 500–17

— *Plebs and Princeps* (Oxford, 1969)

The Army

BOTERMANN HELGA. *Die Soldaten und die Römische Politik in der Zeit von Caesars Tod bis zur Begründung des Zweiten Triumvirats* (Munich, 1968)

BRUNT P. A. 'The army and the land in the Roman revolution', *JRS*, 1962, 69–86

FORNI G. *Il Reclutamento delle Legioni da Augusto a Diocleziano* (Rome, 1953)

GABBA E. 'Ricerche sull' esercito professionale romano da Mario ad Augusto', *Athenaeum*, 1951, 171–272

PARKER H. M. D. *The Roman Legions* (London, 1928)

SCHMITTHENNER W. *The Armies of the Triumviral Period* (D. Phil. thesis, Oxford, 1958, unpublished)

SMITH R. E. *Service in the post-Marian Roman Army* (Manchester, 1958)

(b) *Chapter Bibliographies and References*

Chapter I

ALFÖLDI A. *Studien über Cäsars Monarchie* (Lund, 1953)

BALSDON J. P. V. D. 'The Ides of March', *Historia*, 1958, 80–94

* — *Julius Caesar and Rome* (London, 1967)

EHRENBERG V. 'Caesar's final aims', *HSCP*, 1964, 149–61

GELZER M. *Caesar, Politician and Statesman* (Oxford, 1968)

HEINEN H. 'Cäsar und Kaisarion', *Historia*, 1969, 181–203

p. 1   Plut., *Caes.*, 66
p. 2   Ovid, *Fasti*, 3. 525–6 and 531–2
p. 2   Suet., *Julius*, 80
p. 3   Suet., *Julius*, 80
p. 3   Suet., *Julius*, 80
p. 5   Suet., *Julius*, 77
p. 5   Cic., *ad Fam.*, 7. 30. 1–2
p. 5   Suet., *Julius*, 77
p. 6   Cic., *Phil.*, 2. 87
p. 7   Plut., *Brutus*, 10
p. 12 Nic. Dam., *Vita Aug.*, 25. 91–4

Chapter II

SCHMITTHENNER W. *Oktavian und das Testament Cäsars* (Munich, 1952)

p. 13 Appian, *BC*, 2.119
p. 18 Plut., *Ant.*, 14
p. 18 Cic., *ad Att.*, 14.14.2
p. 21 Cic., *ad Att.*, 14.10.1
p. 21 Pacuvius ap. Suet., *Julius*, 84
p. 25 Cic., *Phil.*, 2.91
p. 26 Cic., *ad Att.*, 14.3.2. and 14.8.1

Chapter III

p. 28 Suet., *Julius*, 83.2
p. 31 Cic., *ad Att.*, 14.12.2
p. 32 Vell., 2.60.2
p. 33 Cic., *ad Att.*, 14.16.2
p. 36 Cic., *ad Att.*, 15.11.1–3
p. 40 Cic., *ad Fam.*, 11.3.2

Chapter IV

FRISCH H. *Cicero's Fight for the Republic* (Copenhagen, 1946)
SMITH R. E. *Cicero the Statesman* (Cambridge, 1966)

p. 43 Cic., *ad Fam.*, 12.2.1
p. 43 Cic., *ad Fam.*, 10.2.1
p. 45 Cic., *ad Fam.*, 12.23.2
p. 49 Cic., *ad Att.*, 16.14.2
p. 50 App., *BC*, 3.42
p. 52 Cic., *Phil.*, 10.10
p. 53 App., *BC*, 3.46

Chapter V
p. 54 Cic., *ad Fam.*, 11.4.1–2
p. 55 Cic., *ad Fam.*, 11.5.2–3
p. 56 Cic., *Phil.*, 3.31
p. 57 Cic., *ad Fam.*, 11.7.2
p. 64 Cic., *Phil.*, 11.28
p. 69 Cic., *ad Fam.*, 10.30
p. 71 App., *BC*, 3.68

Chapter VI
BERCHEM D. VAN. 'La fuite de Decimus Brutus', *Mél. Carcopino*, 941–53
PERROCHAT P. 'La correspondance de Cicéron et de Munatius Plancus', *REL*, 1957, 172 ff.
WALSER G. *Der Briefwechsel des L. Munatius Plancus mit Cicero* (Basel, 1957)
p. 75 Cic., *ad Fam.*, 11.13.2
p. 84 Suet., *Aug.*, 26
p. 84 Cic., *Phil.*, 5.43

Chapter VII
CERFAUX L. and TONDRIAU J. *Le Culte des Souverains dans la Civilisation Gréco-Romaine* (Tournai, 1957)
p. 91 Syme, *Roman Revolution*, 190 n.6
p. 91 Pollio ap. Sen., *Suas.*, 6.24
p. 92 Vell., 2.67.4

Chapter VIII
BABCOCK, C. L. 'The early career of Fulvia', *AJP*, 1965, 1–32
GOODFELLOW, C. *Roman Citizenship* (Lancaster, Pa., 1935)
GILBOA, A. *Viritane Grants of Citizenship* (Diss., Jerusalem, 1958, with English summary)
JONES, G. D. B. 'Southern Etruria 50–40 B.C., an attack on Veii in 41 B.C.', *Latomus*, 1963, 773–6
p. 103 Vell., 2.74.3
p. 103 App., *BC*, 5.12
p. 105 (Virgil, *Eclogues*, 1 and 9)
       (Horace, *Epodes*, 7, cf. 16)
p. 105 App., *BC*, 5.17
p. 110 Sling-bullets: *CIL*, 11.6721
       Octavian's epigram: Martial, 11.20.3–8

Chapter IX

p. 113   Brutus's statue-base: *SEG*, 17.75
p. 113   Plut., *Ant.*, 23
p. 115   Shakespeare, *A. & C.*, II.2
p. 122   Vell., 2.76.4
p. 123   Virg., *Ecl.*, 4.3–17

Chapter X

COMBES R. *Imperator. Recherches sur l'emploi et la signification du titre d'Impérator dans la Rome républicaine* (Paris, 1966)
SYME R. 'Imperator Caesar, a study in nomenclature', *Historia*, 1958, 172–88
p. 138   App., *BC*, 5.92
p. 142   Suet., *Aug.*, 70 (both)

Chapter XI

PAGET R. F. 'The ancient ports of Cumae', *JRS*, 1968, 152–69
INSTINSKY H. U. 'Bemerkungen über die ersten Schenkungen des Antonius an Kleopatra', *Robinson Studies*, II, 975–9
MICHEL D. *Alexander als Vorbild für Pompeius, Caesar, und Marcus Antonius, Archäologische Untersuchungen* (Brussels, 1967)
CERFAUX-TONDRIAU (see under ch. VII above)
p. 154   Plut., *Ant.*, 36

Chapter XII

KROMAYER J. 'Kleine Forschungen . . . VI: Die Vorgeschichte des Krieges von Actium', *Hermes*, 1898, 13–70
SCMITTHENNER W. 'Octavians militarische Unternehmungen in den Jahren 35–33 v. Chr.', *Historia*, 1958, 189–236
p. 165   Plut., *Ant.*, 43
p. 168   Tarn, *CAH*, 10.77
p. 170   App., *BC*, 5.132
p. 170   Virg., *Georgics*, 2.493–502

Chapter XIII

KRAFT K. 'Zu Sueton, Divus Augustus 69.2: M. Anton und Kleopatra', *Hermes*, 1967, 496–9
p. 175   Dio., 49.40.3 (both)
p. 177   Suet., *Aug.*, 69
p. 179   Plut., *Ant.*, 55

p. 182 *Orac. Sibyll.*, 3. 350–61, 367–80
p. 184 Suet., *Aug.*, 69

Chapter XIV

CROOK J. A. 'A legal point about Mark Antony's will', *JRS*, 1957, 36–8
HERRMANN P. *Der römische Kaisereid* (Göttingen, 1968)
KRAFT K. 'Der Sinn des Mausoleums des Augustus', *Historia*, 1967, 189–206
HOLLOWAY R. R. 'The tomb of Augustus and the princes of Troy', *AJA*, 1966, 171–3
p. 189 Suet., *Nero*, 2
p. 192 Plut., *Ant.*, 56
p. 193 Vell., 2.83.1
p. 195 Sallust, *BJ*, 85.4
p. 196 Aug., *Res Gest.*, 25
p. 196 Dio, 51.4.6.
p. 196 (The terms of the oath are a conflation of *ILS* 190 and 8781)
p. 199 Vell., 2.86.3

Chapters XV & XVI

For topography:
HAMMOND N. G. L. *Epirus* (Oxford, 1967)
LEAKE W. M. *Travels in Northern Greece* (4v., London, 1835)

For the campaign:
KROMAYER J. 'Kleine Forschungen...VII: Der Feldzug von Actium und der sogennante Verrath der Cleopatra', *Hermes*, 1899, 1–54
FERRABINO A. 'La battaglia d'Azio', *Riv. Fil.*, 1924, 433–72
KROMAYER J. *Antike Schlachtfelder*, IV (1931), 662–71
TARN W. W. 'The battle of Actium', *JRS* 1931, 173–99
LEVI M. A. 'La battaglia d'Azio', *Athenaeum*, 1932, 3–21
KROMAYER J. 'Actium: ein Epilog', *Hermes*, 1933, 361–83
RICHARDSON G. W. 'Actium', *JRS*, 1937, 153–64
WISTRAND E. *Horace's Ninth Epode and its Historical Background* (Göteborg, 1958)

For the naval side:
ANDERSON R. C. *Oared Fighting Ships from Classical Times to the Coming of Steam* (London, 1962)

BASCH L. 'Un modèle de navire romain', *L'AC*, 1968, 136–71

* CASSON L. *The Ancient Mariners* (London, 1959)

KROMAYER J. 'Die Entwicklung der römischen Flotte vom Seeräuberkriege des Pompeius bis zur Schlacht von Actium', *Philologus*, 1897, 426–91

p. 203   Syme, *Roman Revolution*, 297
p. 204   Virg., *Aen.*, 8.678–88
p. 211   Vell., 2.84.2
p. 221   Plut., *Ant.*, 66
p. 224   Virg., *Aen.*, 8.710
p. 226   Plut., *Ant.*, 68

Chapter XVII
p. 233   App., *BC*, 5.136
p. 234   Plut., *Ant.*, 85

Chapter XVIII

* EARL D. C. *The Age of Augustus* (London, 1968)

GRENADE P. *Essai sur les Origines du Principat* (Paris, 1961)

HAMMOND M. 'The sincerity of Augustus', *HSCP*, 1965, 139–62

* ROWELL H. T. *Rome in the Augustan Age* (Univ. of Oklahoma, 1962)

MILLAR F. 'The emperor, the Senate, and the provinces', *JRS*, 1966, 156–66

SALMON E. T. 'The evolution of Augustus' principate', *Historia*, 1956, 456–78

SATTLER P. *Augustus und der Senat. Untersuchungen zur römischen Innenpolitik zwischen 30 und 17 v. Chr.* (Göttingen, 1960)

p. 238   Tac., *Ann.*, 1.3
p. 238   Aug., *Res Gest.*, 34
p. 239   Ennius ap. Suet., *Aug.*, 7
p. 241   Vell., 2.89.3
p. 241   Tac., *Ann.*, 3.56

ABBREVIATIONS USED ABOVE
(apart from ancient authors, for whom see Lewis and Short's *Latin Dictionary* or Liddell and Scott's *Greek-English Lexicon*)

AJA   American Journal of Archaeology
AJP   American Journal of Philology
CAH   Cambridge Ancient History
CIL   Corpus Inscriptionum Latinarum

HSCP   Harvard Studies in Classical Philology

ILS   Inscriptiones Latinae Selectae (ed. H. Dessau, Berlin, 1892)

JRS   Journal of Roman Studies

L'AC   L'Antiquité Classique

Mél. Carcopino   Mélanges d'Archéologie d'Epigraphie, et d'Histoire Offerts a Jérôme Carcopino (Paris, 1966)

REL   Revue des Etudes Latines

Riv. Fil.   Rivista di Filologia

Robinson Studies   Studies Presented to David Moore Robinson on his Seventieth Birthday (2v. St. Louis, 1951–3)

SEG   Supplementum Epigraphicum Graecum

ACKNOWLEDGEMENTS

MY formal obligations are few, and are set out below; but a book of this sort would be impossible to write without making use of the lifetime's work of other men. I could not begin even to count obligations of this kind, let alone record them here. There are, however, two books I cannot pass over: Sir Ronald Syme's great work *The Roman Revolution*, which itself marked a revolution in the study of Roman history in this country, and has been both an inspiration to me and an indispensable work of reference; and H. Buchheim's *Die Orientpolitik des Triumvirn M. Antonius*, which has confirmed and illuminated from a different angle the picture drawn by Syme.

I am most grateful to Dr. W. Schmitthenner for permission to consult his unpublished doctoral thesis *The Armies of the Triumviral Period* (see p. 251). My thanks are likewise due to the Mansell Collection for permission to publish the photographs of Agrippa (*facing p.* 122) and the Vatican warship sculpture (*facing p.* 123); to the Ministry of Defence (Air Force Department) for permission to publish the air photograph of Actium (*facing p.* 154); and in a more personal way to M. J-M. Rouquette, Conservateur des Musées d'Arles, for his assistance and generosity in procuring new photographs of the Arles bust of Octavian (*frontispiece*), and making them available to me.

I should also like to thank my wife for her encouragement and assistance, and her brothers for their help in the later stages. Finally, I wish to record my gratitude to the Master and Council of Ormond College in the University of Melbourne for my tenure of the Seymour Readership which first gave me the opportunity to work on this topic.

Royal Holloway College
September 1969

INDEX

Abbreviations: *cos.*, consul; *pr.*, praetor; *q.*, quaestor; *tr. pl.*, tribune of the plebs; *desig.*, designate; *suff.*, suffect (i.e. a magistrate appointed to replace another who had resigned or died during the year). For first names. see Appendix.

References in italics, after place-names, indicate the page number of the map on which the place is marked.

The names of men who attained one of the regular major magistracies of the state are followed by the highest office held and year (the first year, in the case of those who held the consulship more than once). All dates are B.C. unless otherwise stated.

f. after a page number indicates the one page following, ff. the two pages following; longer references are given in the form 165–71.

INDEX OF PASSAGES CITED FROM ANCIENT AUTHORS

(Page numbers in italics indicate a direct quotation; others that the author in question is there named as the source for a statement.)

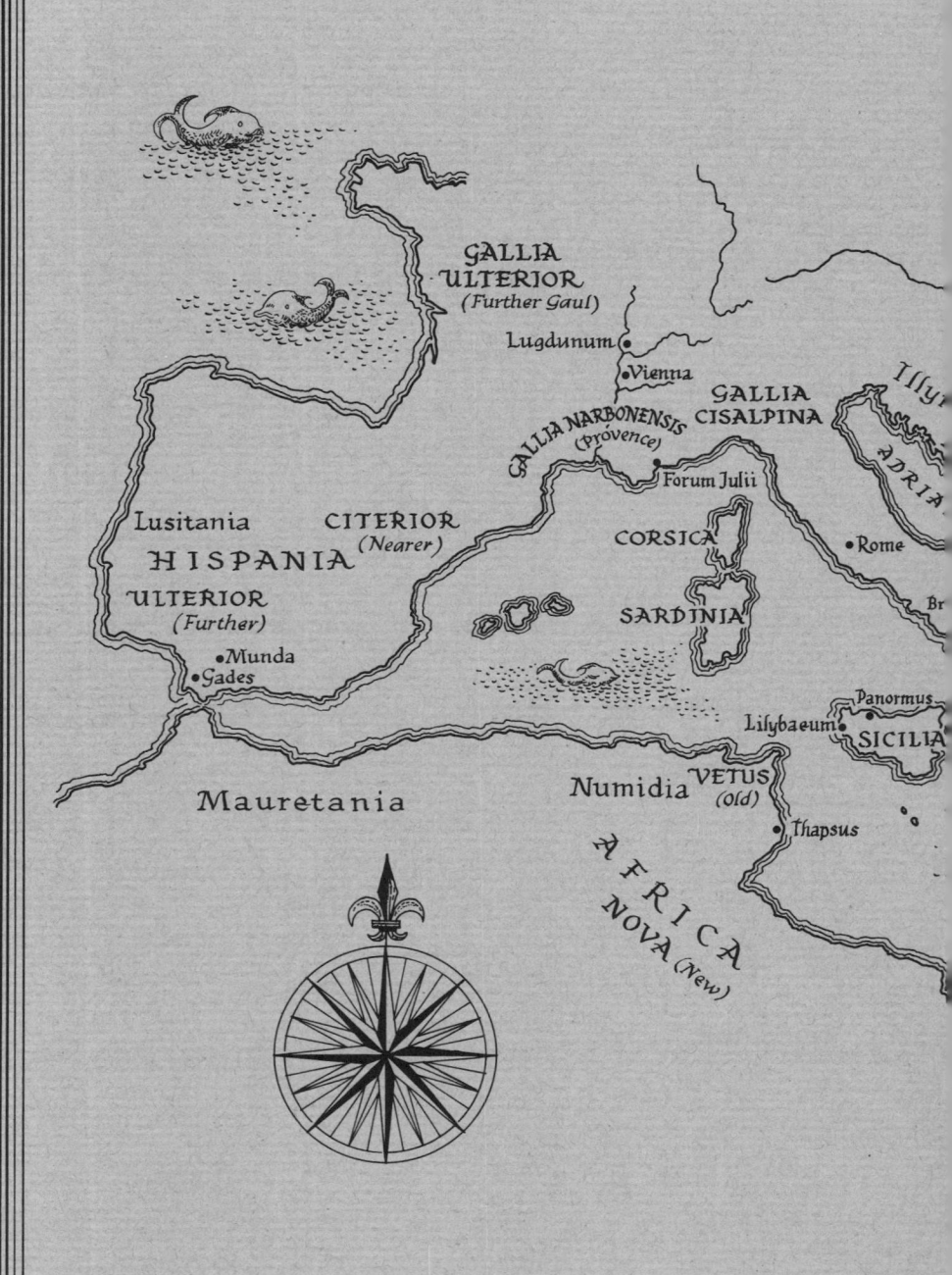